CW00664676

A deeply penetrating study of a movement that shatters conventional ideas of left/right and racist/antiracist. Busher's skilled and sensitive ethnography provides new insight into how the EDL created a shared world of anti-Muslim activism, and how this world unraveled in a cycle of resentments, infighting, and skepticism.

Kathleen Blee, *Distinguished Professor of Sociology, University of Pittsburgh, USA*

Approachably written and closely observed, this book gets inside the life world of EDL activists – a bunch of people more complicated and varied than commonly imagined. Anyone wishing to understand the complexity and the contradictions at the heart of the English Defence League should read Joel Busher's fascinating book.

Tim Bale, *Professor of Politics, Queen Mary University of London, UK*

Political causes emerge, change, cross-breed, and subside in complex ways. The English Defence League is a fascinating case, which emerged from networks of football hooligans, became a lightning rod for anti-Muslim sentiment, and yet resisted the racist slogans of the far Right. This fine book takes us inside the heads – and hearts – of the League's participants.

James M. Jasper, *The Graduate Center of the City University of New York, USA*

Stepping in the shoes of English Defence League activists, Joel Busher paints an insightful inside-picture of the British anti-Islam movement. Years of carefully documented fieldwork yield a thick and rich description of a movement that rocked Great Britain for some time.

Bert Klandermans, *Professor of Applied Social Psychology, VU-University Amsterdam, the Netherlands*

The English Defence League has been labelled fascist, racist, and extremist; its foot-soldiers have been disparaged as mindless thugs. Joel Busher is no EDL-sympathizer, and yet confronts such glib generalizations in this lucid and penetrating book. Busher really gets up close to reveal the essential heterogeneity of those who took to the streets and marched under the EDL banner. This is a superlative study. Everyone with an interest in anti-Muslim activism should read it.

Nigel Copsey, *Teesside University, UK*

Busher's *The Making of Anti-Muslim Protest: Grassroots Activism in the English Defence League* is a masterful piece of story-telling, sewn together with solid theoretical insights into the individual and ecological dynamics that help to explain the rise, fall, and continuity of the EDL. This 'boots on the ground' approach allows us to hear clearly how members at once distanced themselves from 'racist' identities while nonetheless avowing 'racist' sentiments.

Barbara Perry, *University of Ontario Institute of Technology, Canada*

The Making of Anti-Muslim Protest

Activism in any social movement group is, as Deborah Gould observes, a project of collective 'world-making'. It is about changing the world out there by influencing policy and public opinion, but is also about the way it transforms the lives of participants – activists generate new identities, cultures, social ties, rich and varied emotional experiences and interpretations of the world around them. Movements are more likely to be able to attract and sustain support when as projects of collective world-making they feel compelling to activists and would-be activists.

In this book, Busher explores what has made activism in the English Defence League (EDL), an anti-Muslim protest movement that has staged demonstrations across the United Kingdom since 2009, so compelling to those who have chosen to march under its banner. Based on 16 months of overt observation with grass-roots activists, he explores how people became involved with the group; how they forged and intensified belief in the EDL cause; how they negotiated accusations that they were just another racist, far right group; and how grassroots EDL activism began to unravel during the course of 2011 but did not do so altogether. Providing a fresh insight as to how contemporary anti-minority protest movements work on the inside, this book will be of interest to students, scholars and activists working in the areas of British politics, extremism, social movements, community relations and current affairs more generally.

Joel Busher is a Research Fellow at the Centre for Trust, Peace and Social Relations, Coventry University, UK.

Routledge Studies in Extremism and Democracy

Series Editors: Roger Eatwell
University of Bath
and
Matthew Goodwin
University of Nottingham

Founding Series Editors: Roger Eatwell
University of Bath
and
Cas Mudde
University of Antwerp-UFSIA

This new series encompasses academic studies within the broad fields of 'extremism' and 'democracy'. These topics have traditionally been considered largely in isolation by academics. A key focus of the series, therefore, is the (inter-)*relation* between extremism and democracy. Works will seek to answer questions such as to what extent 'extremist' groups pose a major threat to democratic parties, or how democracy can respond to extremism without undermining its own democratic credentials.

The books encompass two strands:

Routledge Studies in Extremism and Democracy includes books with an introductory and broad focus which are aimed at students and teachers. These books will be available in hardback and paperback. Titles include:

Varieties of Right-Wing Extremism in Europe
Edited by Andrea Mammone, Emmanuel Godin and Brian Jenkins

Revolt on the Right
Explaining support for the radical right in Britain
Robert Ford and Matthew Goodwin

Right-Wing Radicalism Today
Perspectives from Europe and the US
Edited by Sabine von Mering and Timothy Wyman McCarty

Routledge Research in Extremism and Democracy offers a forum for innovative new research intended for a more specialist readership. These books will be in hardback only. Titles include:

The Making of Anti-Muslim Protest

Grassroots activism in the English Defence League

Joel Busher

Routledge
Taylor & Francis Group

LONDON AND NEW YORK

First published 2016 by Routledge

2 Park Square, Milton Park, Abingdon, Oxon OX14 4RN
711 Third Avenue, New York, NY 10017, USA

Routledge is an imprint of the Taylor & Francis Group, an informa business

First issued in paperback 2016

Copyright © 2016 Joel Busher

The right of Joel Busher to be identified as author of this work has
been asserted by him in accordance with sections 77 and 78 of the
Copyright, Designs and Patents Act 1988.

All rights reserved. No part of this book may be reprinted or
reproduced or utilised in any form or by any electronic, mechanical, or
other means, now known or hereafter invented, including
photocopying and recording, or in any information storage or retrieval
system, without permission in writing from the publishers.

Notice:
Product or corporate names may be trademarks or registered trademarks,
and are used only for identifi cation and explanation without intent to
infringe.

British Library Cataloguing in Publication Data
A catalogue record for this book is available from the British Library

Library of Congress Cataloging-in-Publication Data
Busher, Joel.
  The making of anti-Muslim protest : grassroots activism in the
English Defence League / Joel Busher.
     pages cm. — (Routledge studies in extremism and democracy)
  1. English Defence League.   2. Right-wing extremists—Great
Britain.   3. Islamophobia—Great Britain.   4. Protest movements—
Great Britain.   5. Nationalism—Great Britain.   6. Great Britain—
Ethnic relations.   7. Great Britain—Emigration and
immigration—Public opinion.   8. Great Britain—Emigration
and immigration—Government policy.   I. Title.
  HN400.R3B87 2016
    305.6 970941—dc23
    2015021330

ISBN: 978-0-415-50267-2 (hbk)
ISBN: 978-1-138-22316-5 (pbk)

Typeset in Times New Roman
by Apex CoVantage, LLC

Contents

Acknowledgements

First of all, I would like to acknowledge the generosity of the English Defence League and March for England activists who allowed me to spend time with them. I was always made to feel welcome and well looked-after during meetings and demonstrations.

I have been fortunate to have a number of encouraging and engaging colleagues who have been willing to share and discuss ideas with me during the course of this research, among them Anthony Richards, Michael Skey, John Morrison, Anthony Gunter, Paul Thomas, Michelle Rogerson, Kris Christmann and Harris Beider. My particular thanks to Gareth Harris for his unbounded enthusiasm and probing questioning, and to Graham Macklin, whose considered scholarship and friendship have been invaluable.

There have been various others along the way who I must also thank: Charlie Flowers and Jamie Bartlett for helping me to build contacts with the EDL activist community; Joel Goodman for his companionship and insight while in the field; Caroline Quinn and Hilary Pilkington for their reflections from their own experiences of conducting research with the English Defence League; Esther Molina Costa and the Biblioteca de la Fundació Pilar i Joan Miró for providing such a peaceful workspace; Sally Sutton for her forensic reading of earlier drafts of this book; Roger Eatwell and Matthew Goodwin for their insights into how to refine the final versions of the text; and the team at Routledge for their considerable patience.

Finally, my thanks to my family and friends for their enduring support and above all to Jessica, whose love and kindness is truly humbling.

Abbreviations

ASBOs	anti-social behaviour orders
ASWJ	Ahlus Sunna wal Jamaah
BFP	British Freedom Party
BNIM	biographic narrative interpretive method
BNP	British National Party
BPA	British Patriotic Alliance
BPS	British Patriots Society
CRASBOs	criminal anti-social behaviour orders
CXF	Combined Ex-Forces
EDL	English Defence League
ENA	English Nationalist Alliance
EVF	English Volunteer Force
IOB	Infidels of Britain
IPCC	Independent Police Complaints Commission
ISIS	Islamic State of Iraq and Syria
LGBT	Lesbian, Gay, Bisexual and Transgender
MAC	Muslims Against Crusades
MDL	Muslim Defence League
MFE	March for England
NEI	Northeast Infidels
NF	National Front
NPA	New Patriot Alliance
NPOIU	National Public Order Intelligence Unit
NWFF	Northwest Frontline Firm
NWI	Northwest Infidels
PEGIDA	*Patriotische Europäer gegen die Islamisierung des Abendlandes*
PVV	*Partij voor de Vrijheid* (Freedom Party, Netherlands)
RO	Regional Organiser
SDL	Scottish Defence League
SEA	Southeast Alliance
UAF	Unite Against Fascism

UBA	United British Alliance
UBP	United British Patriots
UPL	United People of Luton
UKIP	UK Independence Party
WDL	Welsh Defence League

1 Introduction

It's not, you know, it's not just running around screaming 'E – E – EDL'. You know, there's a lot more to it than just running around doing that.

(Tony)[1]

An introduction to the English Defence League

Saturday 9th April 2011 was a gloriously sunny spring day in Chadwell Heath, on the borders of the eastern London boroughs of Barking and Dagenham and Redbridge. Like much of London's periphery, in the last two decades, the area has undergone a dramatic demographic transition with rapid inward migration transforming the face (and faces) of what was until fairly recently a predominantly white British and working-class area. On this particular morning, it was playing host to the third in a series of four demonstrations by English Defence League (EDL) activists over plans to build a Muslim community centre on the high street.

The rendezvous point for the demonstration was, as usual for such events, a pub near the allocated protest site. When I arrived there at a little before 11 AM, there was already a crowd of about 40 activists. Most were in the beer garden enjoying the sunshine; a couple were outside talking with police officers, finalising arrangements for the demonstration. Every few minutes, another group of activists arrived: the East Anglia Division, the Portsmouth Division, the Southend Division and so forth. As each group arrived, there were handshakes and embraces and shouts of 'Oi-oi!' As a few more pints of beer were knocked back, the activists chatted in increasingly animated tones, sang their songs and had photographs taken with Tommy Robinson[2] and Kevin Carroll, the EDL's most recognised spokespersons, who by this point, more than two years after the first EDL demonstrations, had acquired something of a celebrity status. After a short while, one of the stewards, a well-known and popular figure in the local activist community, climbed up onto one of the pub benches with a portable loudspeaker. The march, we were told, would be getting under way in about 10 minutes. As was customary, he called on everybody to follow the instructions of the event stewards and the police, and signed off with a 'NO SURRENDER!' that drew cheers from the 250 or so demonstrators now assembled.

The activists finished off their drinks and made pre-march trips to the toilet. Flags were hoisted aloft or draped over shoulders, and some people wrapped scarves over their faces or pulled down their baseball caps, although most didn't see the need to do so. As the march began the event stewards, dressed in fluorescent jackets, directed the activists, trying to ensure that they kept to the road so that the pavements were left clear for passers-by. There was scant police presence: the two previous demonstrations in the area had both passed off with only very limited public disorder.

The first port of call was the train station. After the first of this series of demonstrations, a young activist had stepped off the platform, apparently to retrieve something he had dropped on the tracks, and had been killed by a train. At each of the subsequent demonstrations, the EDL activists went to the station to pay tribute to their deceased colleague. On the way to the station, some marchers sang and chanted, and a group of activists heckled a young man of Asian background cycling on the other side of the road; others walked along fairly quietly talking amongst themselves. All the while, a couple of men – one wearing a pig-head mask – buzzed around the edges of the procession handing out flyers to passers-by.

On our arrival at the station, there was a marked change of mood. The stewards shepherded the activists inside, and a hush came over the group. Kevin Carroll made a short speech about how the 'young patriot' must not be allowed 'to have died in vain'. Wreaths were laid, and a minute's silence was meticulously observed. Then they all filed back out onto the street, where the volume levels were soon rising again.

The activists continued in the direction of the demonstration site approximately half a mile away. There was no set formation to the procession, although as usual most of the younger activists surged towards the front with most of the older activists and some with limited mobility bringing up the rear. The demonstration elicited a mixed response from onlookers. Some appeared curious, some bemused, some afraid, some irritated: a group of young white men outside a hairdresser's paid no attention whatsoever to the spectacle; an elderly gentleman walked past muttering 'Oh, give it up!' and others hurried past about their business; some residents waved St. George's flags from their front gardens; some motorists hooted their horns in support; small groups of women from black and minority ethnic communities looked on with concern etched on their faces, and a family of Asian origin peered nervously from behind net curtains as a group of young EDL activists pointed and chanted at them until a local EDL organiser intervened: 'No! No! Stop! They're Sikhs! We like Sikhs!'

The demonstration site was at a crossroads on the high street on which the community centre was to be built. Here there was a larger police presence of at least a couple of dozen officers, most of whom positioned themselves between the EDL activists and a small Dagenham Peace & Unity counterdemonstration of fewer than 10 people on the opposite side of the road who sang songs, made peace signs and shook maracas. Most of the EDL demonstrators either ignored them or asked each other whether these were people from Unite Against Fascism

(UAF), an anti-fascist group that had organised several demonstrations against the EDL in the past and with which several EDL activists had already had run-ins.

Coincidentally, there was an open-backed breakdown truck parked on the other side of the road, and some activists were soon clambering over it, dancing and jigging around to the usual selection of EDL anthems that were being blasted out over a loudspeaker set up beforehand by EDL stewards. After a couple of songs, it was time for the speeches. Some activists listened intently to what was being said on the platform, while others continued to chat amongst themselves. As was usually the case, the speaker who received the warmest welcome and the most attention from the activists was Tommy Robinson. There was solemn applause when the speakers referred to British troops, and pantomime boos at the mention of the local council and Margaret Hodge, the local MP for Labour.

Within 20 minutes of arriving, the marchers were on their way again. To leave the demonstration site, they had to pass the Dagenham Peace and Unity counterdemonstration. Here tempers flared, and despite police efforts to keep the groups separate, insults were exchanged, and an EDL activist threw a full can of beer that struck one of their opponents. Soon, however, the EDL activists drifted away in dribs and drabs in the direction of another pub.

Once there, event stewards herded all the activists around the back into the beer garden, where a barbeque had been laid on. After the previous event in March, some activists had been involved in minor altercations with young Muslim men outside the pub, and the organisers and the pub landlord did not want a repeat of this. Once in the beer garden, there were no more speeches, mass songs or chants. Instead, they soaked up spring sunshine and beer while the local organisers reflected on what they saw as a successful day. Almost every activist I spoke with wanted to convey a similar message: I heard again and again about how the EDL is not a racist, extremist or far right group but a single-issue protest movement campaigning against (militant) Islam and (extremist) Muslims[3] in the United Kingdom. As I left to walk back to the station listening to a group of activists from Southend, Essex, earnestly cataloguing a litany of injustices inflicted on 'ordinary English people' by 'muzzies' and the 'liberal elite' we passed another activist on the other side of the road, drunk, head shaved, leaning back, arms in the air, belly thrust out, bellowing 'England till I die!' in the direction of a middle-aged black man no more than two metres away, whose expression showed a mixture of surprise, fear and bewilderment.

The EDL coalesced into a social movement group[4] out of a series of protests that took place in Luton, a town about 30 minutes' train ride north of London, during the spring of 2009. The protests had been sparked[5] by an incident in the town on 10th March when a small group of Islamist activists calling themselves Ahlus Sunnah wal Jammah (ASWJ, Adherents to the Sunnah and the Community) – one of several iterations of the now-proscribed Al-Muhajiroun (the Emigrants) – staged a protest during which they heckled British soldiers of the Royal Anglian Regiment taking part in a homecoming parade after a tour of duty in Iraq.

In the first instance, James Yeomans, a former member of the Royal Anglian Regiment, called a 'Respect our Troops' march in Luton for 28th March. He cancelled the event when anti-fascist campaigners warned him that far right groups were intent on hijacking it (Copsey 2010), but there soon followed an application for another march on St. George's Day (23rd April).[6] This time the application came from the blogger Paul 'Lionheart' Ray, a local man with links to what has come to be widely referred to as the counter-jihad movement, a fairly loose network of bloggers, commentators, small groups, and intellectuals mobilising against what they claim is the Islamification or Islamisation of Europe and North America (see Archer 2013, Denes 2012, Kinnvall 2013a, Williams and Lowles 2012),[7] in collaboration with a group of Lutonians calling themselves United People of Luton (UPL). When the request was declined,[8] UPL activists, incensed by the decision, announced that they would instead hold an unofficial 'Reclaim our Streets' march. On 13th April, approximately 150[9] activists assembled in Luton, many of them young men associated with Luton's football hooligan firm, supplemented by protestors who had travelled from as far afield as the West Midlands and the South Coast, many of whom were also associated with football violence (Blake 2011, 14–16). The protest was quickly dispersed by the police, but there were related incidents of public disorder in the town later that day,[10] and the UPL soon called a further demonstration for 24th May, this time in collaboration with March for England (MFE), a self-identifying patriotic group also comprising mainly former football hooligans. MFE obtained permission from Luton Borough Council to march to the town hall to present a petition calling for Sayful Islam, one of the highest-profile ASWJ activists, to be banned from Luton town centre. Shortly before 24th May however, MFE withdrew as the official organisers, throwing planning for the event into disarray. On the day, about 500 people gathered at the designated meeting point. When the protestors arrived in the town centre, a small group of approximately 20 activists, mostly associated with MFE, did continue with their planned route to the town hall, but the majority broke away from the procession as the police temporarily lost control of the proceedings (Copsey 2010). A man of Asian background was assaulted, some protestors caused criminal damage including smashing car windscreens and a shop front, some hurled stones at the police, and there were reports of protestors making their way to Bury Park, a predominantly Asian-heritage area. Nine people were initially arrested (Copsey 2010, 10), and sixteen people were eventually charged with offences relating to these events.[11]

The launch of the EDL was announced via Facebook on 27th June 2009: representing a loose alliance between people who had been involved in the UPL protests and an assortment of other small groups seeking to mobilise around similar issues, such as Casuals United,[12] established by Jeff Marsh, a Cardiff-based football hooligan of some renown and a founder of the Welsh Defence League, and British Citizens Against Muslim Extremists, a Birmingham-based group also with its roots in the football casuals scene.[13] The EDL's first demonstration took place on the same day in Whitechapel, London, an area with one of the most concentrated Muslim populations in the United Kingdom. The demonstration attracted around 30 to 40 activists and a substantial police escort. As Blake (2011, 39), himself an EDL activist at the time, notes, 'although the protest wasn't an obvious success, more introductions had been made': the event helped to form the national networks of activists that would underpin the subsequent expansion of the movement (see also Marsh 2010). The following week, there were further demonstrations. In Birmingham, 150 people gathered under a combined EDL/Casuals United banner, while in Wood Green, north London, approximately 40 activists gathered to picket a 'Life under Sharia' roadshow being held by Anjem Choudary's now proscribed Islam4UK, another of the plethora of groups that had grown out of Al-Muhajiroun. Little more than a month later, on 8th August 2009, approximately 900 activists participated in an EDL protest in Birmingham,[14] at which there were significant clashes with antifascist campaigners and 35 arrests, mainly for public order offences[15] and, while plans for a further demonstration in Luton were frustrated when the police successfully applied for an order preventing public processions in the town for a three-month period,[16] further demonstrations soon followed in Birmingham (5th September), Manchester (10th October) and Leeds (31st October).

The emergence of the EDL marked a new chapter in the history of anti-minority activism in Britain. Not only had there been little in the way of organised street-based anti-minority activism in Britain since the British National Party (BNP) had turned its attention away from street violence and towards a strategy of community-style politics in the late 1990s (Copsey 2008), but from the outset, there were indications that this was not simply a return to the kind of far right street activism that Britain had experienced in the 1970s, 1980s and 1990s when groups like the National Front (NF), Blood and Honour, the BNP and Combat 18 were most active. First, the group's leadership and a considerable part of its membership sought to distance the EDL ideologically from the conventional far right. There were undoubtedly a number of points of overlap between the protest narratives deployed by EDL activists and those of previous waves of backlash and anti-minority politics in the UK and elsewhere in Europe, such as the prominence of ideas about a looming threat to indigenous British or English culture,[17] and a tendency to apportion at least some of the blame for the perceived encroachment of the dangerous Other to the supposed failings of the 'liberal elite', the nefarious influence of 'the left' and the malady of 'political correctness'.[18,19] From the outset, however, the movement's organisers made it clear that symbols pertaining to known far right groups or to Nazi or Fascist iconography would not be tolerated on EDL demonstrations. Spokespersons for the EDL were, and have remained, at pains to avoid anything hinting at biological racism, maintaining that they are a single-issue group concerned only with (militant) Islam. Early EDL demonstrations offered the initially somewhat surprising spectacle of people sporting 'skins' tattoos and other symbols and insignia associated with racism and the far right walking beside people waving Israeli and gay pride flags (Taylor 2010). On 28th September 2009, trying to prove their point, EDL activists from Luton posted a video of themselves in which 16 men from diverse racial backgrounds clad in balaclavas can be seen burning a swastika flag, with a banner in the background bearing the words 'English Defence League, black and white unite'.[20] The video was not well received by some established far right groups.

Second, while some of those attracted to the EDL also supported and had been activists in more conventional far right groups, it soon became clear this mobilisation was not organisationally associated with the established far right (Copsey 2010). It was instead growing out of the fringes of the football hooligan networks and the counter-jihad movement. While far right groups have long sought to draw support from and mobilise through the football hooligan scene (see Buford 1991, Centre for Contemporary Studies 1981) what was unusual about the EDL was that in this case, the impetus to mobilise came from within the football scene itself. In fact, it was seen by leaders of established far right groups as a threat to their support base, and the national BNP leadership soon mounted a campaign criticising the EDL leadership as 'useful idiots' for the 'ultra-Zionists'.[21]

It is difficult to estimate the scale of the support that the EDL achieved, as is the case for many social movement groups that do not participate in electoral politics. The EDL has never had a formal membership system, and even among activists, there were often differences of opinion over what it meant to be part of the group – did it mean attending demonstrations? If so, how many, and how often? Or was it simply a matter of 'joining' the group on Facebook?[22] What we can say is that at various points the group's Facebook following has touched or even exceeded 100,000 (although it is unclear how many of those joining the EDL on Facebook were in fact supporters of or at least sympathised with the group and how many were trolls from anti-EDL groups, journalists or nosy academics);[23] that from 2010 onwards, there have been EDL divisions active in most major towns and cities across England and Wales;[24] and that by early 2011, the group was attracting some international support, with a number of national Defence Leagues appearing across Europe, some of whose activists I encountered on demonstrations in the United Kingdom.[25]

Since August 2009, the EDL has held national, regional and counter demon-strations[26] at a rate of approximately two per month, ostensibly against (militant) Islam and what activists referred to as the 'Islamification' or 'Islamisation'[27] of Britain. Bartlett and Littler (2011) estimate that by early 2011 roughly 25,000 people had participated in an EDL demonstration at some point. As the EDL developed, activists also explored a range of different forms of collective action: leafleting on their local high streets; attempting to organise legal challenges to the construction or renovation of Islamic buildings; flash demonstrations;[28] physi-cally or verbally disrupting meetings and processions being held by their (militant) Muslim or left-wing opponents; spending many hundreds of hours trying to promote their ideas and arguments online, primarily through social media or in some cases by trolling their opponents; holding fundraising events for veterans' charities; organising St. George's Day parades and memorials for key symbolic events such as the terrorist attacks of 11th September 2001 (New York) and 7th July 2005 (London); and even attempting to coordinate boycotts of shops and fast food restaurants selling halal products.[29]

Activists were organised ostensibly through a network of local 'divisions', each with its own organisers who were usually referred to as 'admins' – a term derived initially from their role as administrators on divisional Facebook pages. As of the summer of 2010, these local divisions were, at least in theory, coordinated by a set of regional organisers or 'ROs', who worked closely with the national leadership; a system introduced in an attempt to provide the expanding group with a clearer structure (Copsey 2010, 19). In addition to the local divisions, there were also various special-interest divisions that were more or less integrated within the EDL including youth divisions, women's divisions (known as the Angels), a Jewish division, a Persecuted Christians division with several of its (online) members based in Lebanon, Syria and Egypt, and a Lesbian, Gay, Bisexual and Transgender (LGBT) Division.[30]

During the latter half of 2011, the EDL began to lose some of its momentum. Throughout 2010, their national demonstrations had regularly attracted more than 1,000 participants, and in February 2011, they managed to mobilise around 3,000 supporters for a demonstration in Luton.[31] Yet in the months that followed, attendances declined: where once national demonstrations had attracted in excess of 1,000 participants, by late 2011 they rarely attracted more than about 500, and the anti-Muslim protest scene came to be characterised by fallings-out between competing factions within the movement that crystallised over time into splinter groups such as the Northwest Infidels (NWI), Northeast Infidels (NEI), Combined Ex-Forces (CXF) and the Southeast Alliance (SEA) among others (see Chapter 6).

As of mid-2015, this wave of anti-minority activism has not however petered out altogether. While the number of people attending events held by the EDL and various splinter groups has declined, they have continued to mobilise on a regular basis and have achieved notable upticks in support after a number of key symbolic events such as the killing of Drummer Lee Rigby by two Islamist militants in Woolwich on 22nd May 2013[32] and the breaking of news stories about systematic child sexual abuse by a network primarily of Muslim men in Rotherham in 2014.[33] On 8th October 2013, Robinson and Carroll left the EDL, but a management committee comprised of nineteen regional EDL organisers was quickly set up to coordinate the group's activities (Pilkington 2014, 118). This committee was initially chaired by Tim Ablitt, who had been the Southwest regional organiser.[34] He was replaced as chairman in February 2014 by Steve Eddowes, previously the West Midland regional organiser and head of security for the group.[35] The first national demonstration of 2015 took place in Dudley on 7th February, attracting somewhere between 600 and 1,000 participants.

About this book

This book is about activism[36] at the grassroots of this wave of anti-minority mobilisation. It is about how people became EDL activists; how they developed and sustained their commitment to the group, to the cause and to one another;

and how and why the fabric of this group started to but did not completely unravel between early 2011 and the time of writing in 2015.

The discussion that I present is theoretically grounded in the idea that social movement activism, regardless of the cause around which people are mobilising, comprises a project of collective 'world-making', a concept that I have taken from Deborah Gould's (2009) landmark study of AIDS activism in the United States. Social movement activism is partly about wanting, and perceiving an opportunity,[37] to change the world *out there*, however well- or ill-defined that change might be – it is a 'politics by other means' (Gamson 1974, Tilly 1978). Yet social movement activism also transforms and can often enrich the lives and lived experiences of those who participate in it. Through their participation in activism, people collectively produce 'sentiments, ideas, values, and practices that manifest and encourage new modes of being' (Gould 2009, 178). In the last 25 years or so, scholars of social movements have documented how participants produce new cultural spaces and codes (Futrell and Simi 2004, Melucci 1996, Polletta 1999), construct collective identities[38] that enable the emergence of both real and imagined communities (Berezin 2001, Casquete 2006, Collins 2001, Melucci 1995), establish, enact and ritualise alternative moral orders (Casquete 2006, Jasper 2007), develop and negotiate cognitive frames through which they interpret and experience the world around them (Benford and Snow 2000, Snow et al. 1986),[39] and achieve and train emotional states and responses that encourage, or discourage, further participation (Gould 2009, Summers Effler 2010, van Troost, van Stekelenberg and Klandermans 2013, Yang 2000).[40] Mobilisation can sometimes be as much if not more about consolidating or creating new identities as it is about affecting public policy[41] and 'The satisfactions of action, from the joy of fusion [with other activists] to the assertion of dignity [can] become a motivation every bit as important as a movement's stated goals' (Jasper 2011, 12).

Social movement groups are more likely to attract and retain participants when 'as projects in world-making, they are *compelling* to participants and prospective participants hungry to construct alternative worlds' (Gould 2009, 178, my emphasis) – when they offer participants and prospective participants subjectively *meaningful* collective identities and *resonant* and *fulfilling* cognitive, moral, cultural and emotional structures. In this book, I discuss how EDL activism came to provide a *compelling* project of collective world-making for those who chose to march under the group's banner. Throughout the discussion, I range across what I conceive of as three broad and intersecting dimensions of this process of world-making: a) the shifting patterns of activists' social interactions; b) the activists' development of beliefs about the world around them and their position within it; and c) the emotional energies generated through EDL activism.

The shifting patterns of activists' social interactions: participation in activism shapes both who individuals come into contact and engage with, and how they do so. Activism brings people into contact with other activists, opponents, state actors, sympathisers, different news sources and so forth. Through their interactions with these actors, rituals and behavioural norms are established that then shape subsequent interactions and might over time crystallise into relationships. I pay particular attention to the personal relationships that shaped and emerged through the activists' interactions. Such relationships are central, not incidental, to activism, especially in largely informal grassroots movements such as the EDL (Blee 2012, 109–133): they shape patterns of recruitment, influence the way that activists organise themselves and are often fundamental to sustaining commitment. Furthermore, participation in activism always entails some degree of reconfiguration of people's personal networks: new relationships and friendships are formed, old ones fade or might be renounced. Exploring these changing relationships can provide us with important insight about the group's social structures, how it manages its boundaries and how activists conceive of their relationship with wider society.

Activists' development of beliefs about the world around them and their position within it: activism alters the way that participants interpret and understand the world around them. Through the course of the their interactions with other actors, activists form and refine beliefs about the nature of the problem that they are ostensibly seeking to address, about who is to blame and what is to be done (Snow and Benford 1988).[42] The development of these beliefs entails and intersects with the evolution of a much wider set of beliefs: about the strategic and tactical opportunities available to them, about who really exercises power within their society, about the parameters of 'us' and 'them', about the moral legitimacy of different courses of action and so forth. My focus in this book is not so much on describing EDL activists' beliefs in aggregate form – as 'a frame' or 'an ideology' – as it is on describing how beliefs emerged, were negotiated and evolved through their everyday practices and experiences.[43]

The emotional energies generated through EDL activism: As well as altering participants' patterns of social interaction and their cognitive processes, activism also entails important changes in people's feelings and emotional responses to the world around them. Activist groups generate what Gould (2009, 10) describes as an 'emotional habitus' – 'socially constituted, prevailing ways of feeling and emoting'.[44] I explore the emotional habitus of grassroots EDL activism, paying particular attention to the group's 'emotional batteries' (Jasper 2011, 2012)[45] – how the impulse to action is generated through the interaction between what we might consider both negative and positive emotions.

In Chapter 2, I discuss the beginnings of people's journeys through EDL activism. I start with a description of the different routes that the activists I knew had followed into the group, before discussing the beginnings of these journeys in terms of the activists' social ties, their initial engagement with the EDL cause and the emotions associated with their first encounters with the EDL. Chapter 3 is about how, once involved in the group, they developed and refined their belief in the EDL cause. Here, as well as exploring the range of materials and experiences that shaped processes of belief formation, I also discuss the social structures of learning within the activist community. In Chapter 4, I concentrate on how activists resisted attempts by their opponents to label them racist and far right, and the implications that this had for the evolution of EDL activism.[46] Chapter 5 is about the partial decline of EDL activism that gathered pace during the spring and summer of 2011. I discuss how EDL activism unravelled at the grassroots of the movement and what this can tell us about the limitations not just of the EDL but more generally of EDL-like groups. In Chapter 6, however, I explore some of the factors that have contributed to ensure that anti-Muslim activism in the United Kingdom has not collapsed altogether, at least as of mid-2015.

Using such an approach in research about groups such as the EDL can of course raise difficult ethical questions for the researcher. Is there a danger that by describing the activists' lived experience one somehow inspires not only empathy but also sympathy for their movement? Is there a danger that one's research simply provides them with further oxygen of publicity? Throughout this research, I have wrestled with such questions.[47] However, like other researchers who have conducted ethnographic studies of anti-minority or far right groups,[48] I believe that such concerns are heavily outweighed by the dangers associated with having only a limited and somewhat stereotyped understanding of activism in these movements and that by exploring the internal logics of anti-minority activism, we become better able to hone our thinking about how we develop appropriate and effective ways of responding to and managing the impacts of anti-minority politics.[49]

There are two ways in particular that detailed description of activists' collective world-making can strengthen our understanding of this wave of anti-minority activism. First, it enables us to develop an account of participation in groups such as the EDL that both avoids simply pathologising activists as angry, white, damaged and vulnerable men seeking to protect their social status and reassert their compromised masculinity,[50] and avoids falling back on rather unsatisfactory accounts of activism in such groups as somehow springing forth from generalised anxieties about how the country is changing, perceptions of declining economic and cultural opportunities, declining trust in the political elite and so forth.[51]

There are of course important kernels of truth in such explanations, but they are analytically limited. During the 16 months that I spent with EDL activists I did on several occasions see the rather clichéd images of angry, shaven-headed, heavily-tattooed men with noses shaped by years of confrontation shouting and snarling at their opposition, at the police and into media cameras. Some activists said and did things that I found deeply unpleasant and sometimes disturbing – miming shooting at Muslim women, slipping into racist caricatures about 'muzz-rats',[52] chanting defamatory slogans about Allah and so on and so forth. Yet the vast majority of the activists that I met were in many respects quite normal and rational people,[53] and while I found some of their arguments and actions difficult to stomach, they were for the most part quite comprehensible as long as one was prepared to situate oneself for a moment within their personal logics and experiences.[54] They were worried about their children's future, anxious about how their neighbourhoods were changing, upset that nobody in the public sphere seemed to represent them or their views and, often, looking to make a bit of sense of and give some meaning to their lives. Likewise, survey data indicate that there are hundreds of thousands, possibly millions, of people in the United Kingdom who are anxious and even pessimistic about the way the country is changing, are sceptical about the compatibility of Islam with Western-style democracy and do not feel that political leaders speak for people like them (Duffy and Lee Chan 2009, Goodwin and YouGov 2013, Harris, Busher and Macklin 2015). Yet only a very small fraction of these people ever seriously think about participating in anti-minority protests, and even fewer will ever become part of a group like the EDL.[55] If we are to explain which of these many thousands of people with ostensibly similar concerns become involved in such groups, when, how and for how long, we need to get closer to the activists themselves and to the interactions that comprised EDL activism.

Second, and at a more meso-level, studying how EDL activism works as a project of collective world-making enables us to develop a more complete analysis than we have at present of how and why such a group has been able to gain and sustain such traction at this particular moment in history. There are several factors that we might point to as enablers of this wave of anti-Muslim protests. Groups such as the EDL can partly be seen as a product of the diffusion of deep and widely held anxieties about Islam and the cultural, political and security implications of a growing Muslim population in Europe. Since at least the late 1980s and the Salmon Rushdie affair, we have seen the relationship between Islam and secular Western democracy repeatedly imagined as a key point of social and political cleavage both nationally and internationally – the (in)famous 'clash of civilisations' thesis advanced by Samuel Huntingdon (1993). While such conceptualisations of the world may find particularly vocal champions in groups associated with the far or radical right, the 'Islam-as-a-threat-to-European-security-and-values frame' (Zúquete 2008, 337) has permeated deep into mainstream political and cultural discourse (Adib-Moghaddam 2011, Allen 2010, 2012, 2013, Bonney 2008, Fekete 2004, 2009, Kundnani 2014).[56] As well as helping to cultivate the kinds of anxiety around which the EDL has mobilised, the proliferation of discourses about a cultural clash have also created discursive opportunities for far right and anti-minority groups in the United Kingdom and elsewhere to distance themselves from, or at least keep at arm's length, traditional and highly stigmatised far right discourses grounded in straightforward biological racism (Poynting and Mason 2007, Rydgren 2005).

Drawing on traditional 'breakdown' theories of support for far right or anti-minority politics,[57] we might also interpret the EDL as a product of collapsing trust in the political classes, particularly among those who find it increasingly difficult to identify political leaders who represent them. Garland and Treadwell (2012, 126) for example attribute the emergence of the EDL at least in part to what they call an era of 'post-politics' in which 'the absence of an authentic working-class political discourse and wider political processes in the United Kingdom has left disadvantaged and marginalised white working-class communities that traditionally supported the Labour Party, with no natural political "home"'[58] – a similar argument to that which Ford and Goodwin have made about the fleeting electoral success of the BNP (Ford and Goodwin 2010) and more recently about the surge of support for UK Independence Party (UKIP) (Ford and Goodwin 2014). Such an argument is lent credibility by Bartlett and Littler's (2011) finding that online supporters of the EDL express strikingly low levels of trust both generally and in some public institutions.[59] Kinnvall (2013b, 146) has added a political psychological dimension to such theorisations by linking the emergence of the EDL and other anti-Muslim groups to what she describes as 'a pervasive sense of existential anxiety' running through contemporary political debate in Europe and North America.

From a subcultural perspective, it could also be argued that the first decade of the 21st century was a particularly opportune moment to mobilise through football hooligan networks. As Garland and Treadwell (2012, 124) note, over the last two decades a combination of domestic football banning orders and 'prohibitive ticket pricing' have combined to 'make the spectator experience of soccer a less attractive arena in which to seek physical confrontations'. Groups such as the EDL, it might be argued, can provide the kind of opportunities to construct and express an aggressive masculinity once provided by football violence (Treadwell and Garland 2011).[60]

Furthermore, like contemporary social movement groups across the political spectrum,[61] the EDL has undoubtedly also benefited from and made deft use of new information technologies which have greatly reduced the financial cost and increased the speed and reach of internal and external communications (Bartlett and Littler 2011, Copsey 2010, Jackson 2011).

Yet it is important not to be seduced into imagining that the emergence of a group such as the EDL was somehow inevitable. It was not. In fact in many ways it has been a rather unlikely social movement group. Shortly after I began the fieldwork for this book in early 2011, I was talking with senior police intelligence officers at a conference about how their understanding of and responses to the EDL had evolved since 2009. One officer recalled somewhat ruefully that in July 2009, their view, and that of most of the professionals they had spoken with at the time both within the police and in central government and academia, was that it would 'probably all blow over when the next football season started'. There were a number of good reasons for such an assessment. First, and quite simply, it was not the first time that there had been mobilisations against (militant) Islam by groups with their roots in football-related public disorder. In 2004, in Luton, a combination of primarily Luton- and Peterborough-based football casuals had sought to organise a 'Ban the Taliban' march in the town (Harris et al. 2015), and a group called United British Alliance (UBA) had carried out a series of demonstrations against the radical cleric Abu Hamza outside the Finsbury Park mosque in London (Copsey 2010, 9). Yet while UBA garnered coverage even in the national media, these protests never escalated into a major or sustained series of mobilisations.

Second, there is a significant difference between going out once or twice to voice anger and frustration and participating in sustained collective action. Social movement activism of any sort may offer multiple benefits and incentives, but it can also be a costly business. Protest, as Oliver and Myers note, 'is not a self-reinforcing behaviour' because it 'inherently disrupts the normal rhythms of people's lives' (2002, 9): it may be financially expensive, almost certainly absorbs a great deal of time, may strain existing personal relationships, can have legal consequences and significant negative implications for participants' employment and career prospects, and at some point or another is likely to entail moments of disappointment and despair. The cost of activism is likely to be particularly high in pariah groups where activists face, or at least expect to face, various forms of social sanction ranging from general public disapproval to exclusion from the labour market and even legal sanctions (Bjørgo 2009, Blee 2003, Klandermans and Mayer 2006, Simi and Futrell 2009). In spite of their efforts to distance themselves from the established far right, EDL activists soon found themselves confronted by massed ranks of opponents from an assortment of anti-racist groups and were routinely labelled 'far right' or 'racist' by most mainstream politicians and media agencies.[62] While such confrontational situations and concomitant deviant identity might have been part of the allure for some people who became involved in the EDL (see Chapter 2), the fact that they were described in this way undoubtedly undermined the ability of the group to gain purchase among people who did not already identify with the far right, and amplified the social costs of participation.

Third, at least until the fallout from the BNP's disastrous general election campaign in mid-2010, it seemed that political space for a movement such as the EDL was actually quite restricted. At the time of writing this book in 2015, the BNP has largely collapsed back into obscurity. In 2009, however, at the time of the EDL's emergence, the BNP not only appeared to be establishing itself as a political force, albeit a relatively marginal one, but was also mobilising around a political discourse that had significant similarities to that of the EDL: like far right groups across Europe the BNP had since at least the early-2000s been attempting to avoid references to biological racism and had been adopting the strategy of targeting Muslims as the dangerous Other (Copsey 2007, 2008, Goodwin 2011, John et al. 2005, Macklin 2015).

Fourth, while it is relatively common for social movements to comprise 'an uneasy coalition between groups favouring different tactics, often with slightly different moral sensibilities [which] have little to do with each other, even dislike each other' (Jasper 2007, 229), the EDL depended on some particularly unlikely alliances. As described above, their demonstrations provided the somewhat surprising spectacle of seasoned far right activists walking alongside people carrying Israeli flags, gay pride flags and banners stating 'Black and white unite against extremism'. How long could these individuals stand alongside one another without the obvious ideological differences coming to the surface?[63] And then there were the football-based rivalries. EDL activists themselves expressed surprise that the truces between rival football firms held as well as they did. As one Southampton-based activist observed to me as we sat around a table in a pub in Fratton, a stone's throw from the home of Portsmouth FC, their arch-rivals, with activists whose footballing affiliations included Southampton, Portsmouth, Plymouth, Chelsea and Millwall, 'before EDL and March for England, we'd all've been trying to kill each other!' before going on to regale us with the tale of his last visit to Fratton, where he had been carted away in a police van for fighting with Portsmouth supporters.

Fifth, and finally, social movement mobilisation, and particularly sustained mobilisation, requires multiple capabilities – communication skills; knowledge about the legal context in which they are operating; experience, or at least links to people with experience of organising similar kinds of events; coordination and management skills and so forth. As resource mobilisation theorists have made clear, outrage and anger alone are not enough (McCarthy and Zald 1977, Zald and McCarthy 1979). One of the striking characteristics of the EDL, particularly early on, was how few of the people associated with the group had any prior experience of social movement mobilisation. In fact during interviews with the national EDL leaders as part of another research project in 2014 (Harris et al. 2015), they laughed about how disorganised and unprepared they had been and how, ironically, they had at least initially learned quite a bit about how to conduct protests by observing their anti-fascist opponents.[64] Although the EDL received some financial, logistical or strategic support from a number of individuals associated with the international counter-jihad movement such as Alan Lake,[65] Pamela Geller and Robert Spencer (Williams and Lowles 2012), there was good reason to doubt whether there would be sufficient wherewithal within the activist community to sustain the group. This situation was exacerbated by the fact that in drawing primarily on politically, economically and culturally marginal working-class communities the EDL was tapping into one of the segments of the UK population that was least likely to be able to supply the kinds of skills or resources historically associated with effective social movement mobilisation.

If we want to develop a comprehensive analysis of movements like the EDL and the 'ebb and flow of [their] organizational viability' (Zald and Ash Gardner 1987, 123), we need to understand how activists negotiate these various challenges. Once again, we can only do this by getting close to these activists and observing their interactions with one another, with their opponents and more generally with various other social and political currents.[66] Doing so can help us to interpret what has happened to date, to reflect on how and why our responses have played out the way they have, and also to think about how this kind of group is more or less likely to evolve in the future, an issue that I return to in Chapter 7. One of the reasons why studies of anti-minority groups tend to overestimate the prospects of such groups is that they do not take fully into account the everyday labour required to sustain them.[67]

Methods

The account of grassroots EDL activism I present in this book is based primarily on overt[68,69] ethnographic observation of and interviews with activists in London and Southeast England, most of which took place between February 2011 and May 2012. A small amount of additional material is drawn from three subsequent studies in which I participated: on public responses to anti-Muslim protest (Busher et al. 2014, Thomas et al. 2014) and on the evolution of anti-Muslim protest in two English towns (Harris et al. 2015), as well as ongoing communication with some EDL activists in the London area until mid-2013 and more sporadic contact after that date via Facebook and telephone.

Participant observation was conducted at 22 public events attended by the activists that I was spending time with.[70] Notes were written up or recorded orally as soon as possible after the event, usually within an hour, longer when attending demonstrations outside of London and the southeast of England.[71] These notes were subsequently cross-checked against footage of the events available on YouTube or being circulated within the EDL activist community. I also informally cross-checked my own observations against those of other actors who were paying close attention to the EDL in that part of the country during this period, including anti-racism campaigners,[72] the police[73] and a freelance photographer, Joel Goodman,[74] who had followed the EDL for some time. Participant observation was supplemented by observation of video footage of other public events attended by EDL activists from London and Essex prior to, during[75] and after the main period of fieldwork.

More general observation of the EDL activist scene in the area was carried out through a combination of participant observation at divisional and regional meetings, telephone conversations with activists, meeting up informally with activists and observation of and interaction with activists via social media. As well as observing the official EDL national and divisional Facebook pages, I also had access to online conversations taking place outside these official spaces as a result of becoming Facebook friends with several activists. After the first six months, there were about 60 people within the local activist scene with whom I was familiar and had multiple conversations. These people were mainly concentrated in the western end of Essex and eastern London, although some were located in Hampshire, Kent, Sussex, Bedfordshire, East Anglia and west London. The somewhat erratic pattern of these contacts was a product of who I had been introduced to during EDL events and, to some extent, where I had been able to build rapport. Approximately 75% of these activists were male, 25% female; approximately 15% were aged 35 or younger, 80% aged 36–65 and 5% over 65.[76]

The emphasis placed on observational data reflects the fact that while I was to some extent interested in the 'big ideas' around which the activists mobilised, I was more interested in how people engaged with, took ownership of, negotiated and lived out these ideas. As Jasper (2010, 967) observes, it is 'the little pieces of strategic interaction' that provide 'the micro-level building blocks' of activism. Whether they are shouting at opponents during a demonstration, sharing a link to a news story with other activists, arguing with police officers, getting drunk with fellow activists or even just sitting in a traffic jam together on a wet Saturday afternoon wanting to get home, it is through their everyday interactions with one another, their opponents and various third parties that activists pick up, adopt and adapt ideas; establish routines and rituals that giving meaning to their actions; and build the often intense personal relationships that can both make and destroy activist groups.

In addition to observational data and the informal interactions with activists that this entailed, interviews were carried out with eighteen core activists. These activists were purposively selected to cover a range of different experiences of EDL activism in terms of the length of time they had been involved and their centrality within the local structures. Of these, 14 were male and 4 female; 3 were 35 years old or younger, 12 were aged 36–65 and 2 were over 65. They were drawn from across the segments of the activist community described in Chapter 2: the football lads, people who had entered the EDL via their involvement in self-identifying patriotic groups, people already associated with far right activism, people already associated with counter-jihad networks, the 'swerveys'[77] and the 'converts'.[78] Interviewees were recruited through established contacts within the activist community.

Interviews were focused on the activists' personal journeys through the EDL and were structured using the biographic narrative interpretive method (BNIM). The BNIM method is a gestalt-based technique developed by Wengraf and colleagues (see Wengraf 2001) in which the interviewer encourages the interviewee to develop an increasingly detailed narrative description of events as they remember them rather than asking them to offer explanations for their actions. Interviewees were first asked to tell the story of their journey through EDL activism in their own words. The initial description lasted anything between 3 and 42 minutes, depending on the respondent, during which time the interviewee was invited to speak without interruption. I then worked my way through this initial response asking progressively for more detail about the events described. The mean length of interview was 101 minutes. Interview data were coded manually, developing codes and nodes[79] organised within three broad categories (relationships, ideas and emotions) that were then stress-tested against observational data.

There were two reasons for using this interviewing technique. The first was because the explicit focus on *describing* events rather than *explaining* their actions lent itself to encouraging the activists to move away from the tramlines of their well-rehearsed narratives about their cause and their concomitant feelings of outrage and injustice. One of the challenges of interviewing activists in groups such as the EDL is that the stories they tell about their lives are saturated with justification and the counter-narrative with which they seek to challenge their opponents and critics – at least partly a product of becoming accustomed to having to defend their involvement in the group in the face of hostile and aggressive opposition. Second, by creating space for the interviewee to narratively explore their own past, the BNIM approach enables the researcher to catch glimpses of the cognitions and emotions of earlier episodes of a person's life – cognitions and emotions that can be hard to access both as a result of interviewees strategic efforts at impression management,[80] but also because of the way that through multiple conversations with friends and family, strangers at the pub, fellow activists and even the occasional researcher or journalist, activists, like humans in general, sieve their past out through their present in a way that helps them to make sense of their today and face their tomorrow.[81]

An overview of the activist communities in London and Essex

The activists

By the summer of 2011, there were approximately 200–300 people[82] in and around London and Essex who regularly attended EDL events, as well as a slightly larger number of more occasional activists who appeared from time to time at EDL events but were not well known in the activist community. The activist community in London, Essex and the Southeast more generally was, as might be expected, overwhelmingly white. The handful of activists from ethnic minority backgrounds acquired something of a celebrity status within the group. It was also predominantly male. During the fieldwork period, I estimated that about 20% of participants at the events and meetings that I attended were female, although it is worth pointing out that several of these women played leading roles within the activist community as divisional admins, delivering speeches and stewarding at demonstrations.[83]

In terms of their socio-economic position, the majority of activists I met were either in low-income jobs or out of work, although again it is worth qualifying this by saying that there were several exceptions. I met an activist who was a skilled professional in the National Health Service, a legal underwriter, a former civil servant, several activists in managerial positions either in the retail or the construction sector, and several activists running their own businesses apparently with considerable success. These activists usually came to hold relatively senior roles within the EDL's local and regional organisational structures. Similarly, while many of the activists I met had not progressed in formal education beyond the end of compulsory schooling, several, particularly younger, activists either had completed or were attending further or higher education.

This general socio-demographic picture is broadly in keeping with the findings of Bartlett and Littler's (2011) online survey of EDL Facebook members undertaken around the time that I commenced my fieldwork.[84] Their survey found that 19% of EDL Facebook members were female, that 30% are educated to college or university level[85] and that those identifying as EDL supporters are on average more likely than the general population to be unemployed (p. 18).[86]

Where my findings differ from those of Bartlett and Littler is with regard to the age-range of the activists. Bartlett and Littler found that 72% of EDL Facebook members were under 30, 21% were aged 31–50 and just 4% were over 51 years old. By contrast, I estimated that people under 30 comprised only 35–45% of people attending demonstrations and only 10–20% of those involved as organisers.[87] This difference may well be due to the different ways in which younger and older people engage with online media; I would hypothesise that older people are less likely to become a member of an online group unless they also intend to engage with the group offline.

Local movement structures

As in the rest of the country, the activists organised themselves through a series of local divisions, which were at least in principle co-ordinated by a network of regional organisers. In London, activists were spread across approximately 20 EDL divisions in different London boroughs – I say approximately because the number rose and fell on a regular basis as new divisions formed, and others merged or collapsed. There was considerable variation across these local divisions. Some of the larger divisions attracted 20–30 people to some of their meetings and organised local leafleting campaigns; some of the smaller divisions never amounted to more than a Facebook page with a handful of 'likes'. At least one of the divisions never held a meeting. These borough divisions were the result of substantial reorganisation during the spring of 2011, when what had formerly been the EDL London Division was divided into a number of smaller divisions; a move undertaken with the aim of facilitating better engagement with the public and achieving a better distribution of what was becoming an unmanageable workload for the London organisers.

In Essex, divisions were established in most of the major towns, with much of the leadership based in and around the Thames Gateway in Dagenham, Ilford, Romford, Tilbury and out towards Southend. Colchester and Chelmsford also had particularly active divisions. Local divisions in Essex were by and large more successful in holding frequent meetings than those in London. Throughout the period of fieldwork for this book, the regional organiser for the EDL in Essex was Paul Pitt,[88] who in 2015 featured in *Angry, White and Proud*, one of several television documentaries about the EDL.

Like activists elsewhere in the country, the activists in London and Essex organised and participated in a range of different activities. The largest demonstration in the area during the main period of fieldwork for this book was a static demonstration on the boundary of Tower Hamlets in east London on 3rd September 2011, attended by approximately 1,500 participants. Activists also organised other local, regional and counter demonstrations. Throughout this time, there was never a period of more than a month without some form of official EDL event in the area. As well as the official demonstrations, core activists also carried out several leafleting campaigns (usually, but not always, associated with a forthcoming demonstration) and organised petitions. Some activists took part in attempts to disrupt the activities of opposition groups. For example, on 19th May 2011, a group of around 25 local activists disrupted a meeting of anti-fascist activists and local councillors in Barking and Dagenham, throwing stones at the building in which the meeting was taking place; on July 9th 2011, around 40 activists, mainly established football lads, had planned to disrupt a Hizb ut-Tahrir conference at the Waterlily Centre in London, but were intercepted at a number of nearby pubs by the police and taken to different police stations for the afternoon;[89] on 28th April 2012, a group of about 15 activists gathered in Lewisham High Street in the hope of carrying out a revenge attack[90] on a UAF rally that they believed was going to pass through the high street, although the UAF rally never materialised due to their truck breaking down; and there were several incidents of low-level altercations with opponents, such as arguments with Islamist groups as Speakers' Corner in Hyde Park, incidents of EDL activists knocking over book or newspaper stalls run by left-wing or Islamist groups and so forth.[91]

The particularities of EDL activism in London and Essex

Conversations with EDL activists, with other people undertaking research on EDL activism elsewhere in the United Kingdom,[92] and with police officers and council officers indicate that there are likely to be some localised variations across the country, particularly in terms of the issue frames that activists used, their tactical tastes and their relationships with the national leaders based in Luton. In this respect, there are three points to which it is worth drawing attention about EDL activism in London, Essex and the Southeast.

The first of these is that, at least when I started my fieldwork, there was a very close relationship between many grassroots activists in London, Essex and the Southeast and the national leaders. The geographic proximity of Luton to London meant that members of the national leadership often attended events in the area – not just demonstrations but also, on occasion, meetings. Almost every core activist I knew in and around London who had been involved with the EDL for more than three months spoke to me at one point or another about a personal conversation that they had had with either Tommy Robinson or Kevin Carroll.[93] This was to some extent also the case in Essex. Both Robinson and Carroll had attended regional demonstrations in the area. During the autumn of 2011, there did, however, emerge tensions between the Essex leaders and the national leaders (see Chapter 5).

A second point concerns the fact that activists in London in particular had some of the most high profile extreme Islamist activists in Europe, such as those associated with Anjem Choudary and Muslims Against Crusades (MAC), another spin-off from Al-Muhajiroun, operating in their area. The activities of Choudary and his colleagues, ranging from small street protests, to holding funeral prayers for Osama bin Laden in London on 6th May 2011, to what they proclaimed were 'Sharia patrols'[94] in Tower Hamlets and Newham, meant that EDL activists in and around London had an almost constant supply of events around which to mobilise and had more opportunity than activists in some other parts of the country to come face-to-face with high-profile Islamist opponents. Several of the London EDL activists came to know MAC activists by name, and vice-versa, and there were even one or two cases of activists on opposing sides clearly developing a certain rapport with one another.

A third point concerns the scale of the black and minority ethnic population in the London area. London is one of the most ethnically diverse cities in world. This basic fact had had a bearing on the lives of all the activists I knew insofar as it was normal for them to have colleagues or neighbours from black and minority ethnic backgrounds, and most also had friends and several had family members (including partners, children and grandchildren) from black and minority ethnic backgrounds. These relationships took on considerable symbolic importance when seeking to reject claims by their opponents that they were racist or far right, as I discuss in Chapter 4. It is possible that they also contributed to the fact that most of the people I knew were more reluctant than activists in some other parts of the country to use or slip into overtly racialised framings of their cause.[95]

A note on terminology: the EDL as an anti-Muslim protest group

Finally, it is worth providing a brief explanation as to why I have chosen to refer to the EDL as an 'anti-Muslim' protest group.[96,97] All ethnographers grapple with difficult questions about the balance they want to strike between adopting the language used by the people they are studying and imposing external conceptual frameworks and categories on them (Atkinson and Hammerlsey 2007, 191–208). These questions are particularly challenging when writing about a group that one does not support personally and that carries a considerable stigma – what Fielding (1993) rather charmingly refers to as 'unloved' groups. How does one find a language to talk about the group which gets close enough to the lived experience of its members as to make that lived experience intelligible to readers, without inadvertently eliciting public sympathy for the group or finding oneself accused of being an apologist for them or even a sympathiser?

My decision not to follow the lead of other academics who describe the EDL as some form of new or alternative manifestation of the far right (Copsey 2010, Jackson 2011, Richards 2013b) is not intended as a statement about whether the EDL is or is not *objectively* a far right group – such terminological debates are not my concern in this book.[98] Instead, it reflects the fact that I found the term 'anti-Muslim' to be the most useful and philosophically consistent terminology for the task of describing activism at the grassroots of the EDL. It offers three specific advantages. First, describing EDL activism as anti-Muslim rather than far right provides a tighter definition of the subject matter of this study. Terms such as 'far right' and 'extreme right' can refer to a highly heterogeneous collection of political parties and protest groups (Davies and Jackson 2008, Mudde 1996, Weinberg 1998).[99] While some of the insights from this study might be applicable to this wider extended family of groups and organisations, other findings are likely to be more specific to anti-minority mobilisations that centre primarily on anti-Muslim protest narratives and that seek explicitly to distance themselves organisationally and ideologically from the established far right.

Second, describing EDL activism as anti-Muslim activism rather than far right activism enables a better rendering of the processes of world-making as they have unfolded at the grassroots of the EDL, because it reflects more closely the arguments and identities around which the group coalesced. This approach is consistent with the tradition of reflexive ethnography, in which this study is broadly grounded, where 'the realities of informants and other subjects within communities studied are characteristically treated as parts of social reality whatever the content of those realities' (Hewitt 2005, 75). As Jasper (2010, 973, emphasis in the original) observes, 'serious efforts to grapple with agency must remain close to agents' *lived experience*'.

Third, referring to the EDL as an anti-Muslim protest group rather than a far right protest group is one way of guarding against overemphasising one particular set of cultural and ideological influences on the group. As I describe throughout the course of this book, the EDL's emergent culture and ideology did partly reflect narratives, social relations and protest tactics associated with the far right. However, as I have described above, the EDL certainly did not emerge out of the existing far right – if anything, traditional far right groups spent the first months after the EDL came on the scene scrambling to work out how to position themselves in relation to it. The EDL's emergent movement culture also owed much to its roots in various other political and cultural currents, including football casuals culture, the growing international counter-jihad movement and even loyalism. At times, it felt more like a convergence of counter-cultural milieux than a 'new far right'.

Notes

1 All of the names used to refer to participants are pseudonyms.

2 Tommy Robinson's official name is Stephen Yaxley-Lennon. 'Tommy Robinson' is in fact the name of a football hooligan of renown from Yaxley-Lennon's hometown, Luton. Throughout this book, I refer to him using his chosen pseudonym as this is how he is best known publicly.

3 Whether people spoke about Islam and Muslims or militant Islam and extremist Muslims varied from activist to activist and across different contexts – during interviews or more reflective conversations, people tended towards the narrower definition; during demonstrations, heated exchanges and moments of bravado they tended towards the broader definition. Throughout the rest of the book, I talk about EDL activists opposing (militant) Islam to convey this ambiguity except where I am talking about specific incidents or individuals where the terminology used was less ambiguous.

4 I conceive of the EDL as a group that sits within overlapping social movements rather than as a social movement in and of itself. Social movements, as Klandermans (1992) observes, can comprise 'multiorganisational fields'. As such, within social movements, we usually 'find a variety of SMOs [social movement organisations] or groups, linked to various segments of supporting constituencies . . . competing among themselves for resources and symbolic leadership, sharing facilities and resources at other times, developing stable and many times differentiated functions, occasionally merging into unified ad hoc coalitions, and occasionally engaging in all-out war against each other' (Zald and McCarthy 1987, 161). Conceiving of the EDL in this way is particularly helpful when talking about the more recent fragmentation of the movement (see Chapters 5 and 6).

5 As Harris and colleagues (Harris et al. 2015) observe, while this event may have provided the spark for this series of protests, the tensions that manifest had been building for some time.

6 St. George is the patron saint of England.

7 'Key aspects of counter-jihad ideology are an assertive cultural nationalism, which portrays Muslims as a threat to Western values, and a belief in the continuation of a centuries-old effort by Muslims to dominate the West, the existence of a conspiracy to Islamise Europe through demographic change and the stealthy implementation of Sharia' (Harris et al. 2015).

8 At the time, Ray was under investigation by the Crown Prosecution Service for inciting racial hatred with articles published in his blog (Copsey 2010, 10).

9 As noted by Harris et al. (2015), 'It is difficult to establish exact attendance figures for demonstrations, and figures are often disputed'. In this instance 150 was the official police estimate (see 'Illegal Protest Ends Peacefully', Bedfordshire Police, 13th April 2009, www.bedfordshire.police.uk/pdf/Annex%20B%202009–00670.pdf). A report in the *Daily Star* however put the number at 200 (see 'Cops halt "reclaim our streets" demo', Ross Kaniuk, *Daily Star*, 14th April 2009, www.dailystar.co.uk/news/latest-news/76784/Cops-halt-reclaim-our-streets-demo), and some participants (Blake 2011, 15) claimed that there had been as many as 500 people.

10 Six people were arrested. See 'Illegal Protest Ends Peacefully', Bedfordshire Police, 13th April 2009, www.bedfordshire.police.uk/pdf/Annex%20B%202009–00670. pdf. On 4th May, there was also an arson attack on Al Ghurabaa Mosque in Luton, which the police suspect was carried out as a revenge attack. See www.independent. co.uk/news/uk/home-news/luton-fights-back-against-rightwing-extremists-1695485. html.

11 See 'Many charged after disturbances as marches are banned in Luton', *Luton on Sunday*, 26th August 2009, www.luton-dunstable.co.uk/charged-disturbances-marches-banned-Luton/story-21692397-detail/story.html

12 The term football 'casuals' is popularly used to refer to a segment of the football violence scene identified by their adoption of 'casual' clothing style, that is, not wearing club colours.

13 See 'English Defence League: chaotic alliance stirs up trouble on streets', Robert Booth, Matthew Taylor and Paul Lewis, *The Guardian*, 12th September 2009, www. theguardian.com/world/2009/sep/11/english-defence-league-chaotic-alliance

14 Birmingham was reportedly identified because it had been the site of an Islam4UK rally at which a video had been made of an 11-year-old boy being converted to Islam: an incident which, as Casciani (2009) notes, 'caused a minor tabloid furore – but a greater reaction on the net, particularly on websites and forums associated with football violence and far-right activity'.

15 '"Patriot" league plots more clashes with anti-fascist activists', Robert Booth and Alan Travis, *The Guardian*, 9th August 2009, www.theguardian.com/uk/2009/aug/09/ defence-league-casuals-birmingham-islam

16 'Luton bans marches amid fears of protests', *The Telegraph*, 21st August 2009, www. telegraph.co.uk/news/uknews/law-and-order/6067813/Luton-bans-marches-amid-fears-of-protests.html

17 The notion that so-called ordinary English people are somehow being stripped of their culture has been a central theme of various waves of far right and more general backlash politics since at least the 1960s (Hewitt 2005).

18 Richards (2013a, 137) claims of the EDL that 'there are no BNP-style savage attacks on the political establishment for allowing this [Islamist] ideology to make itself at home in the UK'. I did not find this: on the contrary, I found that over time activists developed an increasingly sharp focus on and critique of the political establishment (Chapter 3, see also Blake 2011).

19 It was often unclear who qualified as part of the 'left' or the 'liberal elite'. Certainly what activists sometimes called the 'loony left' would have been included – those relatively small groups of activists from organisations like UAF, the Socialist Worker Party (SWP), Antifa and Hope Not Hate who routinely turn out to oppose EDL demonstrations. Trade union groups, Labour and Green Party activists were also usually included, as were certain elements of the media identified by EDL activists as having a particularly strong left-wing bias – *The Guardian*, *The Independent* and the BBC. Other people such as prominent Conservative MPs were rather more difficult to place. On the one hand, actions such as Theresa May's proscription of Muslims

Against Crusades (MAC) on 10th November 2011 and David Cameron's call, during a speech at a security conference in Munich on 5th February 2011, for a 'muscular liberalism' that challenged the 'ideology of extremism' were welcomed by EDL activists. On the other, both were frequently accused of being too 'soft' and activists often urged Cameron to 'grow some balls'.

20 'The English Defence League: will the flames of hatred spread?' Tweedie, N., *The Telegraph*, 10th October 2009, www.telegraph.co.uk/news/6284184/The-English-Defence-League-will-the-flames-of-hatred-spread.html.

21 Nick Griffin, erstwhile leader of the BNP, published an 'in-depth report' on the EDL in an attempt to undermine the group (see Griffin 2013).

22 One of the challenges for those wishing to study and understand activism in the EDL and similar groups is that its absence of formalised group boundaries makes it difficult to define who we are talking about when we discuss the EDL and EDL activism. For the purpose of this book, I describe as activists those who regularly took part in demonstrations, may sometimes have gone out leafleting with other activists and, above all, were acknowledged by other activists as 'proper patriots', as one of them. I do not focus on the 'clictivists' or, as the EDL activists I knew dismissively called them, the 'keyboard warriors'.

23 Bartlett and Littler (2011) estimate that between approximately 10% and 20% of EDL Facebook members could be trolls. It is likely that the EDL Facebook membership also includes a significant number of passive supporters. On the occasions where the EDL Facebook page has been closed down and restarted, it has taken a long time for numbers to return to previous levels.

24 In Scotland, there has been the Scottish Defence League (SDL). The SDL has often supported EDL demonstrations and vice-versa. However, the group has always retained its own identity. Since the fragmentation of the EDL in 2011, the SDL has forged particularly close links with the Northwest Infidels and the Northeast Infidels.

25 Although it is worth noting that attempts to support the emergence of similar Defence Leagues elsewhere in Europe did not gain much support. Approximately 60 EDL activists were opposed and heavily outnumbered by Ajax Amsterdam supporters when they went to the Netherlands (see 'Britons arrested at Amsterdam EDL protest', *The Independent*, 31st October 2010. www.independent.co.uk/news/world/europe/britons-arrested-at-amsterdam-edl-protest-2121551.html), and demonstrations intended to encourage the emergence of Defence League-style groups in Sweden and Norway both attracted pitiably low turnouts (see 'EDL and Swedish Fascists', by Acker Bilk and Pete Norman, EDL News, 25th May 2011. http://edlnews.co.uk/2011/05/25/edl-and-swedish-fascists/ and 'Norwegian Defence League's anti-Islam demonstration flops', Bob Pitt, Islamophobia Watch, 15th April 2011, www.islamophobiawatch.co.uk/norwegian-defence-leagues-anti-islam-demonstration-flops/).

26 Formal demonstrations were organised in consultation with the public authorities and were generally divided into four categories: national demonstrations, regional demonstrations, local demonstrations and counter-demonstrations. The national demonstrations were by far the largest and usually highest-profile of these. They were intended to bring together activists from across the United Kingdom and, once the EDL had started to gain significant momentum and profile, from Defence Leagues and similar groups elsewhere in Europe. The regional and local demonstrations were considerably smaller. The event described at the beginning of this chapter was a regional demonstration. Local demonstrations could involve as few as a dozen or so activists. Because of their smaller size and usually lower media profile these were often low-key affairs with lighter policing and small and often negligible counter-demonstrations. The counter-demonstrations, as the name suggests, were organised in response to events being held by their Islamist opponents.

27 As far as I could tell the two terms were used interchangeably.

28 In contrast to formal demonstrations, flash demonstrations were not organised in consultation with the public authorities. This tactic became increasingly popular among activists in the autumn of 2011 as the EDL fragmented.

29 In Bartlett and Littler's (2011, 19) online survey of people who support the EDL on Facebook, 18% of respondents reported having been out leafleting for the EDL, while 52% reported being involved in online activism, 44% in local demonstrations, 11% in flash demonstrations and 5% in legal challenges.

30 These special-interest divisions were by and large small, sometimes comprising no more than half a dozen people. They did however act as important symbols of the group's heterogeneity and were used by activists to assert their claims about not being racist or far right.

31 Official police estimates for this demonstration range between 1,500–2,000 EDL supporters. The Guardian estimated that 3,000 EDL supporters attended. Estimates from the EDL and some independent observers were significantly higher.

32 'Newcastle EDL march attracts more than 1,500', BBC, 25th May 2013, www.bbc. co.uk/news/uk-england-tyne-22666647

33 'Rotherham EDL child abuse march costs police £750k', BBC 15th Sept 2014, www. bbc.com/news/uk-england-south-yorkshire-29207140

34 See 'EDL Select Dorset's Tim Ablitt as New Leader After Tommy Robinson Quits', Dominc Glover, *International Business Times*, 10th October 2013, www.ibtimes.co.uk/ edl-english-defence-league-tim-ablitt-chairman-512972

35 See 'EDL appoint new leader for moron army', Duncan Cahill, *Hope Not Hate*, 15th February 2014, www.hopenothate.org.uk/blog/insider/edl-appoint-new-leader-for-moron-army-3434

36 Throughout the book, I speak overwhelmingly about what activists said and make very few statements about what 'the EDL' did. As Benford (1997, 418) observes, 'movement scholars often write about social movements as "speaking," "framing," "interpreting," "acting," and the like, that is, engaging in activities that only human beings are capable of doing. Social movements do not frame issues; their activists or other participants do the framing'.

37 See for example McAdam's (1982, 48–51) discussion of 'cognitive liberation'.

38 Following Polletta and Jasper (2001, 284), I understand collective identity to refer to 'an individual's cognitive, moral, and emotional connections with a broader community, category, practice, or institution'. Collective identities are likely to be multi-layered (Gamson 1991, Jasper 2007, Reger 2002). They may form around broad categorical distinctions through which we understand the world around us, for example women, British, academics, working class and so forth; around specific groups (the place one works, the social movement group, the sports club etc.); around sub-groups or cliques (one's specific team in the workplace, the local division of the social movement group or the local church/mosque etc.); and so forth.

39 Frames can be defined as 'an interpretive schemata that simplifies and condenses the "world out there" by selectively punctuating and encoding objects, situations, events, experiences, and sequences of actions within one's present and past environment' (Snow and Benford 1992, 137).

40 While some emotional reactions might be innate, for the most part, a combination of social relations, culture and cognitions shape 'which emotions are likely to be expressed when and where, on what grounds and for what reasons, by what modes of expression, and by whom' (Kemper 2004, 46). See also earlier work by Clark (1990) and Hochschild (1979).

41 A view that can be traced back at least as far as Klapp's (1969) account of social movements as part of broader swathe of practices of identity-searching in the United States of the 1960s. The importance of this search for identity has been given particular prominence within what is often referred to as the 'new social movement' theoretical perspective (Johnston, Laraña and Gusfield 1994, 10)

42 Snow and Benford (1988) refer to these as the diagnostic and prognostic tasks.

43 One of the criticisms of the framing perspective, offered by one of the primary contributors to the literature on frames and framing, is that if we approach frames as 'things' that can be captured and preserved, we risk generating an overly static and homogeneous impression of activism and activists (Benford 1997, 415).

44 In the last two decades, as social movement researchers have sought to flesh out accounts of the motivation for and meaning given to activism they have dedicated increasing attention to the role of emotions (see Goodwin, Jasper and Polletta 2001, Jasper 1998, 2011), an endeavour stimulated and facilitated by the emergence of a much larger body of social and psychological research that has theorised emotions and encouraged the integration of the affective dimension into social and political analysis (Collins 2004, Demertzis 2013, Denzin 2007 [1984], Stets and Turner 2007, Turner 2009). As well as generally providing a thicker description of activism, exploring the emotional energies of activism has, for example, enabled researchers to develop more compelling explanations of how and why particular cognitive frames are more or less effective at generating mobilisation (Robnett 2004, Schrock, Holden and Reid 2004, van Stekelenburg and Klandermans 2013), of the mechanisms through which social ties and collective identities can give rise to or sustain collective action (Goodwin and Pfaff 2001, Nepstad and Smith 2001), of the struggle for attention between competing movements (Collins 2001) and of how even groups that appear, at least from the outside, to be chronically failing can sustain themselves (Summers Effler 2010).

45 Emotional batteries, work 'Just as a battery works through the tension between its positive and negative poles' (Jasper 2011, 7). He cites as examples pride and shame, pity and joy, hope and fear. In his 2011 article, Jasper talks about 'moral' rather than 'emotional' batteries, but the two publications complement one another.

46 Attempts to resist negative definitions imposed on them by opponents have long been identified as an important part of the process through which activists construct collective identities (Taylor and Whittier 1992)

47 Such concerns are one of the reasons why until relatively recently scholarship on the far right has tended to analyse these movements 'from a distance', with a focus on 'the economic, social, attitudinal, or cultural environments that nurture organized racism and right-wing extremism rather than the dynamics of the far right itself' (Blee 2007, 120).

48 Such as Blee's (2003) account of women's participation in race-hate groups in the United States, Simi and Futrell's (2010) account of the 'spaces of hate' through which white power activism operates and Virchow's (2007) description of protest in the German far right. As Barrett-Fox (2011, 16) argues, ethnographers of such groups aim for comprehension, and may use empathy as a tool to achieve it. However, 'the goal is not to create an apologetic portrait of racists or antisemites or homophobes, but one that captures the complexities of their lives'.

49 When we don't fully understand the internal dynamics of a group, we run the risk that intervention might have negative unintended consequences. In the case of groups such as the EDL, these might include radicalising elements within the group, making it more difficult to police or reinforcing in-group solidarity (Klandermans and Mayer 2006, Linden and Klandermans 2006). I return to these issues later in the book. A similar point is made by Klein (1995) in relation to street-gangs.

50 Several early studies of participation in far right activism, informed by a psychoanalytical tradition, explored it as a form of personality disorder and emphasised the irrationality of participants (see Adorno et al. 1954, Lasswell 1933). Such approaches have largely been eschewed in more recent accounts of activists involved in far right and anti-minority groups (see especially Blee 2003, Caiani, della Porta and Wagemann 2012, Klandermans and Mayer 2006). As Cohen (1988, 88) observes, there are 'plenty of "rigid authoritarian personality types"' to be found in other walks of life, including 'the anti-racist movement, for example'.

51 As Githens-Mazer (2010) argues in his critique of debates about 'Islamic radicalisation', one of the underlying conceptual challenges for much research on participants
in radical political or religious movements is that they tend to draw conclusions based
on what are actually outlying cases of the much broader categories, such as 'Salafists',
'Islamists' or 'Muslims' that nonetheless are sometimes given prominence within
explanatory frameworks. The same can be said about 'white working-class'. See
especially Rhodes (2011) for a considered critique of discourses about the 'white
working class' in the context of debates about extremist politics.

52 A derogatory term used by some activists to refer to Muslims.

53 A finding also in keeping with accounts of activism in more traditional far right groups
(Billig 1978, Blee 2003, Klandermans and Mayer 2006, Simi and Futrell 2010).

54 As Goffman (2009 [1961], xviii) observes, the behaviour and arguments of most
people can be made to seem 'meaningful, reasonable, and normal' if one is willing
'to submit oneself in the company of the members to the daily round of petty con-
tingencies to which they are subject'.

55 This distinction between people who share similar views and those who actually
become activists is the reason for my scant reference in this book to Goodwin and
colleagues' work on EDL 'sympathisers' (Goodwin 2013, Goodwin, Cutts and Janta-
Lipinski 2014).

56 The reasons for this go beyond the scope of this book, but are discussed extensively
in the materials referenced in the main text. For a fascinating and quite disturbing
discussion of the mechanisms through which this has happened in the United States,
see Bail (2012).

57 Explanations of support for far right and reactionary movements have often emphasised
the role of social, economic and political crisis and how the impacts of these crises
have been most keenly felt among the 'losers of modernization', thereby making them
particularly vulnerable to the allure of extremist politics (Arendt 1951, Kornhauser
1959, Minkenberg 2001).

58 See also Treadwell (2013), in which he argues that if we are to understand activism
in groups such as the EDL, we must explore the feelings of precariousness of those
who become involved in them.

59 Only 32% of EDL supporters reported that they tend to agree with the statement
'people can be trusted' compared with a national average of 55%. There was also a
significant difference in trust reported in some public institutions: the government
(EDL supporters, 13%; national average, 28%); police (37% as opposed to 71%);
justice and the legal system (24% as opposed to 50%). It is worth noting, however,
that we cannot know the extent to which the exceptionally low levels of trust expressed
by Bartlett and Littler's respondents pre-dated their participation in EDL activism.

60 A similar idea can be found in Kimmel's (2007) description of how skinheads were
attracted to right-wing violence because it provides an opportunity to assert and enact
a compromised masculinity.

61 Castells (2012, 9) is one of several authors who have highlighted that online networks
provide considerable opportunities for social movements to exercise what he calls
'counterpower' by enabling activists to engage in 'autonomous communication, free
from the control of those holding institutional power'.

62 The exception to this was some sympathetic coverage of the group in the *Daily Star*
at the beginning of 2011. In the final line of an article titled 'EDL to go political'
published on 9th February, it reported that 'In the *Daily Star* phone poll yesterday,
98% of readers said they agreed with the EDL's policies'. www.dailystar.co.uk/news/
latest-news/175956/EDL-TO-GO-POLITICAL

63 Multiple researchers of collective action have stressed the importance of explaining
rather than simply assuming the unity and continuity of movements (Blee 2012, 52–80,
Gongaware 2003, Klandermans 1992, Melucci 1988, 1995, Reger 2002)

64 A claim also made to me by some London organisers.

65 'Alan Lake' is also a pseudonym. His name is Alan Ayling.

66 Even the most apparently extreme movements emerge out of and continue to develop in relation to more mainstream social and political currents (Blee 2003, Cohen 1988, della Porta 1995, Mann 2004). They evolve in response to changes in political, economic and social structures (della Porta 2008, Kriesi et al. 1995); their protest narratives and action repertoires will reflect, or at least be shaped by, existing cultures of protest and deeper ideas and beliefs about what is or is not a legitimate form of collective action (Tilly 1986, 2008); the ways in which they frame their cause will always be at least partly a product of the cultural tools made available to them by the webs of symbols and meaning already spun by other actors (Snow and Benford 1992, Tilly 1986, Whittier 2004, Williams 1995, 2004); and their evolution will be shaped by their interactions with opposition groups, rival groups and the state (della Porta 1995, della Porta and Tarrow 2012, McAdam 1983, Macklin and Busher 2015, Oliver and Myers 2002).

67 See for example studies by Ford and Goodwin (2010), Goodwin (2011) and Garland and Treadwell (2012). Other reasons are likely to include a quite understandable desire to ensure that dealing with such issues does not disappear from policy agendas, as well as a certain degree of risk management – we all hedge our bets when talking about the future trajectories of these groups (for example Busher 2013).

68 Whenever I made new contacts, I introduced myself to them as a researcher. I recognise however that the distinction between overt and covert research is not always clear cut. As Bourgois (2007, 296–297) notes, 'we are taught in our courses preparatory to fieldwork that the gifted researcher must break the boundaries between outsider and insider. We are supposed to "build rapport" and develop such a level of trust and acceptance in our host societies that we do not distort social interaction. Anything less leads to the collection of skewed or superficial data. How can we reconcile effective participant/observation with truly informed consent? Is rapport building a covert way of saying "encourage people to forget that you are constantly observing them and registering everything they are saying and doing?"' Calvey (2008) offers a particularly thought-provoking discussion of this problematic.

69 Access to the EDL activist community was initially achieved through Charlie Flowers, who had briefly flirted with EDL activism, with whom I was put in contact by Jamie Bartlett, an extremism expert at Demos. I am sincerely grateful to both of them. It is important to emphasise how easy it was to gain access to the EDL activist community, in part because of the common assumption that activists in groups like the EDL are unlikely to welcome the presence of an academic researcher. After I made contact with the EDL London Division, one of the admins came to visit me at the University of East London. We had a lengthy conversation about the group and my research plans, and he invited me to attend a forthcoming demonstration. When I arrived at the demonstration, he presented me to several other activists. While some activists were initially suspicious of me, during the 16 months I spent attending EDL events only one initially refused to speak to me.

70 In chronological order: three demonstration in Dagenham (12/03/2011, 9/04/2011, 18/06/2011); protest in support of Tommy Robinson at Hammersmith Magistrates' Court (11/05/2011); Casuals United/EDL demonstration in Blackpool (28/05/2011); EDL demonstration in Telford (13/08/2011); British Patriots Society march in London (20/08/2011); EDL demonstration on the edge of Tower Hamlets, London (3/09/2011); gathering in support of Paul Pitt at Westminster Magistrates Court (15/09/2011); EDL demonstration in Birmingham (29/10/2011); assorted 'patriots' gathering in Whitehall, London (11/11/2011); counter-demonstrations against United Ummah (a follow-on group from MAC) in Grosvenor Square, London (2/12/2011, 20/01/2012); EDL demonstration in Barking, London (14/01/2012); EDL demonstration in Leicester (4/02/2012); a charity walk organised by MFE activists, (6/04/2012); MFE St. George's Day parade, Brighton (22/04/2012); gathering to disrupt UAF event in Lewisham

(28/04/2012); EDL demonstration in Luton (5/05/2012); EDL demonstration, central London (27/10/2012); EDL demonstration in Norwich (10/11/2012) (NB. This was observed from outside the demonstration after meeting up with demonstration organisers immediately prior to the event); flash demonstration outside Abu Qatada's house (17/11/2012).

71 Audio and audio-visual recordings were not made during the course of these events due to concern that doing so would further augment the impact of my presence on the behaviour of the activists I was with: the activists tended to play to the presence of cameras in one way or another.

72 Primarily through monitoring the reporting on websites such as Hope not Hate, Searchlight, EDL News, EDL Criminals and Islamophobia Watch.

73 I had a series of informal conversations with police officers at the National Public Order Intelligence Unit (NPOIU) during the course of this research. This took the form purely of an exchange of general ideas about the EDL and the way the group was evolving at the time. No information was sought or shared between us about forthcoming events and operations or, following these, about the roles of individuals who had attended.

74 Joel Goodman was one of the few photographers or journalists believed by the EDL activists I knew to be genuinely impartial in his coverage of the group and had therefore had better access to the group than most. As well as photographing the EDL, he had also spoken at length with a number of activists.

75 During the main 16-month period of fieldwork, there were a number of events that I was unable to attend due to other work commitments, a serious cycling injury I sustained, and in two instances being away on holiday.

76 See the following section for a description of the socio-demographics of the EDL activist community in the area. Younger activists are under-represented in my sample because my primary contact points were through the network of local organisers, the majority of whom were in their 40s and 50s.

77 People who had come to EDL activism with a background in other forms of radical political activism outside the far right (see Chapter 2).

78 People who had come to EDL activism without prior involvement in any of the aforementioned groups (see Chapter 2).

79 Clusters of codes.

80 For example, in order to pre-empt anticipated criticisms that they are irrational hate-mongers and peddlers of prejudice they might emphasise the rational logic of their decision-making or how their decision stemmed from feelings of love towards their in-group rather than hatred and anger towards the out-group (see Ahmed 2004).

81 As della Porta and Diani (2006, 96) put it, 'in constructing their own identity, individuals attribute coherence and meaning to the various phases of their own public and private history', what Spence (1986) discusses as 'narrative smoothing'.

82 Estimate based on my own observation of local EDL events and meetings and the more conservative estimates offered by local organisers.

83 Their doing so was of considerable symbolic importance, used by the activists as a point of contrast with what they claimed was the subservient and second-class position of women in Muslim societies.

84 I had initially considered conducting my own survey, but decided not to once I learned of Bartlett and Littler's survey and once it became apparent that their results broadly coincided with my own observations.

85 Bartlett and Littler (2011, 18) note that the current national rate of higher education participation is approximately 45%.

86 They find that this is particularly the case among 25- to 64-year-olds, where 28% of EDL supporters within this age range were unemployed, compared with a national average of 6%. Among 16- to 24-year-olds, 27.5% of EDL supporters in this age

range were unemployed compared with a national average of 19.7% at the time of the survey.

87 Pilkington (2014) also finds that the EDL activist community in the West Midlands is not as young as Bartlett and Littler's findings suggest.

88 His official name is Paul Podromou, but as with Tommy Robinson, for the purpose of this research, I use his chosen name.

89 Tommy Robinson, who was among those held, claimed that he just happened to be in London for his stag do. A group of 15 MFE activists also happened to be the area that day. They had been holding a memorial event for the 7/7 bombings, something that they did each year. They had then gone to the Blind Beggar pub in Whitechapel near to the Waterlily Centre where they had also been picked up by the police. They maintained that they had no connection with the plans to disrupt the Hizb ut-Tahrir event. Whether this was true I do not know – there is no way for me to verify these claims. However, their detention for the afternoon became something of a cause celebre among activists in the area, coming to be referred to as 'the Bromley 15'.

90 A week earlier, EDL activists from the area had attended an annual St. George's Day parade organised by MFE. The march had been disrupted by an assortment of anti-racist and anti-fascist campaigners, some of whom had thrown objects ranging from coins and plastic bottles to horse manure, full drinks cans and glass bottles at the MFE and EDL marchers. On 28th April, when UAF did not turn up, some of the EDL activists turned over a Socialist Worker Party Stall and assaulted the two men attending the stall.

91 Right- and left-wing activists knocking over one another's stalls has been a staple of street politics for several decades. See for example Pearce (2013, 54–55) for an account of such activities in the 1970s.

92 Caroline Quinn, Leeds University, at the time of my fieldwork, and later also Hilary Pilkington, Manchester University.

93 The only exceptions to this were some of the people who had come to the EDL from traditional far right groups, and who by and large showed far less admiration or enthusiasm for the EDL leaders, and two of the younger activists who were both very shy and tended not to speak with more senior activists unless they were introduced to them by other activists whom they already knew.

94 Vigilante groups claiming to that they are acting to impose the Sharia, see for example 'Muslim "vigilantes" confront Londoners in name of Islam', *The Telegraph*, 17th January 2013, www.telegraph.co.uk/news/uknews/law-and-order/9808539/Muslim-vigilantes-confront-Londoners-in-name-of-Islam.html

95 Harris and colleagues (Harris et al. Macklin 2015) make a similar point about Luton.

96 I prefer the term 'anti-Muslim' to 'Islamophobic' because it is more consistent with the language that I would use to talk about mobilisations organised against other groups, that is, I would talk about anti-immigrant protests, anti-semitic protests, anti-Roma protests or more generally anti-minority protests. Using the term 'Islamophobic activism' would also, I believe, hint at a pathologisation of activists (phobias are irrational fears) that would be contrary to my aims in writing this book: I broadly agree with Bowen's (2005) assertion that the term Islamophobia is more 'polemical' than it is analytical (cited in Zúquete 2008, 323).

97 It is important to acknowledge that for some of the activists I knew their focus was very much on 'militant Islam' rather than on Muslims more generally. However, I believe that such activists represented a relatively small proportion of the activist community. It was common during demonstrations, meetings and online conversations to find commentaries about 'muzzies' and 'muzzrats'.

98 Definitional issues are discussed at length by Copsey (2010), Jackson (2011), Kassimeris and Jackson (2015), Pilkington (2014), Pupcenoks and McCabe (2013) and Richards (2013b).

99 As Eatwell (2004, 14) has argued, at best terms such as 'far right' and 'extreme right' comprise 'a convenient but flawed shorthand'.

References

Adib-Moghaddam, A. 2011. *A Metahistory of the Clash of Civilisations: Us and Them Beyond Orientalism.* New York: Columbia University Press.

Adorno, T. W., E. Frenkel-Brunswick, D. Levinson and R. N. Sandford. 1954. *The Authoritarian Personality.* New York: Harper.

Ahmed, S. 2004. "Affective Economies." *Social Text* 22 (2):117–139.

Allen, C. 2010. "Fear and Loathing: The Political Discourse in Relation to Muslims and Islam in the British Contemporary Setting." *Contemporary British Religion and Politics* 2 (4):221–235.

Allen, C. 2012. *A Review of the Evidence Relating to the Representation of Muslims and Islam in the British Media.* Birmingham: Institute of Applied Social Studies, University of Birmingham.

Allen, C. 2013. "Passing the Dinner Table Test: Retrospective and Prospective Approaches to Tackling Islamophobia in Britain." *SAGE Open* 3 (2):1–10.

Archer, T. 2013. "Breivik's Mindset: The Counterjihad and the New Transatlantic Anti-Muslim Right." In *Extreme Right-Wing Political Violence and Terrorism*, edited by M. Taylor, P. M. Currie and D. Holbrook, 169–186. London: Bloomsbury.

Arendt, H. 1951. *The Origins of Totalitarianism.* New York: Harcourt.

Atkinson, P., and M. Hammerlsey. 2007. *Ethnography: Principles in Practice.* 3rd ed. Abingdon: Routledge.

Bail, C. 2012. "The Fringe Effect: Civil Society Organizations and the Evolution of Media Discourse about Islam since the September 11th Attacks." *American Sociological Review* 77 (6):855–879.

Barrett-Fox, R. 2011. "Anger on the Picket Line: Ethnography and Emotion in the Study of Westboro Baptist Church." *Journal of Hate Studies* 9 (1):11–32.

Bartlett, J., and M. Littler. 2011. *Inside the EDL: Populist Politics in a Digital Age.* London: Demos.

Benford, R. D. 1997. "An Insider's Critique of the Social Movement Framing Perspective." *Sociological Inquiry* 67 (4):409–430.

Benford, R. D., and D. A. Snow. 2000. "Framing Processes and Social Movements: An Overview and Assessment." *Annual Review of Sociology* 26:611–639.

Berezin, M. 2001. "Emotions and Political Identity: Mobilizing Affection for the Polity." In *Passionate Politics: Emotions and Social Movements*, edited by J. Goodwin, J. M. Jasper and F. Polletta, 83–98. Chicago: University of Chicago Press.

Billig, M. 1978. *Fascists: A Social Psychological View of the National Front.* London: Academic Press.

Bjørgo, T. 2009. "Processes of Disengagement from Violent Groups of the Extreme Right." In *Leaving Terrorism Behind: Individual and Collective Disengagement*, edited by T. Bjorgo and J. Horgan, 30–48. London: Routledge.

Blake, B. 2011. *EDL: Coming Down the Road.* Birmingham: VHC.

Blee, K. M. 2003. *Inside Organized Racism: Women in the Hate Movement.* Paperback Edition. Berkeley: University of California Press.

Blee, K. M. 2007. "Ethnographies of the Far Right." *Journal of Contemporary Ethnography* 36 (2):119–128.

Blee, K. M. 2012. *Democracy in the Making: How Activist Groups Form*. Oxford: Oxford University Press.

Bonney, R. 2008. *False Prophets: The Clash of Civilizations and the Global War on Terror*. Witney: Peter Lang.

Bourgois, P. 2007. "Confronting the Ethics of Ethnography: Lessons from Fieldwork in Central America." In *Ethnographic Fieldwork: An Anthropological Reader*, edited by A. C. G. M. Robben and J. A. Sluka, 288–297. Oxford: Blackwell.

Bowen, J. 2005. "Commentary on Bunzl." *American Ethnologist* 32 (4):524–525.

Buford, B. 1991. *Among the Thugs*. London: Random House.

Busher, J. 2013. "Anti-Muslim Populism in the UK: The Development of the English Defence League." In *The Changing Faces of Populism: Systematic Challengers in Europe and the U.S.*, edited by H. Giusto, D. Kitching and S. Rizzo, 207–226. Brussels: Foundation for European Progressive Studies.

Busher, J., K. Christmann, G. Macklin, M. Rogerson and P. Thomas. 2014. *Understanding Concerns About Community Relations in Calderdale*. Huddersfield: The University of Huddersfield.

Caiani, M., D. della Porta and C. Wagemann. 2012. *Mobilizing on the Extreme Right: Germany, Italy, and the United States*. Oxford: Oxford University Press.

Calvey, D. 2008. "The Art and Politics of Covert Research: Doing 'Situated Ethics' in the Field." *Sociology* 42 (5):905–918.

Casciani, D. 2009. "Who Are The English Defence League?" *BBC Magazine*, 11th September.

Casquete, J. 2006. "Protest Rituals and Uncivil Communities." *Totalitarian Movements and Political Religions* 7 (3):283–301.

Castells, M. 2012. *Networks of Outrage and Hope: Social Movements in the Internet Age*. Cambridge: Polity Press.

Centre for Contemporary Studies. 1981. *Football and the Fascists*. London: Centre for Contemporary Studies.

Clark, C. 1990. "Emotions and Micropolitics in Everyday Life." In *Research Agendas in the Sociology of Emotions*, edited by T. D. Kemper. Albany: SUNY Press.

Cohen, P. 1988. "The Perversions of Inheritance: Studies in the Making of Multi-Racist Britain." In *Multi-Racist Britain*, edited by P. Cohen and H. S. Bains, 9–118. Basingstoke: Macmillan Education.

Collins, R. 2001. "Social Movements and the Focus of Emotional Attention." In *Passionate Politics: Emotions and Social Movements*, edited by J. Goodwin, J. M. Jasper and F. Polletta, 27–44. Chicago: Chicago University Press.

Collins, R. 2004. *Interaction Ritual Chains*. Princeton, NJ: Princeton University Press.

Copsey, N. 2007. "Changing Course or Changing Clothes? Reflections on the Ideological Evolution of the British National Party, 1999–2006." *Patterns of Prejudice* 41 (1):61–82.

Copsey, N. 2008. *Contemporary British Fascism: The British National Party and the Quest for Legitimacy*. 2nd ed. Basingstoke: Palgrave Macmillan.

Copsey, N. 2010. *The English Defence League: Challenging Our Country and Our Values of Social Inclusion, Fairness and Equality*. London: Faith Matters.

Davies, P. J., and P. Jackson. 2008. *The Far Right in Europe: An Encyclopedia*. Oxford: Greenwood.

della Porta, D. 1995. *Social Movements, Political Violence, and the State: A Comparative Analysis of Italy and Germany*. Cambridge: Cambridge University Press.

della Porta, D. 2008. "Research on Social Movements and Political Violence." *Qualitative Sociology* 31 (3):221–230.

della Porta, D., and M. Diani. 2006. *Social Movements: An Introduction*. Oxford: Blackwell.

della Porta, D., and S. Tarrow. 2012. "Interactive Diffusion: The Coevolution of Police and Protest Behavior with an Application to Transnational Contention." *Comparative Political Studies* 45 (1):119–152.

Demertzis, N., ed. 2013. *Emotions in Politics: The Affect Dimension in Political Tension*. Basingstoke: Palgrave Macmillan.

Denes, N. 2012. "'Welcome to the Counterjihad': Uncivil Networks and the Narration of European Public Spheres." *Journal of Civil Society* 8 (3):289–306.

Denzin, N. K. 2007 [1984]. *On Understanding Emotions*. 2nd ed. New Brunswick: Transaction.

Duffy, B., and D. Lee Chan. 2009. *People, Perceptions and Place*. London: IPSOS Mori.

Eatwell, R. 2004. "Introduction: The New Extreme Right Challenge." In *Western Democracies and the New Extreme Right Challenge*, edited by R. Eatwell and C. Mudde, 1–16. London: Routledge.

Fekete, L. 2004. "Anti-Muslim Racism and the European Security State." *Race and Class* 46:3–29.

Fekete, L. 2009. *A Suitable Enemy: Racism, Migration and Islamophobia in Europe*. London: Pluto.

Fielding, N. G. 1993. "Mediating the Message: Affinity and Hostility in Research on Sensitive Topics." In *Researching Sensitive Topics*, edited by C. M. Renzetti and R. M. Lee, 146–159. Newbury Park: Sage.

Ford, R., and M. J. Goodwin. 2010. "Angry White Men: Individual and Contextual Predictors of Support for the British National Party." *Political Studies* 58 (1):1–25.

Ford, R., and M. J. Goodwin. 2014. *Revolt on the Right: Explaining Support for the Radical Right in Britain*. Abingdon: Routledge.

Futrell, R., and P. Simi. 2004. "Free Spaces, Collective Identity, and the Persistence of US White Power Activism." *Social Problems* 51 (1):16–42.

Gamson, W. A. 1974. "The Limits of Pluralism." In *CRSO Working Papers*. Ann Arbor: The Center for Research on Social Organisation.

Gamson, W. A. 1991. "Commitment and Agency in Social Movements." *Sociological Forum* 6 (1):27–50.

Garland, J., and J. Treadwell. 2012. "The New Politics of Hate? An Assessment of the Appeal of the English Defence League Amongst Disadvantaged White Working-Class Communities in England." *Journal of Hate Studies* 10:123–142.

Githens-Mazer, J. 2010. "Rethinking the Causal Concept of Islamic Radicalisation." In *Political Concepts Working Paper Series*. Exeter: University of Exeter.

Goffman, E. 2009 [1961]. *Asylums: Essays on the Social Situation of Inmates and Other Patients*. New Jersey: Transaction.

Gongaware, T. B. 2003. "Collective Memories and Collective Identities: Maintaining Unity in Native American Social Movements." *Journal of Contemporary Ethnography* 32 (5):483–520.

Goodwin, J., J. M. Jasper and F. Polletta, eds. 2001. *Passionate Politics: Emotions and Social Movements*. Chicago: University of Chicago Press.

Goodwin, J., and S. Pfaff. 2001. "Emotion Work in High-Risk Social Movements: Managing Fear in the U.S. and East German Civil Rights Movements." In *Passionate Politics: Emotions and Social Movements*, edited by J. Goodwin, J. M. Jasper and F. Polletta, 282–302. Chicago: University of Chicago Press.

Goodwin, M.J. 2011. *New British Fascism: Rise of the British National Party*. Abingdon: Routledge.

Goodwin, M.J. 2013. *The Roots of Extremism: The English Defence League and the Counter-Jihad Challenge*. London: Chatham House.

Goodwin, M.J., D. Cutts and L. Janta-Lipinski. 2014. "Economic Losers, Protestors, Islamophobes or Xenophobes? Predicting Public Support for a Counter-Jihad Movement." *Political Studies* [Early View].

Goodwin, M.J., and YouGov. 2013. *Extremism in Britain*. Edited by YouGov. http:// d25d2506sfb94s.cloudfront.net/cumulus_uploads/document/fbvrufy6ra/Dr-Matthew-Goodwin-University-of-Nottingham-YouGov-Survey-Results-Extremism-In-Britain-130526.pdf.

Gould, D.B. 2009. *Moving Politics: Emotion and ACT UP's Fight Against AIDS*. London: University of Chicago Press.

Griffin, N. 2013. *What Lies Behind the English Defence League: Neo-Cons, Ultra-Zionists and Their Useful Idiots*. British National Party.

Harris, G., J. Busher and G. Macklin. 2015. *The Evolution of Anti-Muslim Protest in Two English Towns*. Coventry: Coventry University/The University of Huddersfield.

Hewitt, R. 2005. *White Backlash and the Politics of Multiculturalism*. Cambridge: Cambridge University Press.

Hochschild, A.R. 1979. "Emotion Work, Feeling Rules, and Social Structure." *American Journal of Sociology* 85 (3):551–575.

Huntington, S. 1993. "The Clash of Civilizations?" *Foreign Affairs* 72 (3):22–49.

Jackson, P. 2011. *The EDL: Britain's New 'Far-Right' Social Movement*. Northampton: Radicalism and New Media Group Publications.

Jasper, J.M. 1998. "The Emotions of Protest: Affective and Reactive Emotions In and Around Social Movements." *Sociological Forum*.

Jasper, J.M. 2007. *The Art of Moral Protest: Culture, Biography, and Creativity in Social Movements*. Paperback Edition. London: University of Chicago Press.

Jasper, J.M. 2010. "Social Movement Theory Today: Toward a Theory of Action?" *Sociology Compass* 4 (11):965–976.

Jasper, J.M. 2011. "Emotions and Social Movements: Twenty Years of Theory and Research." *Annual Review of Sociology* 37:285–303.

Jasper, J.M. 2012. "Choice Points, Emotional Batteries, and Other Ways to Find Strategic Agency at the Microlevel." In *Strategies for Social Change*, edited by G.M. Maney, R.V. Kutz-Flamenbaum, D.A. Rohlinger and J. Goodwin, 23–42. Minneapolis: University of Minnesota Press.

John, P., H. Margetts, D. Rowland and S. Weir. 2005. *The Far Right in London*. York: The Joseph Rowntree Reform Trust.

Johnston, H., E. Laraña and J.R. Gusfield. 1994. "Identities, Grievances, and New Social Movements." In *New Social Movements: From Ideology to Identity*, edited by E. Laraña, H. Johnston and J.R. Gusfield, 5–35. Philadelphia: Temple University Press.

Kassimeris, G., and L. Jackson. 2015. "The Ideology and Discourse of the English Defence League: 'Not Racist, Not Violent, Just No Longer Silent'." *British Journal of Politics and International Relations* 17 (1):171–188.

Kemper, T.D. 2004. "Social Models in the Explanation of Emotions." In *Handbook of Emotions*, edited by M. Lewis and J.M. Haviland-Jones, 45–58. New York: The Guildford Press.

Kimmel, M. 2007. "Racism as Adolescent Male Rite of Passage: Ex-Nazis in Scandinavia." *Journal of Contemporary Ethnography* 36 (2):202–218.

Kinnvall, C. 2013a. "Rightwing Nationalism, Counter-Jihad Movements and Radical Islam in Europe." In *The Palgrave Handbook of Global Political Psychology*, edited by T. Capelos, H. Dekker, C. Kinnvall and P. Nesbitt-Larking. London: Palgrave.

Kinnvall, C. 2013b. "Trauma and the Politics of Fear: Europe at the Crossroads." In *Emotions in Politics: The Affect Dimension in Political Tension*, edited by N. Demertzis, 143–166. Basingstoke: Palgrave Macmillan.

Klandermans, B. 1992. "The Social Construction of Protest and Multiorganizational Fields." In *Frontiers in Social Movement Theory*, edited by A.D. Morris and C.M. Mueller, 77–103. New Haven: Yale University Press.

Klandermans, B., and N. Mayer, eds. 2006. *Extreme Right Activists in Europe: Through the Magnifying Glass*. London: Routledge.

Klapp, O.E. 1969. *Collective Search for Identity*. New York: Holt, Rinehart, & Winston.

Klein, M.W. 1995. *The American Street Gang: It's Nature, Prevalence and Control*. Oxford: Oxford University Press.

Kornhauser, W. 1959. *The Politics of Mass Society*. New York: Free Press.

Kriesi, H., R. Koopmans, J.W. Duyvendak and M.G. Giugni. 1995. *New Social Movements in Western Europe: A Comparative Analysis*. London: UCL Press.

Kundnani, A. 2014. *The Muslims are Coming!: Islamophobia, Extremism and the Domestic War on Extremism*. London: Verso.

Lasswell, H.D. 1933. "The Psychology of Hitlerism." *Political Quarterly* 4 (3): 373–384.

Linden, A., and B. Klandermans. 2006. "The Netherlands. Stigmatized Outsiders." In *Extreme Right Activists in Europe: Through the Magnifying Glass*, edited by B. Klandermans and N. Mayer, 172–203. London: Routledge.

Macklin, G. 2015. *White Racial Nationalism in Britain*. Abingdon: Routledge.

Macklin, G., and J. Busher. 2015. "The Missing Spirals of Violence: Four Waves of Movement-Countermovement Contest in Post-War Britain." *Behavioral Studies of Terrorism and Political Aggression* 7 (1):53–68.

Mann, M. 2004. *Fascists*. Cambridge: Cambridge University Press.

Marsh, J. 2010. *From Seasiders to Casuals United*: The Mashed Swede Project.

McAdam, D. 1982. *Political Process and the Development of Black Insurgency, 1930–1970*. Chicago: University of Chicago Press.

McAdam, D. 1983. "Tactical Innovation and the Pace of Insurgency." *American Sociological Review* 48 (6):735–754.

McCarthy, J.D., and M.N. Zald. 1977. "Resource Mobilization and Social Movements: A Partial Theory." *American Journal of Sociology* 82 (6):1212–1241.

Melucci, A. 1988. "Getting Involved: Identity and Mobilization in Social Movements." *International Social Movements Research* 1:329–348.

Melucci, A. 1995. "The Process of Collective Identity." In *Social Movements and Culture*, edited by H. Johnston and B. Klandermans, 41–63. London: UCL Press.

Melucci, A. 1996. *Challenging Codes: Collective Action in the Information Age*. Cambridge: Cambridge University Press.

Minkenberg, M. 2001. "The New Right in France and Germany: Nouvelle Droite, Neue Rechte and the New Right Radical Parties." In *The Revival of Right-Wing Extremism in the Nineties*, edited by P.H. Merkl and L. Weinberg, 65–90. London: Frank Cass.

Mudde, C. 1996. "The War of Words Defining the Extreme Right Party Family." *West European Politics* 19 (2):225–248.

Nepstad, S. E., and C. Smith. 2001. "The Social Structure of Moral Outrage in Recruitment to the U.S. Central America Peace Movement." In *Passionate Politics: Emotions and Social Movements*, edited by J. Goodwin, J. M. Jasper and F. Polletta, 158–174. Chicago: University of Chicago Press.

Oliver, P. E., and D. J. Myers. 2002. "The Coevolution of Social Movements." *Mobilization* 8 (1):1–24.

Pearce, J. 2013. *Race with the Devil: My Journey from Racial Hatred to Rational Love.* Charlotte, North Carolina: Saint Benedict Press.

Pilkington, H. 2014. 'Loud and Proud': Youth Activism in the English Defence League. Report on Work Package 7 of MYPLACE Project. www.fp7-myplace.eu.

Polletta, F. 1999. "'Free Spaces' in Collective Action." *Theory and Society* 28 (1):1–38.

Polletta, F., and J. M. Jasper. 2001. "Collective Identity and Social Movements." *Annual review of Sociology*, 283–305.

Poynting, S., and V. Mason. 2007. "The Resistible Rise of Islamophobia: Anti-Muslim Racism in the UK and Australia Before 11 September 2001." *Journal of Sociology* 43 (1):61–86.

Pupcenoks, J., and R. McCabe. 2013. "The Rise of the Fringe: Right Wing Populists, Islamists and Politics in the UK." *Journal of Muslim Minority Affairs* 33 (2):171–184.

Reger, J. 2002. "More than One Feminism: Organizational Structure and the Construction of Collective Identity." In *Social Movements: Identity, Culture, and the State*, edited by D. S. Meyer, N. Whittier and B. Robnett, 171–184. Oxford: Oxford University Press.

Rhodes, J. 2011. "'It's Not Just Them, It's Whites as Well': Whiteness, Class and BNP Support." *Sociology* 45 (1):102–117.

Richards, B. 2013a. "Extreme Nationalism and the Hatred of the Liberal State." In *Emotions in Politics: The Affect Dimension in Political Tension*, edited by N. Demertzis, 124–142. Basingstoke: Palgrave Macmillan.

Richards, J. 2013b. "Reactive Community Mobilization in Europe: The Case of the English Defence League." *Behavioral Sciences of Terrorism and Political Aggression* 5 (3): 177–193.

Robnett, B. 2004. "Emotional Resonance, Social Location, and Strategic Framing." *Sociological Focus* 37 (3):195–212.

Rydgren, J. 2005. "Is Extreme Right-Wing Populism Contagious? Explaining the Emergence of a New Party Family." *European Journal of Political Research* 44 (3):413–437.

Schrock, D., D. Holden and L. Reid. 2004. "Creating Emotional Resonance: Interpersonal Emotion Work and Motivational Framing in a Transgender Community." *Social Problems* 51 (1):61–81.

Simi, P., and R. Futrell. 2009. "Negotiating White Power Activist Stigma." *Social Problems* 56 (1):89–110.

Simi, P., and R. Futrell. 2010. *American Swastika: Inside the White Power Movement's Hidden Spaces of Hate.* Plymouth: Rowman & Littlefield.

Snow, D. A., and R. D. Benford. 1988. "Ideology, Frame Resonance, and Participant Mobilization." *International Social Movement Research* 1 (1):197–217.

Snow, D. A., and R. D. Benford. 1992. "Master Frames and Cycles of Protest." In *Frontiers in Social Movement Theory*, edited by A. D. Morris and C. McClurg Mueller, 133–155. London: Yale University Press.

Snow, D. A., E. B. Rochford Jr, S. K. Worden and R. D. Benford. 1986. "Frame Alignment Processes, Micromobilization, and Movement Participation." *American Sociological Review* 51 (4):464–481.

Spence, D.P. 1986. "Narrative Smoothing and Clinical Wisdom." In *Narrative Psychology: The Stories Nature of Human Conduct*, edited by T.R. Sarbin. Westport: Praeger.

Stets, J.E., and J.H. Turner, eds. 2007. *Handbook of the Sociology of Emotions*. New York: Springer.

Summers Effler, E. 2010. *Laughing Saints and Righteous Heroes: Emotional Rhythms in Social Movement Groups*. London: University of Chicago Press.

Taylor, M. 2010. "English Defence League: New Wave of Extremists Plotting Summer of Unrest." *The Guardian*, 28th May 2010.

Taylor, V., and N.E. Whittier. 1992. "Collective Identity in Social Movement Communities: Lesbian Feminist Mobilization." In *Frontiers in Social Movement Theory*, edited by A.D. Morris and C.M. Mueller, 104–129. New Haven: Yale University Press.

Thomas, P., M. Rogerson, G. Macklin, K. Christmann and J. Busher. 2014. *Understanding Concerns About Community Relations in Kirklees*. Huddersfield: University of Huddersfield.

Tilly, C. 1978. *From Mobilization to Revolution*. Reading: Addison Wesley.

Tilly, C. 1986. "European Violence and Collective Action since 1700." *Social Research* 53 (1):159–184.

Tilly, C. 2008. *Contentious Performances*. Cambridge: Cambridge University Press.

Treadwell, J. 2013. "The English Defence League and the Counter Jihad." *Criminal Justice Matters* 93 (1):8–9.

Treadwell, J., and J. Garland. 2011. "Masculinity, Marginalization and Violence: A Case Study of the English Defence League." *British Journal of Criminology* 51 (4): 621–634.

Turner, J.H. 2009. "The Sociology of Emotions: Basic Theoretical Arguments." *Emotion Review* 1 (4):340–354.

van Stekelenburg, J., and B. Klandermans. 2013. "The Social Psychology of Protest." *Current Sociology Review* 61 (5):886–905.

van Troost, D., J. van Stekelenberg and B. Klandermans. 2013. "Emotions of Protest." In *Emotions in Politics: The Affect Dimension in Political Tension*, edited by N. Demertzis, 186–203. Basingstoke: Palgrave Macmillan.

Virchow, F. 2007. "Performance, Emotion, and Ideology: On the Creation of 'Collectives of Emotion' and Worldview in the Contemporary German Far Right." *Journal of Contemporary Ethnography* 36 (2):147–164.

Weinberg, L. 1998. "An Overview of Right-Wing Extremism in the Western World: A Study of Convergence, Linkage, and Identity." In *Nation and Race: The Developing Euro-American Racist Subculture*, edited by J. Kaplan and T. Bjørgo, 3–33. Boston: Northeastern University Press.

Wengraf, T. 2001. *Qualitative Research Interviewing*. London: Sage.

Whittier, N. 2004. "The Consequences of Social Movements for Each Other." In *Blackwell Companion to Social Movements*, edited by D.A. Snow, S.A. Soule and H. Kriesi, 531–551. Oxford: Blackwell.

Williams, D., and N. Lowles. 2012. *The 'Counter-Jihad' Movement: The Global Trend Feeding Anti-Muslim Hatred*. London: Hope Not Hate.

Williams, R.H. 1995. "Constructing the Public Good: Social Movements and Cultural Resources." *Social Problems* 42 (1):124–144.

Williams, R.H. 2004. "The Cultural Contexts of Collective Action: Constraints, Opportunities, and the Symbolic Life of Social Movements." In *The Blackwell Companion to Social Movements*, edited by D.A. Snow, S.A. Soule and H. Kriesi, 91–115. Oxford: Blackwell.

Yang, G. 2000. "Achieving Emotions in Collective Action: Emotional Processes and Movement Mobilization in the 1989 Chinese Student Movement." *The Sociological Quarterly* 41 (4):593–614.

Zald, M. N., and R. Ash Gardner. 1987. "Social Movement Organisations: Growth, Decay, and Change." In *Social Movements in an Organizational Society*, edited by M. N. Zald and J. D. McCarthy, 121–141. New Brunswick: Transaction.

Zald, M. N., and J. D. McCarthy. 1979. *The Dynamics of Social Movements: Resource Mobilization, Social Control and Tactics*. Cambridge: Winthrop.

Zald, M. N., and J. D. McCarthy. 1987. "Social Movement Industries: Competition and Conflict Among SMOs." In *Social Movements in an Organizational Society*, edited by M. N. Zald and J. D. McCarthy, 161–181. New Brunswick: Transaction.

Zúquete, J. P. 2008. "The European Extreme-Right and Islam: New Directions?" *Journal of Political Ideologies* 13 (3):321–344.

2　Journeys into EDL activism

Six routes into EDL activism

This chapter is about *how*[1] people became involved with the English Defence
League (EDL). I discuss the social ties associated with the beginnings of their
journeys into activism, their initial engagement with the EDL cause, and the
emotions that they experienced during their initial contacts with the group. Before
doing so, however, it is useful to sketch out the range of different routes that
the people I spent time with had followed into EDL activism. Of course, to some
extent, every activist's route was unique, but there were a number of broadly
definable pathways: via the football hooligan scene, via other self-identifying
patriotic groups, through the traditional far right, through counter-jihad networks,
and what I describe as the 'swerveys' (see below) and the converts (see below).[2]

The football lads: As described in Chapter 1, the EDL emerged at least partly
out of the fringes of the UK's football hooligan scene, and from the outset, the
group's national leadership was dominated by people with a background in football-
related violence. It is not surprising therefore that people from this scene, often
referred to by themselves and fellow activists as 'football lads', also comprised
a significant proportion of the activist community in London and Essex. I estimate[3]
that approximately 30–40% of the core activist community in the area between
March 2011 and May 2012 had entered EDL activism directly from the football-
related public disorder scene, although their involvement waned more quickly
than that of some other segments of the activist community when the group started
to lose momentum in the course of 2011.[4] All of these activists were male. They
ranged in age from teenagers, at least some of whom were still active in football
violence, to older men who had 'retired'[5] from football violence either because
they had grown tired of it and drifted away or as the result of a banning order.
Most of them had had little or no prior involvement with any form of social
movement activism, although there were some who had had a brief involvement
with established far right groups[6] and some who had attended the United British
Alliance (UBA) protests against Abu Hamza in Finsbury Park in 2004.

Those already engaged in 'patriotic'[7] activism: As described in Chapter 1, the
EDL was pre-dated by a number of small self-identifying patriotic groups or
'groupuscules'[8] that had mobilised around similar issue frames and using protest

tactics similar to those that would be taken up by the EDL. This scene included groups such as UBA and March for England (MFE), which, drawing heavily on the football casuals scene, might be seen as prototypes of the EDL. There were also smaller groupuscules. For example, one activist, Andy, described having been part of a group called UK Patriots, a Facebook-based group whose participants did not identify especially with the football scene but sought to mobilise around issues cognate with those of groups such as MFE and UBA. Part of what characterised these groups was their attempt to distance themselves from established far right groups such as the BNP and the NF and their preoccupation with (militant) Islam – although, like the EDL, known far right activists were spotted at a number of their events.[9] The people who had come to EDL activism through these groups were often particularly critical of some of the newer recruits to the cause for their involvement in public disorder incidents during EDL demonstrations (see Chapter 5).[10] I estimate that between February 2011 and May 2012, people who had become EDL activists via such self-identifying patriot groups comprised approximately 10–20% of the activist community in London and Essex. Based on my field observations, discussions with other researchers who have carried out work with the EDL and police intelligence officers, I believe that this figure is considerably higher in London, Essex and the Southeast than in other parts of the country, principally due to the fact that groups such as MFE and UBA were active in this region.

Those coming from traditional far right groups: While there has been considerable antagonism between the national leadership of the EDL and that of established far right groups such as the British National Party (BNP) and the National Front (NF),[11] at the grassroots these supposedly clear organisational boundaries tended to fade. I estimate that approximately 20–30% of core EDL activists in London and the Southeast between February 2011 and May 2012 had come to the EDL via their involvement[12] in established far right groups of one sort or another – in most cases political parties such as the BNP,[13] English Democrats and the NF, and a handful had also been associated with more ideologically and tactically radical groupuscules such as Combat 18. When support for EDL demonstrations began to ebb in the autumn of 2011, people from this segment of the activist community tended to be among the slowest to distance themselves from the EDL, thereby becoming an increasingly significant proportion of the then dwindling activist community.

There was some variation in the extent to which activists who had previously been involved in traditional far right groups continued to identify with such groups and their ideas. Some still identified with them very strongly. As I was coming to the end of my period of fieldwork, Dave kindly offered to introduce me to some 'proper far right people' for my next research project, and on several occasions I saw Jim, one of the few activists I had met who identified himself as 'racist', sneak out a straight-armed salute during demonstrations. Other activists however had sought to disassociate themselves from what they often euphemistically referred to as 'nationalist' groups. For example Tony, a former BNP activist, claimed that part of what had persuaded him to become involved with the EDL was that it was *not* a nationalist group like the BNP, and was one of several former BNP supporters who told me that he had not supported the BNP out of a general ideological affinity but out of hostility towards the main parties and, in his case in particular, because of their Bring the Troops Home campaign (I return to this in more detail below).

Those who entered EDL activism was via the counter-jihad network. People who came to EDL activism through their involvement in this scene – mainly comprising participation in various online discussion forums, but in two cases also attending conferences and small-scale protest events – constituted a very small proportion of the EDL activist community. I estimate that between February 2011 and May 2012, they never amounted to more than about 5% of the activist community. However, these activists exerted considerable ideological influence within the movement, primarily because they were identified by fellow activists as relative experts on (militant) Islam. They were already familiar with and able to talk about prominent counter-jihad authors and their core arguments, and this acted as a form of 'cultural capital'[14] within the anti-Muslim activist scene (see Chapter 3). They were particularly keen to distance themselves from the traditional far right, a fact that later saw them playing a prominent role in the intra-movement arguments that contributed to the unravelling of EDL activism (see Chapter 5).

Swerveys: The activists who came to the EDL through the four routes that I have described above – via the football violence scene, patriotic groups, the traditional far right and the counter-jihad networks – had the greatest influence on what emerged as the EDL movement culture. There were, however, two other routes into the EDL. One of these was the pathway of what I refer to as the swerveys.[15] At first glance, Terry did not seem to fit in the EDL: he dressed more like the people from the assorted anti-racist groups who usually gathered to oppose EDL demonstrations, was a staunch anti-royalist, loved and played blues music, and often dipped into Marxist economic and social theories when explaining his arguments about the global diffusion and threat of Islam.[16] I soon learned that he had been involved in revolutionary socialist politics during his early adult life – something he had fallen into when, after going to listen to Tony Benn speaking at Brixton Town Hall he had found himself in conversation with some radical left-wing activists from a Trotskyite group. He had gradually exited the revolutionary socialist scene when he had a family to raise. About 20 years later, when his daughter was grown up and attending college, he had found himself drawn to the EDL. There were several activists with similar stories. Not all had been involved in radical socialist politics, but they had all been involved in some form of radical[17] political or religious scene other than, and sometimes opposed to, the far right, had for one reason or another left that scene and then connected, sooner or later, with anti-Muslim or 'patriotic' activism.

I estimate that the swerveys comprised around 5% of the core activist community in London and Essex area during 2011–2012. What stood out about these activists was that they were all highly articulate, very engaged with the intellectual arguments swirling around the anti-Muslim protest scene and were prolific contributors to discussions taking place on EDL Facebook pages and the online EDL discussion forum. They and other activists frequently used their prior involvement in other, often overtly anti-racist or anti-fascist, activism to evidence their assertions that neither they nor the EDL were racist or far right (see Chapter 4).

The converts:[18] This, to some extent, is something of an 'other' category comprising people who did not have a background in football violence, traditional far right activism, 'patriotic' mobilisations, counter-jihad activism or some other form of radical political activism. Some of those whom I refer to as converts had been involved in collective social or political action such as supporting animal welfare groups, fundraising for veterans' charities, campaigning on behalf of mainstream political parties or representing a workplace union. Others, from what I was able to ascertain, had never previously engaged in any form of overt political or social movement activism. I estimate that between February 2011 and May 2012, these individuals comprised 20–30% of the core activist community in London and the Southeast. I estimate that the number was considerably higher among the younger activists.

In practice, as I have already intimated above, these are prototypical routes and are not mutually exclusive. For example, several people who had come to the EDL from self-identifying patriotic groups had also been football lads, and while most of these claimed to have retired from football violence – either of their own volition or as a result of a football banning order – they remained networked into this scene. Similarly, as described above, several of the football lads had also dabbled with the far right. Outlining these routes is however useful on two levels. First, it provides a reminder about the heterogeneity of the EDL activist community. The different routes that people had followed into the EDL often shaped their experiences as activists, particularly at the beginnings of their involvement with the EDL.[19] For example, none of the football lads I spoke with expressed a great deal of surprise or alarm about the scale of policing operations that they encountered on their first demonstrations, yet this was a recurring theme among activists who had previously neither been involved in football violence nor participated in large scale protests of any sort. Likewise, while the traditional far right activists all expressed enthusiasm for the EDL as an opportunity to get out on the street, none that I met shared the kind of optimism about the group's prospects that was described to me by some of the people who were new to political activism. Second, these different routes and activists' awareness of these different routes contributed to the crystallisation of sub-groups within the activist community that would later shape patterns of intra-group confrontation.

Activists' social ties

The prominence of recruitment through existing personal networks

> How it started, my two best friends at the time joined the EDL a few months before me, and I knew nothing about it. I used to go on their Facebook, it used to be 'EDL this', and 'Sharia law that' . . . This was getting on my nerves, I

never used to read it. So I went around [to their house] one day and I went, 'What is all this shit about this Sharia law and all of that stuff? You're going to have to educate me because I haven't got a clue'. So she told me all about Sharia law and I was disgusted with some of the things she said about it. I went home, thought about it and started doing a bit of research myself, then I joined the Dagenham Division; she added me to the Dagenham Division.

(Bev)

Originally I got into the EDL through Casuals United, which I joined first, talking to Joe Cardiff[20] who ran it. When we were talking I said I was from London and he said, 'Do you know about the EDL?' He said, 'It's only really just started'. I said 'No, I've not really heard of them'. He said, you know, 'You want to get into them, it sounds like your kind of thing', he said, 'I'll give you the number of a fella called Joel Titus,[21] he's only young but he's a real good bloke. Give him a ring and make a meeting with him'. So I phoned Joel up . . .

(Mark)

Among the EDL activists I knew, three themes relating to their social ties during their journeys into the movement stood out. The first of these concerned the prominence of existing personal ties in their accounts of how they initially entered the group. Research on social movements has long stressed the importance of existing social ties in the process of mobilisation, whether personal ties or ties to other cognate organisations (della Porta and Diani 2006, 114–134, Snow et al. 1986, Snow, Zurcher and Ekland-Olson 1980). Such ties are often particularly important for recruitment into high-risk activism, where prospective activists might anticipate high emotional, reputational, legal, physical or financial costs (Atran 2010, della Porta 1988, McAdam 1986, Nepstad and Smith 1999).[22]

Of the eighteen activists from whom I collected extended activist life-history interviews, only four did not describe existing social ties as playing an important role in their recruitment. Conversations with other members of the local activist community indicate that this may well overestimate the proportion of cases in which prior social ties did not play an important role in their recruitment.[23,24] Among the converts, these ties tended to be personal in nature. Ben, for example, was one of three activists I met who had started going to EDL events with their parent(s); Maggie, an occasional presence at local and regional rather than national demonstrations, had got involved through her husband; Phil had become involved with the EDL when his girlfriend introduced him to some MFE organisers;[25] and as described above, Bev initially came into contact with the EDL through two close friends who were already involved with the group and who often posted information about the group on their personal Facebook pages. Among the other activists, the social ties that featured in stories about their journey into the EDL were usually associated with the various social scenes out of which the EDL had emerged: the traditional far right, the football casuals' network, the patriotic scene and the counter-jihad network.

These personal ties facilitated entry into activism in a number of ways. Most simply, as in the cases of Bev and Mark above, they initially became aware of the group through personal contacts. Andy, for example, recalled how he had first heard about the EDL via the UK Patriots Facebook page – 'someone put a link up one day and it had EDL on it; I clicked on that and I started talking to a few people'. The fact that they received information about the EDL from people that they already knew and trusted and, in many cases, with whom they already had some sense of affinity, helped to persuade prospective activists about the claims being made and made it easier for them to identify with the group (see Passy 2003). Among those who did not identify themselves as far right or racist, it was common for them to make comments about how somebody they knew had been part of the EDL and 'I knew that [name] was definitely not a racist or far right or anything like that, he wouldn't be in a group like that'.[26]

Existing ties also eased prospective activists' first encounters with the EDL. Even some activists who had been part of the football casuals networks or the far right scene described a certain anxiety about attending their first EDL event – would they know anybody there? Would they get on with them? Would the EDL be what they were looking for? Would they feel that they fitted in? Going with somebody already known in the activist community who could introduce them and vouch for them – 'This is [name], a mate of mine, he's alright' – made it a lot easier for new activists to settle in and feel welcomed. On many occasions during the first couple of months of fieldwork I was the person being vouched for, although I was usually presented as 'a researcher' rather than a mate. As the vouched-for person, it was easy for me to imagine how important such introductions had been in helping new activists to feel at home in the scene.

While not necessarily surprising, the prominence of existing ties in people's journeys into EDL activism is interesting on two levels. First, it provides a useful reminder that participation in such groups is at least partly predicted by the social circles in which people move. Patterns of participation in groups like the EDL are to some extent at least socially structured, but this might not be so much about belonging to abstract categories such as 'the white working class' or 'the losers of modernisation' as it is about the micro-structures through which people come into contact and identify with those in groups like the EDL. Second, these existing social ties also facilitated the emergence of bonds of solidarity and intra-group trust, a point which leads me to the next theme.

The ease and speed of entry into the activist community

> I met a few people [at the demonstration], not a lot of people, but I met a few people and then I just got added to the Dagenham Division page and I just took it from there and I just got right involved.
>
> (Bev)

Every activist I spoke with told a similar story of being welcomed at the first demonstration they attended, of being invited to be Facebook friends with more established activists (two older activists who didn't use Facebook had been offered phone numbers), and of quickly finding themselves made to feel part of the activist community. There may be a question here of a sampling bias – I was after all speaking with people who had gone on to become core EDL activists and were therefore likely to have had a positive first experience of contact with the group. However, such accounts were generally borne out by ethnographic observation.[27] At public EDL events, several organisers and more established activists took it upon themselves to speak with newcomers, introducing them to other activists from their local area and encouraging them to make further contact through Facebook.

As well as it being fairly easy to attend public demonstrations and to be added to public Facebook groups, prospective new recruits were also quickly invited to attend less public events such as divisional meetings and social gatherings. Within only a few weeks of their first contact with the EDL, most new recruits were included in what were referred to as 'trusted only' mobile phone communication networks used to organise activities under the police radar. Some had even been asked if they would like to help to run or set up a local EDL division.

Some activists, particularly those who had come to the EDL without prior personal ties into the activist community, reported being 'screened' before they were invited to group meetings. Terry, for example, was invited to meet with a divisional organiser before attending his first meeting and recalled feeling concerned that his appearance and prior involvement in Trotskyite movements might make him unwelcome in the EDL. He observed however that the screening was 'not particularly lengthy', comprising little more than a fairly casual conversation with a local EDL organiser who reassured him that he was not the only person in the group with a past in socialist activism.

In some respects, the ease and speed with which they were accepted into and recognised as part of the activist community may seem surprising. Activists in radical political groups are often gripped by feelings of anxiety and paranoia (Bjørgo 1998, 2011, Clough 2012, Klatch 2004). In some ways the EDL was no different. Within the activist scene there was a swirling fug of rumours about who might or might not be a police informant or a left-wing 'troll' which became increasingly toxic as the EDL started to unravel in the summer and autumn of 2011 (see Chapter 5). Yet somehow this anxiety did not translate into the adoption of more clandestine modes of organisation or into increasingly tightly managed group boundaries.

A number of factors might help to explain this. First, by early 2011, most of the activists that I knew appeared to be somewhat resigned to the fact that they could be identified in any number of videos and images available online, and took it as read that they were under some form of police surveillance. When I first met Kevin Carroll and asked if I could participate in the demonstration he response was: 'Feel free – we've already got police informants here, we know that'. Second, operating as a largely unbounded group offers strategic advantages. EDL activists were acutely aware of the need to attract supporters if they were to command the attention of the media and public authorities. Tightly controlled boundaries would have been incompatible with their aspiration to get several thousands of people out on the street. Third, it is possible that at least to some extent established activists had simply got used to there being a high turnover of people participating in EDL events. It was normal for about 10–30% of the people at any given demonstration to be attending an EDL event for the first time, with the figure towards the higher end of this range for national demonstrations and the lower end for local or regional demonstrations.[28] Fourth, and perhaps most importantly, most activists sincerely believed that they had nothing or at least very little to hide. Although the identities that they constructed for themselves often centred on their imagined bravery and heroism and the fact that they were among the few willing to speak out in order to save the nation (Busher 2013, Treadwell and Garland 2011), they also saw themselves as 'ordinary English people' who used primarily legal methods of protest to get their point across (see Chapter 4). As one contributor put it during a Facebook discussion about whether a former activist might have been a police informant:

> . . . Anyway we don't do anything wrong but challenge militant Radical scum so hopefully if he was plod he might have put a good word in for us lol.[29]

The relative absence of social bridge-burning on entry

A third theme relating to the activists' social ties concerns the general absence of social bridge-burning by new activists. Research on socialisation into radical political movements often describes a process by which, as people become activists and forge bonds of solidarity within the group they also increasingly loosen and in some cases entirely cut off previous social contacts (Blee 2003, Bjørgo 2009, Husain 2007, Klatch 2004, Wasmund 1986). This kind of bridge-burning has a number of functions: it may help to maintain security, facilitates immersion in the world-view of the group and reinforces in-group solidarity and identification;[30] it also raises the cost of leaving by making the group the centre of the activist's social and personal life (Miller McPherson, Popielarz and Drobnic 1992). What is interesting about people's journeys into EDL activism is that this kind of bridge-burning was not prevalent.

Standing outside Abu Qatada's house during a flash demonstration on 17th November 2012, I mentioned to Debbie that one of the things I was interested in was how EDL activism affected participants' everyday lives. She laughed and exclaimed 'When you join the EDL it takes over your life!' Her comment was echoed by every other core activist I spoke with. Most estimated that they spent between ten and 35 hours a week on EDL business such as planning, preparing for and attending demonstrations and meetings, leafleting, making promotional materials, researching and posting relevant news stories on their Facebook page, managing divisional Facebook pages, and scouring national and local newspapers for 'EDL issues' to mobilise around. On top of this there was the social side of activism. Becoming involved in the EDL entailed new friendships, social events and many hundreds of hours exchanging all manner of stories, images, jokes, grievances and gossip on Facebook. This inevitably meant that the EDL increasingly became the focal point of the activists' social life, often at the expense of other relationships. A minority of activists reported that their participation in the EDL had created strains and stresses in their relationships with friends and neighbours, in the workplace and even at home. Joe was one of several activists who claimed to have lost his job as a result of his involvement in the EDL:[31] having been spotted wearing a company jumper on an EDL demonstration, he was asked to leave the company on the grounds of jeopardising its reputation. Pete described how several of his friends at college had distanced themselves from him since he had told them that he was involved in the EDL, and several other activists spoke about family members expressing disapproval of their association with the group.[32]

What the activists did not encounter however, at least in the cases that I was able to observe, was any encouragement of, let alone insistence on, bridge-burning on the part of other activists. I never encountered stories of EDL activists being told that they should, let alone had to, sever ties with work colleagues, friends or family due to their religious or political beliefs. It was also common for activists who had come to the EDL through participation in other political or social movement groups to continue to associate with those groups *as well as* the EDL, placing more emphasis on their association with one group or another at different times, depending on the specific situation. For example, most people who had come to EDL activism via MFE continued to identify themselves as MFE activists, even when marching under an EDL banner. The same applied to affiliation with groups such as Casuals United. It was not uncommon for somebody to have both a Casuals United t-shirt and an EDL hoodie. Such identities only started to rub against one another when, during the spring of 2011, rumours started circulating of friction between the Luton-based EDL leaders and the Casuals United leadership (see Blake 2011) and as the EDL began to lose momentum and fragment in the summer and autumn of 2011 (see Chapter 5). Similarly one long-term BNP (and prior to that, NF) activist observed to me that he knew that as a BNP activist, he was not supposed to attend EDL demonstrations and vice-versa but that this was of little concern to him; and nor did it seem to be of much concern to the other people attending EDL events, most of whom were well aware of his political affiliations, provided that he did not start chanting 'BNP' during EDL events.

As well as reiterating the idea that the EDL comprised what Bjørgo (2009) would describe as a largely 'unbounded' group,[33] this absence of bridge-burning also points to the fact that there was scant impulse within the EDL activist community to isolate themselves socially from their wider social and political milieux, a point that I will return to in the following two chapters.

Activists' initial engagement with the EDL cause

The second aspect of people's journey into EDL activism concerns their engagement with the EDL cause – what we might call their ideological engagement. Not surprisingly, all the activists I knew were keen to talk with me about their cause, and when asked directly about *why* they had become involved in the EDL, they usually reeled off various lengthy commentaries about what they saw as the cultural and security threats posed to *their* country, culture or way of life,[34] primarily by militant Islam, or about how 'ordinary English people' were being ignored by the political elite. These were straightforward stories of activism proceeding from common feelings of injustice. However, once I started asking activists to narrate their journeys into the EDL step by step, a more complex picture began to emerge.

The EDL as a 'lightning rod'[35] for different interests

What quickly became clear was that, once beyond generic and much repeated statements about believing in the need to defend or preserve their culture, there was considerable variation in terms of how the activists described what it had been about the EDL protest narrative that had initially resonated with them. For example, Steve, one of the older members of the group, described having had an interest in English heritage and local history for some time before coming into contact with the EDL and was one of several activists who spoke about his initial attraction to the group in terms of the opportunities it offered to claim and celebrate his national identity. He described his first encounter with the EDL as follows,

> I was on the Internet one day and, er, I came across the English Defence League and thought 'Who are they?' I thought I was the only person in this country that was proud to be English, and I've always said it – I'm an Englishman, I'm not anything else but English, that's my country, that's my birthright and I thought 'Oh hold on a minute – who are these?'
>
> (Steve)

It was only since coming into contact with the EDL that he had developed a keener interest in the issue of (militant) Islam and Islamisation. John, by contrast, claimed that nationalism, England and Englishness had little to do with his involvement. He did not even consider himself particularly 'patriotic' and never joined in the 'Ing-er-land!' chants during demonstrations. In fact, he didn't particularly like that aspect of EDL activism. His connection with the EDL cause had been via an interest he had developed in the precarious social and political position of Christians in a number of Muslim-majority countries; an interest that he had partly developed through contact with the counter-jihad networks. He was particularly taken by the writings of Ali Sina, an Iranian ex-Muslim,[36] the founder of Faith Freedom Initiative, a well-known counter-jihad website, and a board member of Pamela Geller's Stop Islamization of Nations. He had forged friendships with Christians in Lebanon and Egypt and set up a Facebook group called EDL Persecuted Christians Living under Islam. Meanwhile, although Terry described a deep sense of personal national attachment – the entrance to his home was dominated by an English flag, and he explained how he always liked to have a flag with him, even if it was only as a pin-badge – he was keen to frame his nationalism not only as a celebration of his own nation but also as a more abstract commitment to nations as a bulwark against the supra-national diffusion of Islam. Like John, what had resonated with Mark was the idea of a global struggle against Islam, but unlike John he saw this as a struggle between secularism and religion rather than between Christianity and Islam.[37] Even though he considered Islam a particularly unpleasant belief system – 'I consider it to be the most vile, evil doctrine that exists so far in the history of mankind' – he identified himself as a militant atheist, explaining that 'for all of my life, religion has been my enemy and I detest *all* religions' (his emphasis).

Similarly, most activists I met, among them the majority of the London leadership, claimed to have been attracted to the EDL precisely because of the narrowness of its focus on (militant) Islam and the fact that it explicitly claimed not to be a racist or far right group – several were keen to describe how their anxiety about mixing with 'racists' and 'hooligans' had soon dissipated when they met 'just ordinary people' on EDL demonstrations. Some activists, however, hankered for a wider platform. One of the reasons Andy was so enthusiastic about plans in the autumn of 2011 to forge a loose alliance with the British Freedom Party (see Chapter 5) was, he told me as Kevin Carroll delivered a speech at a demonstration in Luton in May 2012, that he believed it would give people like Carroll the opportunity to talk about a wider set of issues, including immigration. Some of those who had come to the EDL from the traditional far right also lamented the EDL's insistence on positioning itself as a non-racist group. The second time I spoke at length with Jim he remarked 'I don't agree with everything the EDL says'. When I asked him what he didn't agree with and whether he could give me an example of anything specific, he responded 'Well, they say that they're not racist, but I am a racist – at least that's what they call it these days. I like living with other white people, with other British people'. The reason he was attending EDL events was that they were 'the only people doing anything'.

Over time these different interests did converge, but only to a limited extent. In Chapter 3, I explore how the EDL was able to accommodate people with these apparently difficult to reconcile interests and identities, and in Chapter 5, I discuss how these points of ideological tension developed into sites of intra-movement conflict during the course of 2011.

The role of critical events in processes of ideological engagement

A second point where there was considerable variation across the activists' accounts of how they had connected with the EDL cause concerned the role of critical events in their journeys. I met some activists who traced their involvement with the EDL back to specific traumatic events in their own lives. Pete was 18 years old when I interviewed him. From an Irish traveller background, he had spent a large proportion of his life in east London and had close friends with black and minority ethnic backgrounds – as he pointed out, growing up where he did, it would have been difficult not to have such friends. He reported one or two run-ins with young people of South Asian background: he and some friends, not all of whom were white, had been attacked and beaten up by what he described as 'a group of Asian lads' while playing football. But he was adamant that these incidents had not led him towards the EDL. He pointed out that he had also had run-ins with young people of other ethnic and religious backgrounds, including being mugged by white English lads, but saw this just as part of having grown up where he did. The event he identified as moving him to make contact with the EDL had taken place a few months before our interview. He and his grandmother had noticed that his sister had become quiet and uncommunicative. Initially she was unwilling to talk about what was upsetting her and they became increasingly concerned. Eventually, however, she explained that she was feeling harassed by encounters with a young Muslim man on the bus to school who had been telling her that she should convert to Islam. The next day, Pete caught the bus with his sister, sat a couple of rows behind her and waited for the young man. When he arrived and started talking to his sister Pete confronted him. He maintained that it was not a violent confrontation: that he simply told the young man to stop pestering his sister. He had heard about the EDL a few weeks earlier when they held a demonstration in his neighbourhood. Shortly after this incident, he contacted his local division via Facebook.

Tony's story was inextricably bound up with the death of his son in Afghanistan. Tony was in his 40s, and he too had grown up in the East End of London. As a young man, he had had little interest in politics, being far too busy trying to make ends meet and raise a family, although he had a friend of many years who did some campaigning for the BNP. From time to time, he had helped this friend to fold campaign leaflets, but nothing more, 'I wasn't interested'. Tony's life changed when his son joined the armed forces. Looking back, he mused:

> Before [my son signed up and went to Afghanistan] we were an average family going about our own thing . . . but when the events happen like that, the reality comes real, this is actually happening. 'Course you wish this was just a dream, that you can just wake up and that's a bad old dream: it's not. You feel different and you think different.

When the BNP started its Support Our Troops, Bring Them Home! campaign, it 'just struck a chord – on a personal level' and for a short while Tony was a BNP activist. He claimed that he didn't agree with everything they said, but 'who does agree with everything their party says?'[38] His focus was on his son. When his son was killed his own life started to unravel: he had to leave work, his family fell apart, he left the BNP and largely cut himself off from the outside world. However, 'as time went on I went back on the computer'. He came across the EDL while browsing the Internet, watched several videos about them and was interested in what they might have to offer. He didn't want to go back to the BNP and what he referred to as 'nationalism', but did want to do something that he felt would honour his son. When he heard that the EDL was holding a demonstration in Dagenham not far from where he lived, he decided to go and observe it from the other side of the street. During the course of the day, he got talking to some of the local EDL activists, and things progressed from there.

Pete and Tony's stories are striking and moving. They were important not only for their personal journeys into EDL activism, but also for the wider activist community insofar as they became potent symbolic material that all the activists could make use of. Tony's son and Pete's sister were the kind of 'innocent victim' of (militant) Islam around which the EDL's protest narrative has been built,[39] and activists who featured in such stories acquired a form of celebrity status within the activist scene. The fact that activists were able to trace a clear relationship from themselves to these victims – 'my mate's son', 'my mate's sister' – accentuated both the credibility and the emotional force of the claims that these events were used to make about the supposed threat of (militant) Islam. Such stories were few and far between, however.

Far more common were two rather different types of story. The first of these, told to me by a little under half of the activists with whom I spoke on a regular basis, was of activists tracing their engagement with the EDL cause back to specific public events that had functioned as the kind of 'moral shock'[40] which social movement researchers have posited as possible catalysts for participation in political or social movement activism even when people don't have social ties that might facilitate engagement (see Jasper and Poulsen 1995). Four events in particular were frequently cited as starting points for their eventual engagement with the EDL: the attack on New York of 11th September 2001; the London bombing on 7th July 2005; an event in Barking on 15th June 2010 when, similar to the incident in Luton that had triggered the United People of Luton (UPL) demonstrations, approximately 25 Muslims Against Crusades (MAC) activists gathered to heckle a homecoming parade by British soldiers of the Royal Anglian Regiment;[41] and an incident in London on 11th November 2010 when MAC activists burnt three remembrance poppies at a public Remembrance ceremony.[42]

The first two events, which predated the emergence of the EDL, were described by several of the activists as moments that prompted them to start 'doing their research'.[43] The importance of the second two events was also underlined during conversations with senior activists in the area. Organisers in east London and Essex in particular saw the events in Barking on 15th June as the moment when the EDL activist community 'really came together' in the area, while several activists including Jack, the London RO at the time, told me that the poppy-burning incident had 'really launched us in London; it just took off'.[44,45]

However, approximately half the activists with whom I conversed on a regular basis told me another type of story, one in which they were unable, or perhaps reluctant, to identify any particular event as a key moment.[46] Their accounts of coming to feel a connection to the EDL cause were not so much stories of moments of moral shock as of activism born out of chronic moral outrage nourished by anecdotes about shops in their area changing and pubs closing down; rumours about a neighbour being asked to take down his St. George's flag; recurrent news stories about the extent of anti-Western sentiment among radical

Muslims; reading about the plight of Coptic Christians in Egypt and Lebanon, mutterings about immigrants taking jobs and benefits and wilfully not fitting in, and of course references to the Taliban and Al-Qaeda. Lofland and Skonovd (1983, 9) encourage us to be cautious about slipping into 'the fallacy of the uniformly profound' – whereby 'if someone makes a dramatic change of life-orientation . . . we are likely to feel that there must be equally dramatic, deep and strong forces which have brought it about'. The stories of a large proportion of the EDL activists I knew suggest that we would do well to bear this in mind. As Blee (2003, 33) observes, 'dramatic political outcomes', such as the decision to dedicate one's time to organised anti-minority activism, can have 'quite mundane beginnings'.

Levels of ideological engagement
on entry into the EDL

A third issue concerns the timing of the activists' engagement with the EDL cause in relation to the beginning of their journeys into activism. There were some who had a fairly high level of what we might call 'ideological proficiency' (Fangen 1998) when they first came into contact with the EDL. As might be expected, this applied particularly to activists who came to the EDL with a background in the counter-jihad network, but was also the case for most of the swerveys and those who had come to the EDL via their involvement in the smaller patriotic groups. Terry and John, for example, both reported having spent several months taking a growing interest in what they would eventually think of as EDL issues prior to making contact with the group. John was already interested in and reading up on ideas about the threat posed by Islamisation when, while browsing online, he first came across an interview given by the leaders of the then newly formed EDL in 2009. Prior to engaging with the EDL, Terry was already visiting counter-jihad sites and reading critiques of Islam by people such as Sam Harris and Robert Spencer (see Chapter 3).

More common, however, were stories such as Steve's and Bev's. While Steve was already interested in issues about local heritage and patriotism when he came into contact with the EDL, as described above, he only started looking into issues about Islam and militant Islam after he became involved with the EDL in 2009. Even in 2011 when I met him he described himself as being 'just a novice', and spoke appreciatively of other activists whom he considered 'really know their stuff'. Bev was one of several activists who by her own admission had thought very little and known even less about Islam, militant or otherwise, until about a month before becoming involved in the EDL. She had had some general concerns about the way the country was changing and the futures of her children and grandchildren – 'like anyone really' – but she couldn't recall particular concern about (militant) Islam. She first heard about the EDL via friends; one of her best friends and the friend's husband were involved in the group and were always 'banging on about Islam this and EDL that'. Eventually she decided to ask them to tell her more about the group, prompted by the fact that the EDL had held a demonstration in her local high street and were planning another in the near future. After talking with them over a cup of tea she followed up a couple of the websites that they had recommended and was shocked at what she read. As there was a protest taking place locally, she decided to go along and find out more about the group. On the demonstration she met several activists who were very welcoming – 'Really, you know, not like the hooligans and racists you read in the newspapers' – who had Facebook-friended her and added her to the local EDL division's Facebook page. It was only after this event that she 'started reading all sorts of things'[47] and really began to engage with the EDL cause. Bev was far from alone in telling a story like this. In other words, at least prior to involvement in the EDL, many would-be activists' political ideas were neither particularly developed nor sometimes even especially radical.[48]

The emotions associated with entry into EDL activism: beyond outrage, anger and fear

> I think on one of them Muslim websites [further questioning indicates it was probably the MAC website], I was reading one of them and it said, 'Don't forget about the Holocaust – you haven't seen anything yet'. You know what I thought, 'You bunch of bastards'. That done me, and I thought no, that's horrible because that holocaust was fucking atrocious.
>
> (Bev)

The third aspect of people's journeys into EDL activism concerns the emotions associated with entry into the group and its social scene. As might be expected, EDL activists' explanations of their decisions to become involved with the group were almost always at least to some extent tales of outrage and indignation,[49] fear and anger – about how their 'mum doesn't feel safe in her own neighbourhood anymore' (Mark), how the schools were teaching their children more about Islam than they were about English culture, how the culture of 'political correctness' was ruining the country, how they had felt incensed when they saw images of people shouting at and threatening British military personnel, fears that 'in 50 years' time my grandchildren will be wearing burkas' (Bev) and so forth. Such emotions have often been identified as conducive to processes of mobilisation (Castells 2012, Jasper 2014, Jasper and Poulsen 1995, van Troost, van Stekelenberg and Klandermans 2013), and such emotions and their conversion into hatred have been closely associated with anti-minority activism (Futrell and Simi 2004, Simi and Futrell 2010, Virchow 2007, among many others). In the following two chapters, I discuss at length these emotions and how they were generated, sustained and amplified.

There were however other more positive emotions that featured in people's accounts of their journey into the EDL and that provide us with valuable clues as to what it was that attracted people to EDL activism. Four positive emotional themes in particular stood out: the 'buzz' of demonstrations, feelings of belonging, feelings of pride, and feelings of agency and possibility.[50] To some extent these themes come as no great surprise. While there was a period during the 1970s and 1980s when social movement researchers tended to shy away from talking about the emotions associated with the act of protest – largely in an attempt to emphasise the rational aspects of protest and as a reaction to the descriptions of impulsive and irrational crowd behaviour inspired by people such as LeBon (1960 [1895]) and Blumer (1951) – today many researchers working on social movements highlight how the emotional intensity associated with protest events contributes to processes of generating and sustaining mobilisation (Collins 2001, Gould 2009, Häberlen and Spinnet 2014, Virchow 2007). Similarly, feelings of belonging associated with achieving collective identities have long been identified by social movement researchers as one of the attractions of activism (Hunt and Benford 2004, Klandermans and Mayer 2006): Goodwin et al. (2001, 9) go so far as to propose that 'strong feelings for the group' can 'make participation pleasurable in itself, independently of the movement's ultimate goals and outcomes'. Feelings of exercising agency and confidence have also been identified as 'one of the deepest satisfactions of collective action' (Jasper 2011, 8, see also Summers Effler 2010, Wood 2001). For some theorists, such as Castells (2012), perceptions of efficacy and attendant feelings of hope are a necessary prerequisite for mobilisation.[51] Feelings of pride, and the conversion of feelings of shame into pride, have also often been identified both as a common emotional reward for activism and as an emotion that may be particularly important in catalysing and sustaining participation (Gould 2002, Jasper 2010, Scheff 1994, Whittier 2001, 2012) – indeed, other than hate, anger and fear, pride is one of the emotions that most often features in academic accounts of mobilisations associated with far right, or more general backlash politics (Fangen 1998, Goodwin 2011, 153–170, Pilkington 2014). It is however useful to elaborate on the specific contours of these emotions in the context of the beginnings of would-be activists' journeys into the EDL.

The 'buzz' of demonstrations

Bev: [When we got back from the demonstration in Tower Hamlets] we all got off the coach at the [pub name] down in Dagenham and we all went in the pub. We were all on such a high, no one wanted that day to end. Even when I was going home at eleven o'clock, I still didn't want to go home because I wanted to be with them all still and it was just the best feeling ever. I couldn't stop talking. [Shifting excitedly in her seat and becoming increasingly animated] I went home and I was like, 'Yeah, this, that and the other!' I was like a nutty woman; I just didn't want to go to bed. You know, if I could have paid to do that again the next day I would have done it.

Susan: I'm getting excited just thinking about it.

Bev: That was, my highlight was that probably, it was just the nuts.

Every person I talked to about their journey into EDL activism spoke about the excitement or the 'buzz' of the demonstrations. National demonstrations in particular could provide highly charged days out. Activists from the same town or borough generally travelled together to the event, and during the journey, the mood was usually buoyant, almost festive, as if they were going to a football match. Conversations were punctuated by outbursts of singing and flag-waving until, on arriving at whichever town the demonstration was taking place in, the activists caught the first glimpses of police motorbikes or, if travelling by train, the British Transport Police. At this point the mood would change to one of a mixture of apprehension and nervous excitement. At the rendezvous point the mood would pick up again, with activists milling around, many drinking, arms draped around the shoulders of fellow-activists posing for photographs and a hum of chitchat and banter.

The announcement of the beginning of the march always generated a wave of adrenaline that coursed through the crowd. There would be chanting, singing and clapping and an almost palpable frisson of expectation of what was to come. There was considerable variation across the activists in terms of how they participated in the demonstration rituals. Some drank heavily and some took cocaine, while others preferred to remain drug- and alcohol-free; some chanted and sang, others walked quietly holding their placards or taking photographs of what was going on around them; some listened intently to the speeches, while others busied themselves with their own conversations; some sought ways of getting past the police line, while others readily complied with the directions of the event stewards and police; some sought to goad and antagonise their opponents, and others encouraged their fellow activists to ignore them; some played up to cameras pointed in their direction, shouting and sneering, but others shied away from the limelight; some described quite bluntly how they saw the EDL as an opportunity to 'go and kick off' against 'Muzzies' or 'lefties',[52] while others were anxious about and sought to avoid physical confrontations.[53] Common to all the activists however were references to 'the buzz' of these events.

The confrontations (which did not usually entail direct physical contact) between EDL activists and counterdemonstrators provided some of the moments of greatest emotional intensity. Even some of those who spent much of the day talking quietly and calmly, of whom there were plenty, at least in the Essex and London Divisions, broke off their conversations to participate in these moments of collective invective. It was at these points, when the crowd was at its most volatile or in the immediate aftermath of demonstrations as the activists dispersed, that public disorder was most likely to occur.

Yet it was not only these encounters and their concomitant feelings of indignation, outrage and anger that comprised the 'buzz' of demonstrations: as Blee (2007) and Virchow (2007) note, even in the context of some of the most far right groups collective action is characterised by a complex array of different emotions that extend well beyond anger or hate. Shared protest rituals – the singing, chanting, marching together or the minute's silence generated moments of emotionally charged 'collective effervescence' (Durkheim 1915). During speeches, it was not uncommon to see activists welling up. I remember at one of the earlier demonstrations I attended in Blackpool being struck by what at the time seemed to me a rather surprising image of two male skinheads with arms around each other and tears in their eyes listening to a speech by the sister of Charlene Downes, the Blackpool girl whose death had become a focus of attention for the EDL, Casuals United and the BNP.[54] Activists also experienced feelings such as the satisfaction at 'getting one over'[55] their various opponents or the police. Accounts of EDL demonstrations were laced with gleefully told anecdotes of minor triumphs and amusement at mishaps that had befallen their opponents – how they had managed to commandeer a police helmet during a melee and have their photograph taken wearing it; how they had caught the police unaware by going to another town for a drink en route to a formal demonstration;[56] how a co-activist had managed to wind up MAC activists by infiltrating their pen[57] and jumping up and down amongst them waving two Union Jacks; how a group of young EDL activists had managed to 'slip past' Scotland Yard on the morning of a demonstration in Tower Hamlets in spite of major police effort to keep activists concentrated in a handful of rendezvous points; or the look of blind panic on the face of two anti-EDL activists in Cardiff who realised all of a sudden that the EDL activists that they had been taunting actually were not, as they had believed, safely behind either a barrier or police cordon. On the way home and in the days following the event, activists resuscitated these emotions, exchanging photographs and anecdotes, both offline and online.

It is worth noting however that while the 'buzz' of these events was described by almost all the activists as having been one of the attractions of the EDL, as the EDL started to fragment during the summer and autumn of 2011, the fact that some people were seen to treat these events as 'a bit of a jolly'[58] became a source of concern and tension within some sections of the EDL activist community (see Chapter 5).

Feelings of belonging and solidarity

> I recall heading in the direction of the meeting point for the demo, turning the corner and seeing a pub with the crosses of St George flying proudly in the air. And the effect on me was instantaneous and I felt totally at home in the situation. I walked into a pub that I'd never been to before that was absolutely packed with people I'd been told were violent thugs and racists and so on. But once I saw the flags and felt the atmosphere and the feeling of the people there, I just felt totally at home, in every sense.
>
> (Terry)

How the activists explained their initial feelings of identification with the EDL varied from person to person, largely as a function of their sense of personal identity when they first came into contact with the group. For example, activists who did not identify with the far right, such as Terry and Bev (above), emphasised how important it had been to them that the EDL did not look like 'violent thugs and racists'. This was not the case for those who did identify with the far right. Similarly, several of the football lads referred to how they had felt at home with the EDL once they saw that there were some 'proper lads' involved with the EDL, while activists such as Andy, a middle-aged professional who was always keen to dissociate himself from football violence, emphasised the presence at his first demonstrations of people who, to his mind, helped to make the EDL a more respectable group:

> You know we actually walked down towards Parliament Square and I was with a load of city guys! I don't know what organisation they came from but they had like morning dress on, they had the black tie and the grey pinstripe trousers, I don't know, maybe one of the financial organisations, I don't know what but there were six or seven of them and they were very bright lads, and I was quite impressed that, you know, amongst all these pissed up northerners there were these six guys and there was an old Jewish woman and there was this incredible mix of people. There was a couple of black guys, a couple of Asian guys.
>
> (Andy)

Common to every activist's account of their journey into EDL activism however was a description of an initial sense of identity compatibility with the group followed quickly by a sense of solidarity with fellow activists.[59] The initial feelings of belonging with the EDL could have multiple bases. To some extent, they were associated with a sense of finding like minds with similar beliefs and interests,[60] as described for example by Steve, the activist who was so pleased to find a protest group mobilising around notions of Englishness and the need to preserve English culture. Yet the bases of these feelings were also more diffuse than that, particularly initially. As in Terry's description above of feeling 'totally at home' in the situation, it was often just as much about somehow feeling comfortable with the people, the surroundings and the shared formal and informal rituals – the chants and songs, but also the drinking culture and the tenor of the interactions between activists – that characterised EDL events. In fact, one of the characteristics of the EDL that seems to have facilitated recruitment is the extent to which it was culturally accessible to the broad demographic to which it sought to appeal. The protest rituals and the 'tie signs' (Goffman 1971) – the songs, the flag-waving, the minutes of silence, the clothing, the pub culture – all felt familiar because they imitated and appealed to already-established cultural practices and norms for most of the people who became involved in the group. The EDL songs were mainly adaptations of football chants already known to most new recruits;[61] the verbal register was more or less that of their everyday lives, with everyone 'mate' or 'bruv'; the aesthetic of the activist community largely imitated that of the football casuals scene; and the core symbols used to mark the in-group – such as the St. George's flag, remembrance poppies and crusader knights – were already the focus of strong affective attachments. Most activists would have bought and felt moved wearing their remembrance poppy for years and would at some point have had the St. George flag painted on their faces, tattooed on their arms or wrapped around them as they watched football.

This was some way removed from adopting the Nordic runes or adorning one's person with the deeply stigmatised symbols of the Third Reich that often act as 'tie signs' for people in some of the most extreme right-wing groups.

What helped to thicken these initial feelings of identity compatibility into feelings of solidarity was partly the simple fact that new recruits quickly accumulated shared experiences with other activists (see Chapters 3 and 5). As I have described above, new recruits soon found EDL activism taking up a growing proportion of their day-to-day lives. As well as demonstrations, there was the social side of activism – the often boozy meetings and social events, and the ongoing Facebook communication through which they quickly established personal ties with other activists. These nascent relationships with co-activists were not only about drinking and general raucousness. Several activists spoke about how the people they met through the EDL had come to provide them with a much-valued support network. Tony, for example, whose son had been killed in Afghanistan, spoke with deep emotion about how EDL activists in his area had supported him at that difficult time in his life. He remained convinced that the Ministry of Defence and the local authorities were wary of him due to his prior involvement with the BNP, whereas he had been welcomed even at his first EDL demonstration. He appreciated tremendously the fact that he could 'pop round, sit around and have a chat' with some of his fellow activists. While Tony's story was exceptional due to the depth of the tragedy that he had experienced, the feeling that the EDL, and particularly the local division, provided a tight support network was common to most activists, with the exception of some of the older established far right activists who tended to move primarily in their own circles. Most people had a story to tell about the emotional and in some cases financial support that had at some point been afforded to them by their co-activists.

What also helped to consolidate feelings of belonging was the way that new recruits could quickly acquire status within the activist community.[62] Almost every person who had been with the EDL for more than a couple of months had some kind of formal role, whether it was as an admin of their local division or an organiser of one of the special-interest divisions. Beyond these there was a host of semi-formal or informal roles. One activist with a passion for photography and a willingness to put herself in the middle of things if and when trouble arose was identified as the group photographer; another, who sang and played guitar, volunteered their skills as a songwriter; a tattoo artist contributed graphic design skills and knowhow; an activist who had worked in the pub trade arranged meeting venues and music; a handful of activists with a reputation for having studied more than most about Islam and militant Islam provided information, advice and arguments to others to help in their campaigns (see Chapter 3); and some younger 'lads' took on the role of providing security for some of the older activists.[63] This helped to promote feelings of self-worth among activists and cultivate a perception that their movement was characterised by bonds of mutual respect,[64] a theme I return to several times during the next four chapters.

Feelings of collective agency and possibility

> We're challenging our governments! We're challenging local councils! We're challenging the local community leaders!
>
> (Tony)

In 2009 and 2010, when most of the activists that I knew had taken their first steps into EDL activism, the EDL felt like a movement that, as several put it, was 'going somewhere', or at least had more chance of going somewhere than other groups mobilising around similar issues. To some extent, this sense of momentum was simply a function of the number of people that the EDL was able to mobilise.[65] For example, recalling his early optimism about the group, Mark told me:

> One thing that surprised me about [the demonstration in] Manchester was the numbers. I mean there was like two to three thousand,[66] I would have thought, at Manchester. Now that was an early demo [10th October 2009] and you thought to yourself, 'EDL has apparently only just started, and we're getting this many people at a demo: give it a year, it'll be massive'.

The scale of the EDL's support helped to make the group attractive to people in established far right groups, small patriot groups and the counter-jihad network, many of whom had spent months or even years feeling frustrated by their group's inability to generate anything similar. As described above, Jim, a former BNP and NF activist, had been drawn to the EDL because it seemed to him like 'the only group doing anything', while Andy, who had been running the UK Patriots Facebook group, decided to get involved with the EDL after taking part in a particularly poorly-attended UK Patriots event – 'I turned up and there was only 30 people there . . . then I kind of worked out that the only people that were going to have the numbers to do things, to do events like that, were going to be the EDL'.

What helped to accentuate these perceptions of the EDL's support was the growth of the EDL's Facebook following and various rumours of wider support networks that were circulated both by members of the EDL activist community and, somewhat ironically, by some counter-EDL campaign groups. The activists were forever sharing tales of possible forthcoming support for the EDL from mysterious financial backers or high-profile international counter-jihad leaders and intellectuals; of how Tommy Robinson and Kevin Carroll had met somebody – a lawyer, an image management consultant, a counter-jihad expert, etc. – who was going to help the EDL to advance; or of growing levels of clandestine support for the EDL from UK police officers, politicians, lawyers and business leaders who, the activists claimed, were 'on the EDL's side'.[67]

In early 2011, when I started spending time with EDL activists this sense of possibility was still in the air. They had been buoyed up by their largest demonstration to date in Luton on 5th February, which had attracted in the region of 3,000 supporters, and many activists took David Cameron's speech in Munich in which he criticised the 'doctrine of state multiculturalism' and called for a 'muscular liberalism' to challenge the 'ideology of extremism' as an indication that somehow their message was getting through. This sense of possibility was largely to fade during the course of 2011. However, as I discuss in Chapter 6, it did not give way to despair.

Pride and dignity

I don't think St George's day is celebrated enough in this country and it's a real shame, so to go to an event about that and to see, well to be fair there was only probably 80 of us, but to see 80 of us coming out and celebrating a national day is what we're about, I'm proud to be English, you know what I mean?

(Phil)

I felt the need to do more than just discuss the matter with someone. I felt the need to go out and make some kind of political protest.

(Terry).

When I first started [with the EDL] I used to – I was like everybody else, I was sat in my nice three-bedroom house, sitting there nice and comfortable, had a beer in the fridge, food in the cupboard, I was making a reasonable living and I wasn't concerned about anything else. I was just sat there watching Big Brother and all the other – then I started checking the EDL forum and everything else and – for once in my life I actually sat up and watched the [2010] General Election Results come in! I mean politics, me and politics, I'd never even have thought about it before.

(Steve)

The activists described several types of pride. One of these was feelings of pride associated with the various collective identities invoked and developed by activists. Like Phil, most activists spoke about how the EDL had provided them with opportunities to express feelings of attachment to and pride in their national or cultural identity. To some extent, this was about the loud and assertive performance of national identity at demonstrations, parades and memorials. Yet the cultivation of feelings of cultural pride also extended into their everyday life, for instance by ensuring that they always had the English flag around the house or on their person (see Terry, above), or by taking an increasingly keen interest in exploring what could be considered their cultural heritage. During meetings or demonstrations and on Facebook, the activists often shared stories about British military history[68] and local history – usually dewy-eyed reminiscences about local pubs, shops, or sporting venues that have closed down and tales of famous London gangsters (see Chapter 4 for an example). On 20th November 2011, I was intrigued to receive a Facebook message wishing me a happy St. Edmund's Day – St. Edmund, I learned, was the patron saint of Saxon England.[69]

As people became more involved in the group they also developed feelings of pride associated both with the EDL as a group and with their local divisions. Activists' in all local divisions felt proud when demonstrations or other events that they organised ran according to plan or attracted a good turnout, or when their division was particularly well represented at a national demonstration, either in terms of the number of people in attendance, the amount of noise they made or the catchiness of their banners. In the spring of 2011, London activists considered themselves to be one of the most active and well-organised divisions in the country – a function both of the frequency of the events that they were organising and the high profile of these events (see Chapter 1). Essex activists were also proud of what they had achieved:

> *Susan:*   Dagenham! What other town has three demos? There's no other town in the country that's had three successful demos and Dagenham is – everyone says, 'When's the next?' Even up north they'll go, 'When's the next Dagenham coming up?' Know what I mean?
>
> *Bev:*   A lot of people mention Dagenham, they find us welcoming as well, don't they, a lot of people have said it's very welcoming over here.
>
> *Susan:*   Dagenham and Essex are very patriotic people.

Another type of pride described to me by activists was more akin to feelings of personal dignity[70] and self-realisation.[71] Here there were two sub-themes: the first was what could be described as feelings of moral pride – a sense of fulfilling responsibilities and assuming one's duties, whether that duty was to the nation, one's family or, once they felt part of the community, one's fellow activists. Being an EDL activist transformed them into 'proper patriots',[72] setting them apart from 'people who just don't give a shit about what is happening' (Mark) and from the much maligned 'keyboard warriors' – people who contributed a great deal to online discussions without taking to the street. In a particularly moving exchange, Tony reflected on the importance to him of feeling that he was 'doing something':

> Maybe I'm looking for answers, maybe I'm saying why me? Why does it have to be me? Um, I wish it wouldn't because everything would be alright, but it's not and the only way I can, er, address that is by becoming an activist, because by becoming an activist that means you are doing something. That means you are out there saying something, you are doing something about it. It does take away some of the pain. I do come home [from demonstrations], I do feel good, I feel I've done something. Um, I look at the picture and I think that's the best I can do, [name of son], you know what I mean? I can't – [addressing the picture of his son] you've done more than I could ever do, you know, er, we're both men, you're a man. You're a lot braver than I ever am, make no mistake on that. So I guess, er, I'm doing it because of what's happened.

As I discuss further in Chapters 3 and 4, these feelings of moral pride often expanded as the activists experienced and endured the costs of activism, providing them with rich narratives of personal sacrifice and duty performed.[73] What threatened these feelings of moral pride for those that did not identify either with the far right or with racism, was the possible encroachment of shame associated with these stigmatising labels. In Chapter 4 I discuss how the activists managed this threat.

The other sub-theme concerned feelings of pride associated with an enhanced sense of their capabilities and knowledge – feelings that in part intersected with their sense of efficacy. With the exception of some who had long been involved in far right or counter-jihad activism, almost all the activists emphasised how becoming part of the EDL had been a 'steep learning curve' (Sarah) for them.[74] In part this involved learning about the cause (see Chapter 3) – as described above, relatively few activists considered themselves particularly knowledgeable about EDL issues when they first came into contact with the group. It was also about gaining new skills and know-how; for example Andy described how he had felt rather nervous and taken aback by the scale of policing when he attended his first EDL demonstration. However, he had become increasingly well-informed about the legal regulations governing protest policing and was one of several activists who gained a certain satisfaction from pointing it out to the police when he believed they were overstepping the line.

> I personally have never had any problem with the police, I've always spoken to them in a civil manner but I'm quite aware of my rights and I'm quite aware of what they're allowed to do and what they're not allowed to do and if they try to take liberties I will stop them, but I've never had any problem with the police to be honest, never been shoved around, never been handcuffed, never been arrested. Erm, even in, they've been, they were very upset with me at Newcastle because we got off the train and they stopped a load of us as we were getting off the train, and they were trying to line us up and take video footage of us and asking us our names and addresses and I sort of said, 'Actually guys you're not meant to do this, you know you're not, so we're all just going to cover our faces, if you'd like to arrest us, or perhaps you might just find me a more senior officer I can talk to', and they kind of um'ed and ah'ed and they went away. It wasn't the section 60[75] area so they couldn't make us cover up, basically, and they were just chancing it really and the police do take it for granted sometimes that the EDL guys are thick, or that they're not clued up . . .
>
> (Andy)

Mark told me a similar story about pointing out to a police officer that he was not entitled to rifle through his wallet under a Section 27 order.[76] Activists also acquired other skills such as learning the procedures for arranging a demonstration, what kinds of slogans they could or could not use and so on (see also Harris, Busher and Macklin 2015).

Over time, they began to pass on this information and advice to others. Phil, a young man who had spent much of his adolescence in care and left school at

16 with few qualifications, is a particularly good example of this kind of story of personal growth. As a teenager and prior to joining the EDL, he had been involved in several incidents of racially aggravated violence and had been arrested on at least two occasions. He claimed however that after joining the EDL he had learned a great deal from some of the older activists. He had revised some of his previous racist attitudes (see Chapter 4), had enthusiastically thrown himself into learning about (militant) Islam and had also become more strategically aware. He told me:

> I'm not the most educated person, but I feel I know a lot, well I don't know a lot, well I know quite a lot of the older lads you know so I get to, if I ever say something stupid they'll go 'Well no actually this is this and that's that', and then I'm like 'Oh, actually fair enough' and then I know.
>
> (Phil)

In time he became a divisional leader and, particularly with the younger activists, he had to be

> ... like, not a father figure, but I've got to do what the older ones are doing to me and I've got to pass that on like, if they was fucking taking the piss out of a person because they're Chinese on the train or something because they're black or something like that I'd be like 'Sit down and sort yourself out, because if you get nicked I'm getting nicked', and so I'm passing on the information that the older person has told me.

Notes

1 There are a number of reasons why I prefer to focus on describing *how* people became involved in EDL activism rather than attempting to say *why* they did. First, there are serious methodological problems with attempting to establish motivation based on retrospective interviews. The explanations that we offer for why we make the life decisions that we do almost invariably tend towards simplification and 'narrative smoothing' (Spence 1986). This is in part a conscious and strategic process – we have a story of ourselves that we are keen to convey to our listeners – but is also a function of the sheer complexity of our decision-making processes: there are almost certainly impulses that, without extensive self-reflection, we are unlikely to be aware of. As Wright Mill's (1940) famously observes, motives are often furnished 'after the act'. The fact that for activists in groups such as the EDL justifying their participation becomes part of their day-to-day lives makes it particularly difficult to explore the full gamut of motivations post hoc.

Second, I have been keen to avoid ironing out the complexity from activists' accounts of their journeys into the group. Participation in social movement activism is usually associated with multiple motives; 'people may want to change the world they live in, they may want to be part of a group, or they may want to give meaning to their world and express their views' (Klandermans and Mayer (2006, 7), and in practice, most people will describe a combination of these motives, the balance of which is likely to vary during the course of the process of entry (Blee 2003, della Porta and Diani 2006, 98, Sageman 2004).

Third, and perhaps most fundamentally, there is a basic ontological problem with trying to explain why people decided to join the group. Entering into social movement activism is unlikely ever to be the result of just one decision. Rather, it is the outcome of multiple more or less conscious decisions (Blee 2003, 23–109, Horgan 2008) – the decision to ask their friend to tell them a bit more about this thing called the EDL that they keep posting about on Facebook, the decision to spend an evening looking at the web links their friend sent them, the decision to follow additional web links to a jihadist website, the decision to attend their first demonstration, the decision to follow that up by attending a group meeting, the decision to attend their second demonstration, and so forth. Different cognitive, emotional and social processes are more or less important at different points in this journey, that is, the motivation to click on a web link about (militant) Islam is unlikely to be the same as the motivation to agree to attend an EDL demonstration with friends, or to attend a second one. As Snow and colleagues (Snow, Zurcher and Ekland-Olson 1980, 795) argue, '"motives" for joining or continued participation are generally emergent and interactional rather than pre-structured'. If we seriously want to develop an account of why people participate we need to break it down to the multiple smaller decisions.

2 The idea of tracing these different routes is taken from the work of Linden and Klandermans' (2007). I make some use of the typology that they developed. However, I have also sought as far as possible to develop a typology that coincides with EDL activists' own conceptualisation of the social geography of their movement.

3 This estimate and similar estimates that I make below are based on a combination of my field notes and discussions with local and regional EDL leaders in London and the Southeast.

4 A trend widely acknowledged by activists (see Blake 2011). Indeed, the issue was addressed directly by Tommy Robinson at a leadership meeting in West Bromwich on 19th November 2011 when plans to form a partnership with the British Freedom Party were officially announced (Chapter 5).

5 A term often used by respondents to describe quitting football violence.

6 As is the case with Tommy Robinson, who had been an BNP member for a year in 2004 but had chosen not to renew his membership.

7 This was the preferred term of those involved in these groups.

8 Small and often loosely organised pockets of activists who come together around specific issues and events (Griffin 2003).

9 MFE was also not as clearly defined as a 'single issue group' as the EDL has been. MFE mobilised more generally around what activists described to me as events to 'promote English culture and support the armed forces' (conversation with Dave Smeeton, MFE organiser). These included events such as St. George's Day parades and memorial marches for the Gurkhas (https://www.youtube.com/watch?v=IpxrX00TukA).

10 As early as 2009, MFE organiser Dave Smeeton was distancing his organisation from the EDL, describing themselves as a more 'family friendly' organisation (Copsey 2010, 10).

11 Although Robinson was a member of the BNP for a year around 2004.

12 It is likely that a higher number of EDL activists voted for or sympathised with extreme right-wing groups. Bartlett and Littler's (2011, 22) survey found that 34% of EDL supporters expressed a voting preference for the BNP (compared with 2% in the general population at the time of the survey), although as Bartlett and Littler note, this might in part reflect an attempt by anti-EDL campaigners to infiltrate the data set and show the EDL in a bad light. All of the former BNP activists I met during the course of my fieldwork were over 40.

13 In the years prior to the emergence of the EDL, the BNP in particular developed a considerable and, by the far right's standards, well-organised local network of activists, particularly in London's periphery. This activist network had been the basis of notable successes in local elections from 2004–2008 (Goodwin 2008, John et al. 2005).

14 Understood simply as 'high status cultural signals used in cultural and social relations' (Lamont and Lareau 1988, 153). Different signals can function as cultural capital within different social settings and the same signal might be a rich source of cultural capital in one setting but not in another.

15 My thanks to Charlie Flowers for this term. What I refer to as the swerveys are broadly similar to what Linden and Klandermans (2006, 2007) call 'wanderers'. I prefer the term swerveys because it emphasises the change in political direction that was the principle theme in the life-history narratives of the activists to whom this term applied. I also prefer this term because Linden and Klandermans' 'wanderers' label could also conceivably be applied to most of the activists who came to the EDL via the patriotic groups.

16 Here I use 'Islam' rather than '(militant) Islam' because he usually spoke of Islam rather than militant Islam as the 'problem'.

17 Here I use radical in its broad sense. This does not imply recourse to violent action, but only collective action organised around radical ideas that challenge the cultural, political or economic status quo.

18 This term is borrowed from Linden and Klandermans (2007).

19 A finding very much in keeping with the observations of Linden and Klandermans (2007).

20 The Facebook name of Jeff Marsh, the founder of Casuals United and the Welsh Defence League. It was quite common for activists to refer to one another by their Facebook names.

21 Joel Titus had been an early recruit to the EDL and was the Youth Division leader. In April 2011, he was jailed for nine months and given a football banning order for his participation in organised football violence. 'EDL member jailed for Liverpool Street football brawl', BBC, 20th April 2011, www.bbc.co.uk/news/uk-england-london-13140452

22 Although it is important to note there will almost always be many more people who also had personal ties into the movement but did not go on to become involved. Exploring the life trajectories of this latter group alongside those of people who became activists could provide particularly rich theoretical insights about what shapes propensity to participate in activism (see della Porta and Diani 2006, 121).

23 This is likely to reflect the sampling procedures that I used. My aim to conduct life history interviews with activists with as wide a range of experiences as possible meant that people who are somewhat atypical in one way or another are probably over-represented in my interview sample.

24 The idea that existing constellations of personal networks have played an important role in recruitment into the EDL is also borne out by other studies relating more or less directly to EDL activism. Harris, Busher and Macklin (2015), for example, found that in both Luton and Blackburn participation in EDL activism has been heavily concentrated in specific, and in the case of Blackburn quite socially isolated, family, neighbourhood and football-based networks. Similarly, Thomas et al. (2014) and Busher et al. (2014) found participation in EDL activism in West Yorkshire to be concentrated in hyper-local spaces – it was not even specific estates but specific families and streets.

25 Who often attended EDL events.

26 My own paraphrasing of a conversation recorded in my fieldnotes after the first demonstration I attended and noted on several subsequent occasions.

27 Such accounts also resonate with my own experience of meeting activists and attending my first demonstrations. As described in Chapter 1, once it was established that I was neither an undercover journalist nor working for Unite Against Fascism (UAF), most activists were friendly, relaxed and even enthusiastic about my presence at their events, and several were very generous in terms of the amount of time they were willing to spend introducing me to other activists.

28 This estimate is based on a) observations made between June 2011 and May 2012 after I had become familiar with and was therefore able to recognise the core activist community and b) conversations with local EDL organisers at EDL demonstrations.

29 'Lol' stands for laugh out loud.

30 Klatch (2004, 493) talks about the importance of constructing a 'we/they distinction' in radical protest groups.

31 'Colin', one of the protagonists of the documentary *Angry, White and Proud* by Jamie Roberts shown in January 2014 apparently lost his job after the documentary was aired (personal communication with former EDL activist).

32 Pilkington (2014, 114) describes how one activist she knew in the West Midlands had 'been kicked out of the family home because his Mum did not approve of his activities with the EDL'.

33 Unbounded groups may have inner circles to which access is 'restricted to individuals considered reliable and worthy of trust', and there will almost certainly be some form of status hierarchy within the group. However, their boundaries are usually 'relatively fuzzy' – 'who is inside and who is outside' tends to remain ill-defined and there are usually 'a number of people at the margins of the scene who sympathize or share some elements of opinions or style; who mingle socially with activists; and who drift in or out of the scene' (Bjørgo 2009, 30).

34 As will become clear below and in the course of the following chapters, what comprised 'their' culture varied across activists and conversations. Definitions of their culture varied by scale (English, British, Western), were sometimes infused with specific religious identities (e.g. 'our Judaeo-Christian culture'), with class identities and sometimes also with racial identities. What is important at this point is not how it was defined, but that it (whatever 'it' might be) somehow felt as though it was theirs.

35 I have adopted this extremely apt term from Matthew Taylor's (2010) early coverage of the EDL.

36 Now resident in Canada.

37 As Zúquete (2008, 324–327) notes, within the European, far right there has been a move to mobilise around a European *Christian* identity. A recent example of this in the United Kingdom has been Britain First's 'Christian Patrols' (Allen 2014). There has also been sporadic use of Christian identity by some people associated with the EDL (Copsey 2010, Garland and Treadwell 2012), and most activists expressed some sense of Christian heritage even if they did not consider themselves to be Christians. However, in day-to-day discussion of their cause such identities were only used frequently by a handful of the activists I knew. Describing her religious identity, Susan told me 'I'm not religious in any way, shape or form . . . I'm not an atheist though, I'm Church of England', while Bev explained 'I don't even go to church at Christmas. I don't even eat turkey, it's too dry, I don't like turkey'.

38 My paraphrasing of a snippet of conversation after the formal interview ended.

39 See Oaten (2014) for a discussion of the role of victim identities in the mobilisation and justificatory narratives of EDL activism and, as a useful point of comparison, Berbrier (2000) for a discussion of the construction of victim claims in contemporary white supremacist movements in the United States.

40 Defined as 'an unexpected event or piece of information [that] raises such a sense of outrage in a person that she becomes inclined towards political action, with or without the network of personal contacts' (Jasper 2007, 106).

41 'Soldiers heckled during homecoming parade in Barking', BBC, 15th June 2010, www.bbc.co.uk/news/10324027

42 'Muslims clash with police after burning poppy in anti-Armistice Day protest', Andy Bloxham, *The Telegraph*, 11th November 2010, www.telegraph.co.uk/news/uknews/law-and-order/8126357/Muslims-clash-with-police-after-burning-poppy-in-anti-Armistice-Day-protest.html

43 As I discuss in Chapter 3, this phrase was often used by activists to refer to the time they spent reading up on information about (militant) Islam.

44 Such accounts would provide at least anecdotal support for notions of what has come to be referred to as cumulative extremism or reciprocal radicalisation, understood as 'the way in which one form of extremism can feed off and magnify other forms [of extremism]' (Eatwell 2006, 205). As Graham Macklin and I have argued elsewhere, however, there are reasons to be cautious about seeing this as a straightforward tit-for-tat process (Bartlett and Birdwell 2013, Busher and Macklin 2014, Macklin and Busher 2015).

45 The other event often described by activists as a take-off point was a march in support of Dutch MP Geert Wilders, the leader of the Freedom Party, who was in London to present *Fitna,* his controversial anti-Islam film, at the House of Lords. Wilders has repeatedly sought to distance himself from the EDL. 'Dutch MP Geert Wilders' anti-Islam film sparks protests', BBC, 5th March 2010, http://news.bbc.co.uk/1/hi/uk/8551220.stm

46 This is not the same as saying that people were not able to identify some kind of personal connection to the EDL cause. As I discuss in more detail in Chapter 3, part of what helped many activists to engage with and commit to the EDL cause was that they were able to find, or at least to narratively construct, some kind of connection to it, whether it was a friend or family member who had been on the London underground on the morning of 7th July 2005 or a friend or friend of a friend fighting the Taliban in Afghanistan.

47 I discuss this in more detail in Chapter 3.

48 This, again, is quite in keeping with other studies of participation in forms of radical anti-minority politics, or in radical political activism more generally. For example, Mann (2004, 28) observes in his study of Fascism that it was quite possible for people to 'sign up for a movement' when they 'possess only rudimentary knowledge of it' perhaps extending no further than a feeling of 'sympathy for a few slogans'. Similarly, Virchow (2007) notes that while people who become involved in the German far right tend to have some affinity to its worldview and emotional and cultural repertoire, it is through participation in the group's rituals that they go on to develop their ideas and attachment; and a similar picture also emerges from Blee's (2003) account of women's pathways into organised racism in the United States and Fangen's (1998) account of extreme right-wing activists in Norway. See also Bjørgo and Horgan (2009, 3), Jongman (2009) and Veldhuis and Bakker (2009) for similar observations in relation to participation in Islamist extremism, Jamieson (1990) on militant left-wing groups in Italy during the 1970s, or Munson (2009) on participation in pro-life activism. Similarly, in relation to religious cults Collins (2004, 96–97) notes that 'Persons who join religious cults typically are not to any great extent acquainted with, nor committed to, the beliefs of the cult before they join it. They are initially attracted to the cult because they are brought by friends, relatives, and acquaintances. Their belief grows as they take part in the cult activities'.

49 Jasper (2014, 208) describes indignation as 'the morally ground form of anger'.

50 Castells (2012) emphasises the importance of hope in achieving mobilisation. My experience with activists was that their emotions fell some way short of hope. I return to this point in Chapter 6.

51 A view which echoes the long-held view that part of what determines a social movement group's capacity to mobilise support is their ability to persuade participants and prospective participants that there are favourable political opportunities ripe for exploitation (Diani 1996, Gamson and Meyer 1996).

52 In most instances there was also a sizeable counterdemonstration, usually by a combination of formal and broadly defined 'left-wing' opposition groups, with the UAF providing the most regular opposition together with more- or less-organised local community mobilisations. On some occasions, these counterdemonstrations included

overtly aggressive groups from the Anti-Fascist Network and the Muslim Defence League (MDL).

53 A similar observation is made by van der Wal (2011, 127) who describes how, at a demonstration in Dudley in 2010 'the majority of the group was near the stage, listening orderly to the speeches and seriously taking part in the protest. Another group of around 300 were bouncing around the fence, trying to break out. They were not interested in the British national anthem being played, nor in the different speeches. They were just looking for a way to break through the fences and find their way to the UAF protesting area'.

54 Charlene Downes disappeared on 1st November 2003. It is alleged that she was a victim of child sexual exploitation involving a group of Muslim men associated with a local fast food outlet. The first time the case went to trial, the jury failed to return a verdict. The second time, the defendants were found not guilty after the prosecution withdrew the charges. See 'Charlene Downes murder', BBC *Crimewatch*, 4th December 2014, www.bbc.co.uk/programmes/profiles/1W57h1YhDLh49rpQFc4GZw0/charlene-downes-murder

55 My paraphrasing of an expression often used by the activists when reflecting on what they had enjoyed about a recent demonstration.

56 On the way to a demonstration in Leicester on 9th October 2010, approximately 300–400 EDL activists eschewed the official muster point, stopping instead at Market Harborough – a story told to me with some satisfaction by several activists.

57 The EDL activist was of mixed race and had apparently used this to his advantage on a number of occasions to pass through police lines or get closer to MAC activists than would usually have been possible for an EDL demonstrator in this situation.

58 That is, they went there to get drunk and generally have a good time rather than make a serious political point.

59 Following people like Gamson (1992) and Taylor and Whittier (1992), I take solidarity to be not only shared identification but also a feeling of loyalty and affective bond.

60 Such feelings often accompany entry into social movement activism (see for example Klatch 2004).

61 The point is a similar one to that made by Morris (1984), about how Christian hymns and spirituals were so effective within the US Civils Rights movements because participants were already familiar with their cadences.

62 For a similar observation, see Linden and Klandermans' (2006, 188) discussion of far right activists in the Netherlands.

63 Research on other social movements has demonstrated that activists are sometimes able to import cultural capital from other aspects of their lives (Nepstad and Bob 2006), for example Robnett's (1997) discussion of how ministers acquired authority within the civil rights movement. This was also true in the EDL, and was particularly the case with some of the football casuals who brought with them a reputation for being a 'proper lad' or a 'fixer'. This was, for example, the case with Tommy Robinson (Harris et al. 2015) and with Jeff Marsh (Marsh 2010).

64 As Turner (2009, 348) notes, summarising the arguments of Kemper and Collins (1990) 'when persons experience gains in prestige (or receive deference from others), they will feel satisfaction and well-being; and they will give off positive emotions to others, which in turn will increase the flow of positive emotions and bonds of solidarity between the givers and receivers of status'. This feeling of satisfaction and well-being is closely associated with feelings of pride, to which I turn below.

65 Large mobilisations are particularly able to engender confidence and transmit enthusiasm (Koenker 1965, 74 cited in Casquete (2006, pp. 290–291).

66 Official estimates only put the numbers at around 700, although as discussed in Chapter 1, it is difficult to estimate numbers at these events. See 'Dozens arrested during protests', BBC, 10th October 2010, http://news.bbc.co.uk/2/hi/uk_news/england/manchester/8300431.stm

67 See also Busher (2013).
68 As I have already mentioned, there were quite a few activists, particularly older ones, with a keen interest in military history and, to a lesser extent, local history.
69 Speaking with activists I was often reminded of Hewitt's description of how among some young white people living in low-income areas of southeast London there was a sense of almost craving a 'culture' that they could celebrate and call their own, and of Clarke's (1998 [1975]) famous description of how skinheads in east London in the 1960s undertook a 'magical recovery of community' to compensate for the decline of 'real' working class communities.
70 Jasper (2010, 2014) describes dignity as a form of individualised honour. The association of feelings of dignity with participation in political activism is discussed in particular detail by Wood (2001, 2003). Lamont's (2000) work on working class men in the United States and France suggests that vocabularies of dignity may be particularly important among working class men in post-industrial countries.
71 As Gamson (1992) notes, feelings of self-realisation or self-fulfilment are often among the rewards of activism.
72 An expression of respect that the activists often used when talking about one another.
73 Protest performances by social movement activists often emphasise the theme of sacrifice in order to demonstrate commitment and worthiness to external and internal audiences (Tilly 2004).
74 Linden and Klandermans (2007) observe that activists tend to tell narratives of either continuity or transformation. Among the activists I knew, the overwhelming majority told narratives of lives transformed by activism, at least in terms of the practice of activism. This was also the case with national EDL leaders (Harris et al. 2015).
75 'Section 60 of the Criminal Justice and Public Order Act 1994 allows a police officer to stop and search a person without suspicion. Section 60 stops and searches can take place in an area which has been authorised by a senior police officer on the basis of their reasonable belief that violence has or is about to occur, and where it is expedient to prevent it or search people for a weapon if one was involved in the incident'. Liberty, https://www.liberty-human-rights.org.uk/human-rights/justice-and-fair-trials/stop-and-search
76 'Section 27 legislation allows police to move someone from a specified area for a period of up to 48 hours. No offence needs to have been committed for the act to be enforced: the legislation gives police the power to move on people who they say pose a risk of alcohol-related disorder'. Football Supporters Federation, www.fsf.org.uk/campaigns/watching-football-is-not-a-crime/faqs-on-section-27/

References

Allen, C. 2014. "Britain First: The 'Frontline Resistance' to the Islamification of Britain." *The Political Quarterly* 85 (3):354–361.

Atran, S. 2010. *Talking to the Enemy: Violent Extremism, Sacred Values and What it Means to Be Human.* London: Allen Lane.

Bartlett, J., and J. Birdwell. 2013. *Cumulative Radicalisation Between the Far-Right and Islamist Groups in the UK: A Review of Evidence.* London: Demos.

Bartlett, J., and M. Littler. 2011. *Inside the EDL: Populist Politics in a Digital Age.* London: Demos.

Berbrier, M. 2000. "The Victim Ideology of White Supremacists and White Separatists in the United States." *Sociological Focus* 33 (2), 175–191.

Bjørgo, T. 1998. "Entry, Bridge-Burning and Exit Options: What Happens to Young People who Join Racist Groups and Want to Leave." In *Nation and Race: The Developing Euro-American Racist Subculture*, edited by J. Kaplan and T. Bjørgo, 231–258. Boston: Northeastern University Press.

Bjørgo, T. 2009. "Processes of Disengagement from Violent Groups of the Extreme Right." In *Leaving Terrorism Behind: Individual and Collective Disengagement*, edited by T. Bjørgo and J. Horgan, 30–48. London: Routledge.

Bjørgo, T. 2011. "Dreams and Disillusionment: Engagement In and Disengagement From Militant Extremist Groups." *Crime, Law and Social Change* 55 (4):277–285.

Bjørgo, T., and J. Horgan. 2009. "Introduction." In *Leaving Terrorism Behind: Individual and Collective Disengagement*, edited by T. Bjørgo and J. Horgan, 1–13. London: Routledge.

Blake, B. 2011. *EDL: Coming Down the Road*. Birmingham: VHC.

Blee, K. M. 2003. *Inside Organized Racism: Women in the Hate Movement*. Paperback Edition. Berkeley: University of California Press.

Blee, K. M. 2007. "Ethnographies of the Far Right." *Journal of Contemporary Ethnography* 36 (2):119–128.

Blumer, H. 1951. "Collective Behavior." In *New Outline of the Principles of Sociology*, edited by A. M. Lee, 166–222. New York: Barnes & Noble.

Busher, J. 2013. "Grassroots Activism in the English Defence League: Discourse and Public (Dis)order." In *Extreme Right-Wing Political Violence and Terrorism*, edited by M. Taylor, P. M. Currie and D. Holbrook, 65–84. London: Bloomsbury.

Busher, J., K. Christmann, G. Macklin, M. Rogerson and P. Thomas. 2014. *Understanding Concerns About Community Relations in Calderdale*. Huddersfield: The University of Huddersfield.

Busher, J., and G. Macklin. 2014. "Interpreting 'Cumulative Extremism': Six Proposals for Enhancing Conceptual Clarity." *Terrorism and Political Violence*. www.tandfonline.com/eprint/XGyY3ynSqq2BXcNJnDXd/full#.VcNEZvlViko.

Castells, M. 2012. *Networks of Outrage and Hope: Social Movements in the Internet Age*. Cambridge: Polity Press.

Casquete, J. 2006. "Protest Rituals and Uncivil Communities." *Totalitarian Movements and Political Religions* 7 (3):283–301.

Clarke, J. 1998 [1975]. "The Skinheads & the Magical Recovery of Community." In *Resistance Through Rituals: Youth Subcultures in Post-War Britain*, edited by S. Hall and T. Jefferson, 99–102. London: Routledge.

Clough, N. L. 2012. "Emotion at the Center of Radical Politics: On the Affective Structures of Rebellion and Control." *Antipode* 44 (5):1667–1686.

Collins, R. 2001. "Social Movements and the Focus of Emotional Attention." In *Passionate Politics: Emotions and Social Movements*, edited by J. Goodwin, J. M. Jasper and F. Polletta, 27–44. Chicago: Chicago University Press.

Collins, R. 2004. *Interaction Ritual Chains*. Princeton: Princeton University Press.

Copsey, N. 2010. *The English Defence League: Challenging Our Country and Our Values of Social Inclusion, Fairness and Equality*. London: Faith Matters.

della Porta, D. 1988. "Recruitment Processes in Clandestine Political Organizations: Italian Left-Wing Terrorism." *International Social Movement Research* 1:155–169.

della Porta, D., and M. Diani. 2006. *Social Movements: An Introduction*. Oxford: Blackwell.

Diani, M. 1996. "Linking Mobilization Frames and Political Opportunities: Insights from Regional Populism in Italy." *American Sociological Review* 61 (6):1053–1069.

Durkheim, E. 1915. *The Elementary Forms of the Religious Life*. Translated by J. Ward Swain. London: Allen and Unwin.

Eatwell, R. 2006. "Community Cohesion and Cumulative Extremism in Contemporary Britain." *The Political Quarterly* 77 (2):204–216.

Fangen, K. 1998. "Living Out Our Ethnic Instincts: Ideological Beliefs Among Right-Wing Activists in Norway." In *Nation and Race: Developing Euro-American Racist Subculture*, edited by J. Kaplan and T. Bjørgo, 202–230. Boston: Northeastern University Press.

Futrell, R., and P. Simi. 2004. "Free Spaces, Collective Identity, and the Persistence of US White Power Activism." *Social Problems* 51 (1):16–42.

Gamson, W.A. 1992. "The Social Psychology of Collective Action." In *Frontiers in Social Movement Theory*, edited by A.D. Morris and C.M. Mueller, 53–76. New Haven: Yale University Press.

Gamson, W.A., and D.S. Meyer. 1996. "The Framing of Political Opportunity." In *Comparative Perspectives on Social Movement Opportunities, Mobilizing structures, and Framing*, edited by D. McAdam, J.D. McCarthy and M.N. Zald, 275–290. Cambridge: Cambridge University Press.

Garland, J., and J. Treadwell. 2012. "The New Politics of Hate? An Assessment of the Appeal of the English Defence League Amongst Disadvantaged White Working-Class Communities in England." *Journal of Hate Studies* 10:123–142.

Goffman, E. 1971. *Relations in Public*. New York: Basic.

Goodwin, J., J.M. Jasper and F. Polletta. 2001. "Introduction: Why Emotions Matter." In *Passionate Politics: Emotions and Social Movements*, edited by J. Goodwin, J.M. Jasper and F. Polletta, 1–24. Chicago: University of Chicago Press.

Goodwin, M.J. 2008. "Backlash in the 'Hood: Determinants of Support for the British National Party (BNP) at the Local Level." *Journal of Contemporary European Studies* 16 (3):347–361.

Goodwin, M.J. 2011. *New British Fascism: Rise of the British National Party*. Abingdon: Routledge.

Gould, D.B. 2002. "Life During Wartime: Emotions and the Development of ACT Up." *Mobilization* 7 (2):177–200.

Gould, D.B. 2009. *Moving Politics: Emotion and ACT UP's Fight Against AIDS*. London: University of Chicago Press.

Griffin, R. 2003. "From Slime Mould to Rhizome: An introduction to the Groupuscular Right." *Patterns of Prejudice* 37 (1):27–50.

Harris, G., J. Busher and G. Macklin. 2015. *The Evolution of Anti-Muslim Protest in Two English Towns*. Coventry: Coventry University/The University of Huddersfield.

Horgan, J. 2008. "From Profiles to Pathways and Roots to Routes: Perspectives from Psychology on Radicalization into Terrorism." *The Annals of the American Academy of Political and Social Science* 618 (1):80–94.

Hunt, S.A., and R.D. Benford. 2004. "Collective Identity, Solidarity and Commitment." In *The Blackwell Companion to Social Movements*, edited by D.A. Snow, S.A. Soule and H. Kriesi, 433–457. Blackwell: Oxford.

Husain, E. 2007. *The Islamist*. London: Penguin.

Häberlen, J.C., and R.A. Spinnet. 2014. "Introduction." *Contemporary European History* 3 (4):489–503.

Jamieson, A. 1990. "Entry, Discipline and Exit in the Italian Red Brigades." *Terrorism and Political Violence* 2 (1):1–20.

Jasper, J.M. 2007. *The Art of Moral Protest: Culture, Biography, and Creativity in Social Movements*. Paperback Edition. London: University of Chicago Press.

Jasper, J.M. 2010. "Strategic Marginalizations, Emotional Marginalities." In *Surviving Against Odds: The Marginalized in a Globalizing World*, edited by D.K. SinghaRoy, 29–37. Delhi: Manohar.

Jasper, J. M. 2011. "Emotions and Social Movements: Twenty Years of Theory and Research." *Annual Review of Sociology* 37:285–303.

Jasper, J. M. 2014. "Constructing Indignation: Anger Dynamics in Protest Movements." *Emotion Review* 6 (3):208–213.

Jasper, J. M., and J. D. Poulsen. 1995. "Recruiting Strangers and Friends: Moral Shocks and Social Networks in Animal Rights and Anti-Nuclear Protests." *Social Problems* 42 (4):493–512.

John, P., H. Margetts, D. Rowland and S. Weir. 2005. *The Far Right in London.* York: The Joseph Rowntree Reform Trust.

Jongman, A. 2009. "Radicalisation and Deradicalisation: Dutch Experiences." In *Home-Grown Terrorism: Understanding and Addressing the Root Causes*, edited by T. M. Pick, A. Spekhard and B. Jacuch, 32–50. Amsterdam: IOS.

Kemper, T. D., and R. Collins. 1990. "Dimensions of Microinteraction." *American Journal of Sociology* 96 (1):32–68.

Klandermans, B., and N. Mayer. 2006. "Right-Wing Extremism as a Social Movement." In *Extreme Right Activists in Europe: Through the Magnifying Glass*, edited by B. Klandermans and N. Mayer, 3–16. London: Routledge.

Klatch, R. E. 2004. "The Underside of Social Movements: The Effects of Destructive Affective Ties." *Qualitative Sociology* 27 (4):487–509.

Koenker, E. B. 1965. *Secular Salvations: The Rites and Symbols of Political Religions.* Philadelphia: Fortress Press.

Lamont, M. 2000. *The Dignity of Working Men: Morality and the Boundaries of Race, Class, and Immigration.* New York: Russell Sage Foundation.

Lamont, M., and A. Lareau. 1988. "Cultural Capital: Allusions, Gaps and Glissandos in Recent Theoretical Developments." *Sociological Theory* 6 (2):153–168.

LeBon, G. 1960 [1895]. *The Crowd.* New York: Viking Press.

Linden, A., and B. Klandermans. 2006. "The Netherlands. Stigmatized Outsiders." In *Extreme Right Activists in Europe: Through the Magnifying Glass*, edited by B. Klandermans and N. Mayer, 172–203. London: Routledge.

Linden, A., and B. Klandermans. 2007. "Revolutionaries, Wanderers, Converts, and Compliants: Life Histories of Extreme Right Activists." *Journal of Contemporary Ethnography* 36 (2):184–201.

Lofland, J., and N. Skonovd. 1983. "Patterns of Conversion." In *Of Gods and Men: New Religious Movements in the West*, edited by British Sociological Association, 1–24. Macon: Mercer University Press.

Macklin, G., and J. Busher. 2015. "The Missing Spirals of Violence: Four Waves of Movement-Countermovement Contest in Post-War Britain." *Behavioral Studies of Terrorism and Political Aggression* 7 (1):53–68.

Mann, M. 2004. *Fascists.* Cambridge: Cambridge University Press.

Marsh, J. 2010. *From Seasiders to Casuals United*: The Mashed Swede Project.

McAdam, D. 1986. "Recruitment to High-Risk Activism: The Case of Freedom Summer." *American Journal of Sociology* 92 (1):64–90.

Miller McPherson, J., P. A. Popielarz and S. Drobnic. 1992. "Social Networks and Organizational Dynamics." *American Sociological Review* 57 (2):153–170.

Morris, A. D. 1984. *Origins of the Civil Rights Movement: Black Communities Organizing for Change.* New York: The Free Press.

Munson, Z. 2009. *The Making of Pro-Life Activists.* Chicago: University of Chicago Press.

Nepstad, S. E., and C. Bob. 2006. "When do Leaders Matter? Hypotheses on Leadership Dynamics in Social Movements." *Mobilization* 11 (1):1–22.

Nepstad, S. E., and C. Smith. 1999. "Rethinking Recruitment to High-Risk/Cost Activism: The Case of Nicaragua Exchange." *Mobilization* 4 (1):25–40.

Oaten, A. 2014. "The Cult of the Victim: An Analysis of the Collective Identity of the English Defence League." *Patterns of Prejudice* 48 (4):331–349.

Passy, F. 2003. "Social Networks Matter. But How?" In *Social Movements and Networks: Relational Approaches to Collective Action*, edited by M. Diani and D. McAdam, 21–48. Oxford: Oxford University Press.

Pilkington, H. 2014. 'Loud and Proud': Youth Activism in the English Defence League. Report on Work Package 7 of MYPLACE Project. www.fp7-myplace.eu.

Robnett, B. 1997. *How Long? How Long? African American Women in the Struggle for Civil Rights*. New York: Oxford University Press.

Sageman, M. 2004. *Understanding Terror Networks*. Philadelphia: University of Pennsylvania Press.

Scheff, T. J. 1994. *Bloody Revenge: Emotions, Nationalism, and War*. Boulder: Westview Press.

Simi, P., and R. Futrell. 2010. *American Swastika: Inside the White Power Movement's Hidden Spaces of Hate*. Plymouth: Rowman & Littlefield.

Snow, D. A., E. B. Rochford Jr, S. K. Worden and R. D. Benford. 1986. "Frame Alignment Processes, Micromobilization, and Movement Participation." *American Sociological Review* 51 (4):464–481.

Snow, D. A., L. A. Zurcher and S. Ekland-Olson. 1980. "Social Networks and Social Movements: A Microstructural Approach to Differential Recruitment." *American Sociological Review* 45 (5):787–801.

Spence, D. P. 1986. "Narrative Smoothing and Clinical Wisdom." In *Narrative Psychology: The Stories Nature of Human Conduct*, edited by T. R. Sarbin. Westport, CT: Praeger.

Summers Effler, E. 2010. *Laughing Saints and Righteous Heroes: Emotional Rhythms in Social Movement Groups*. London: University of Chicago Press.

Taylor, M. 2010. "English Defence League: New Wave of Extremists Plotting Summer of Unrest." *The Guardian*, 28th May 2010.

Taylor, V., and N. E. Whittier. 1992. "Collective Identity in Social Movement Communities: Lesbian Feminist Mobilization." In *Frontiers in Social Movement Theory*, edited by A. D. Morris and C. M. Mueller, 104–129. New Haven: Yale University Press.

Thomas, P., M. Rogerson, G. Macklin, K. Christmann and J. Busher. 2014. Understanding Concerns About Community Relations in Kirklees. Huddersfield: University of Huddersfield.

Tilly, C. 2004. *Social Movements, 1768–2004*. Boulder: Paradigm.

Treadwell, J., and J. Garland. 2011. "Masculinity, Marginalization and Violence: A Case Study of the English Defence League." *British Journal of Criminology* 51 (4):621–634.

Turner, J. H. 2009. "The Sociology of Emotions: Basic Theoretical Arguments." *Emotion Review* 1 (4):340–354.

van der Wal, R. 2011. "United Kingdom: Policing EDL Manifestations and Demonstrations Across England." In *Managing Collective Violence Around Public Events: An International Comparison*, edited by O. M. G. Adang, 119–152. Apeldoorn: Police Science and Research Programme.

van Troost, D., J. van Stekelenberg and B. Klandermans. 2013. "Emotions of Protest." In *Emotions in Politics: The Affect Dimension in Political Tension*, edited by N. Demertzis, 186–203. Basingstoke: Palgrave Macmillan.

Veldhuis, T., and E. Bakker. 2009. "Muslims in the Netherlands: Tensions and Violent Conflict." In *MICROCON Policy Working Paper*. Brighton: MICROCON.

Virchow, F. 2007. "Performance, Emotion, and Ideology: On the Creation of 'Collectives of Emotion" and Worldview in the Contemporary German Far Right." *Journal of Contemporary Ethnography* 36 (2):147–164.

Wasmund, K. 1986. "The Political Socialization of West German Terrorists." In *Political Violence and Terror: Motifs and Motivations*, edited by P. H. Merkl, 191–228. Berkeley: University of California Press.

Whittier, N. 2001. "Emotional Strategies: The Collective Reconstruction and Display of Oppositional Emotions in the Movement Against Child Sexual Abuse." In *Passionate Politics: Emotions and Social Movements*, edited by J. Goodwin, J. M. Jasper and F. Polletta, 233–250. Chicago: Chicago University Press.

Whittier, N. 2012. "The Politics of Coming Out." In *Strategies for Social Change*, edited by G. M. Maney, R. V. Kutz-Flamenbaum, D. A. Rohlinger and J. Goodwin, 145–169. Minneapolis: University of Minnesota Press.

Wood, E. J. 2001. "The Emotional Benefits of Insurgency in El Salvador." In *Passionate Politics: Emotions and Social Movements*, edited by J. Goodwin, J. M. Jasper and F. Polletta, 267–281. Chicago: University of Chicago Press.

Wood, E. J. 2003. *Insurgent Collective Action and Civil War in El Salvador*. Cambridge: Cambridge University Press.

Wright Mills, C. 1940. "Situated Actions and Vocabularies of Motive." *American Sociological Review* 5 (6):904–913.

Zúquete, J. P. 2008. "The European Extreme-Right and Islam: New Directions?" *Journal of Political Ideologies* 13 (3):321–344.

3 Developing belief in the cause

> We've always been told we were wrong. You know what I mean? If I really thought
> we was that wrong I would not – I wouldn't bother stepping out me – stepping out me
> front door. We have to do it. It takes a lot to like, you know – you have to *believe* in it.
> (Tony, his emphasis)

In Chapter 2, I drew attention to the fact that many of the people who went on
to become core English Defence League (EDL) activists had only a limited level
of ideological proficiency, and some only a limited sense of *the cause,* when
they initially became involved with the group. This is not however to play down
the importance of the EDL's arguments in shaping people's journey through EDL
activism; it is only to say that people's beliefs tended to emerge, intensify and
become more defined as they became involved with the group. Belief in the
EDL cause and engagement with what were often referred to as 'EDL issues'
was an important part of what built and sustained their commitment to EDL
activism, particularly once the novelty and exhilaration of the first adrenaline-
soaked demonstrations started to give way to realisation of the various costs of
participation: the financial cost, the time cost, the effect on relationships with
friends, family and colleagues, and for some, even legal implications. As Goodwin
and colleagues (Goodwin, Jasper and Polletta 2001, 8) observe, while it is possible for feelings of suspicion, hostility, anger and so forth to 'arise even before
blame is allocated through more cognitive processes', it is by developing ideas
about *the problem* and who is to blame[1] that feelings of often rather vague and
undirected disquiet, anxiety, anger, frustration or fear can be transformed into
more directed feelings of hate and into the kinds of sustained feelings of outrage
and injustice that can, to use Gamson's famous phrase, 'put fire in the belly and
iron in the soul' (Gamson 1992, 32):

> The anger of a farmer living near a proposed site for a nuclear plant is the
> intuition that the antinuclear movement tries to build into a systematic ideol-
> ogy of opposition. What a farmer sees first as 'meddlesome outsiders'
> develops into 'technocracy': fear develops into outrage.
> (Goodwin et al. 2001, 19)

This chapter is about how the EDL activists I knew developed the beliefs that underpinned their commitment to the cause and to one another and their increasingly acute feelings of indignation and outrage. In the second section, I discuss the materials that the activists engaged with as they constructed their ideas and what this can tell us about the structures of belief that they develop. In the third section, I explore the social structures of learning. First however it is useful to elaborate on the two basic mechanisms of ideological engagement.

Two mechanisms of ideological engagement

You know Graham? He genned me up on a lot of stuff because where I was a newbie he took me under his wing and he used to post things for me [on Facebook] and he used to tell me about things to read. I had to sit there and read it all out to my family, what he was posting me, to wise them up too.

(Bev)

I started to tell Bev's story in Chapter 2: a woman in her 40s, she became involved in the EDL through close friends who had been 'banging on about' the EDL and sharia law, and had in March 2011 persuaded her to go with them to a demonstration taking place not far from where she lived. Although she had been anxious about the way her neighbourhood and the country were changing, until shortly prior to attending her first demonstration she knew little about Islam, or militant Islam, and took little interest in it. During the months that followed this changed dramatically.

Among the people she met on her first demonstration was Graham. Graham was in his early 60s and had lived all his life in and around east London. He had been involved in the EDL since 2009 and, in spite of being somewhat outspoken and abrasive at times, was widely respected in the local activist scene. Besides the duration of his involvement and his regular attendance at demonstrations and other events, he had gained a reputation as somebody who knew what he was talking about. He was an able orator, and was one of the people who usually said a few words at local demonstrations and meetings. Like several other activists, he was also keenly interested in history, in particular British military history and local history, and had a talent for linking this to his commentaries about the supposed threat of Islam.[2] He was one of the most prolific contributors to Facebook in the region. Bev was one of several newcomers who Graham took under his wing during the period of time that I spent with the EDL.

In the weeks following her first demonstration Bev threw herself into what she, like most of the activists I knew, referred to as 'doing my research'. As well as taking time to speak with and listen to more senior activists, she started to follow up the various links that Graham and other activists posted on the divisional Facebook page or sent directly to her. Speaking about this period some seven months later, she recalled how she suddenly found herself 'reading all sorts of things'. Alongside the various blogs popular within the activist community (see below) she had also started reading newspapers regularly – something she said she had not done before – and visiting websites and blogs run by extreme Islamist groups. She even recalled spending several nights sitting up late reading about topics such as the Second World War in the Pacific and the building of the Thailand–Burma railway.

During the 12 months that I knew Bev, she never came to consider herself an expert on EDL issues. Like other core activists, however, she did start to post what she considered EDL-relevant information on her Facebook page and was keen to share this information with her family and non-EDL friends. By the end of 2011 she had become an admin on one of the local EDL Facebook pages and was helping to identify stories to post on it for the benefit of other activists and supporters.

On March 12th 2012, I spent the day in one of London's Magistrate's Courts, where one of the core London activists, Rob, was facing a charge of assaulting a police officer at an EDL event. This was a serious charge that not only carried a potentially substantial financial penalty but, Rob believed, could well jeopardise his business.

The charge related to events on Remembrance Day, 11th November 2011, on Whitehall in central London. EDL activists had intended to go to the Royal Albert Hall, where Muslims Against Crusades (MAC) activists were reportedly planning to desecrate a remembrance poppy as they had the year before (see Chapter 2). However, on 10th November, Theresa May, the UK Home Secretary, proscribed MAC as an organisation.[3] On hearing this, the EDL activists changed their plans and instead agreed to head to Whitehall to attend the memorial at the Cenotaph. By 10am on 11th November, there were about 200 people more or less closely associated with the EDL and various cognate groups in the vicinity of the Red Lion pub on Whitehall, almost directly opposite Downing Street. Most, particularly the older activists, were dressed smartly – a mark of respect and respectability often assumed by activists at memorial events. They joined in the public remembrance rituals at 11 o'clock – a minute's silence followed by reverent applause for the veterans that filed past – and then returned to the pub. The atmosphere started to change at around 11.30 AM when the activists became aware that police officers were amassing in the middle of Whitehall. It transpired later that the police were acting to prevent what they believed was a plan whereby a large number of EDL activists would proceed from Whitehall to St. Paul's to confront the Occupy protestors camped outside the cathedral – a plan which, as all the activists I knew insisted, involved only half a dozen to a dozen activists at most and about which some, judging from their reactions, were clearly oblivious at the time.[4]

Seeing what was starting to unfold, some activists left the Red Lion and went to St. Stephen's Tavern, just around the corner on Parliament Square. Most, however, stayed in or just outside the Red Lion and soon found themselves within a police cordon that prevented them from leaving the premises. Most continued drinking and socialising, but there was growing anxiety about what was happening. As well as being unsettled by the scale of the policing operation now unfolding before them there were also more mundane concerns – a car parked on a meter, a pre-booked train to catch, and so forth. At approximately 1.30 PM, the police entered the Red Lion to clear the premises. While some activists sought to leave peacefully, others clashed with the police and something of a melee ensued. Eventually 179 activists were detained, of which 176 were released without charge and 3 were bailed.[5] One of these was Rob. His was the only case from that day that went to court.

The news that Rob was facing charges for assaulting a police officer was met with disbelief among the other activists. He was well-known for being astute, and while he had something of a reputation as 'a wind-up merchant'[6] he rarely drank alcohol on demonstrations and most considered him to be one of the 'calmer heads', one of those who usually tried to diffuse rather than inflame a tense situation. Eventually, it transpired that his fellow activists had been right to be surprised – it had been, as the magistrate diplomatically put it, a case of mistaken identity on the part of the police officers in question. Unbeknown to the police, Rob's defence team had secured CCTV footage from the Red Lion and were able to demonstrate that he had not been acting in an aggressive or violent manner as alleged by the officers, that, as he claimed in his initial statement, he had been attempting to prevent a fellow activist with a known heart condition from becoming involved in the scuffle unfolding in the pub and that he had not attacked police officers as he left the building.

The acquittal was an enormous relief for Rob, his family and his friends. In a way, it felt like a minor victory. Talking with me the following day, one activist who had stood as a witness for the defence told me that, once he knew about the CCTV evidence, he had actually 'been looking forward to it'. He, like many activists, felt bitter about what he saw as the police and Crown Prosecution Service's 'stitch-up jobs' over the previous months, which had seen a growing number of EDL activists receiving hefty fines and, in some cases, 'CRASBOS' – Criminal Anti-Social Behaviour Orders. He had submitted letters to the Independent Police Complaints Commission (IPCC) on more than one occasion, each time to no avail. This case, he told me, had been 'a chance to notch one up for us'. Yet it also served to reinforce the activists' feelings of injustice and narratives of victimhood: 179 people, many of whom claimed they had only intended to attend the remembrance service and enjoy a drink to celebrate the proscription of MAC, had suffered the indignity of being hauled into police vans, and Rob and his family had had to go through the ordeal of a court hearing. They asked one another rhetorically, 'would activists from other movements be treated in this way?' and 'what would happen if they were?' Rob's comments were representative of those of many of his fellow activists:

> Where were all – you know, where are Liberty and Amnesty International rushing out screaming 'What about these people's human rights?' you know? If we were students, rioters or black youths, whatever, they'd be bending over backwards: 'Abuse by the police!' and 'The government overstretching their powers!'[7]

Like Bev, all the core activists I knew spent a considerable amount of time doing their research. Exactly what this entailed varied from activist to activist. For some, it comprised little more than speaking with some of the more established activists and reading bits and pieces of information posted up by others on Facebook or the EDL web forum. For most of the core activists, however, it involved more: like Bev, most described spending many hours following up links in online discussions, reading various blogs, and scouring the national and local newspapers for stories related to their cause. Some described working their way through a number of books (see the second section of this chapter), several of the established London leaders were active contributors to Alan Lake's Four Freedoms website, and some attended offline seminars and presentations organised through the counter-jihad network.

Doing their research was an integral part of the activists' world-making on a number of levels. Most obviously, it provided a way of expanding the range of empirical referents around which they spun their protest narrative.[8] Most of the activists I knew were quick to seize on news stories in the national and local media that seemed to coincide with their claims, whether these were about a campaign of 'sharia patrols' carried out by MAC activists in London (see Chapter 1), a woman challenging her employer's decision that she could not wear a visible cross at work, British war graves in Libya being vandalised during the civil war, or Andrew Gilligan's criticisms of Lutfur Rahman, the (now former) mayor of Tower Hamlets, for his association with the Islamic Forum for Europe. In doing their research, particularly where this involved engaging with various counter-jihad materials (see below), activists also picked up a range of phrases and ideas that came to function as interpretive keys and symbolic amplifiers for them and became core components of their framing apparatus. These included expressions such as 'two-tier system',[9] used to connote a systemic bias against 'ordinary English people', and 'cultural Marxism',[10] a phrase used to invoke ideas of nefarious leftist influence over British and Western public life which, if tagged onto the end of any number of stories, could transform them from anecdotes into evidence and explain the perceived injustice of the world around them.

There were also other ways in which doing their research contributed to the activists' world-making. The sharing of information and stories was a collective process in which all of the activists I knew participated in one way or another: forwarding web links to news stories and websites, recommending a book to somebody at a demonstration, or expressing outrage and shock at the stories forwarded or told to them by other activists, whether with a sharp intake of breath and a string of expletives in face-to-face conversation or an 'FFS'[11] or 'NFSE'[12] comment on Facebook. These practices comprised everyday rituals through which activists built and sustained their feelings of common purpose and validated one another's anxiety, loathing, disdain and so forth. There is considerable satisfaction to be gained from seeing that your Facebook post has received multiple 'likes' and numerous comments that broadly sustain and reinforce the point that you make.[13]

These collective processes of learning also helped to enhance the activists' belief in the credibility of their group. The extent to which an issue frame or a set of arguments is likely to gain traction is shaped not only by the availability of empirical referents, but also by the credibility of the claim-makers (Benford and Snow 2000).[14] The circulation of and ongoing commentary on information, particularly that which went beyond the mainstream media to various sources that claimed expert knowledge of (militant) Islam, provided valuable performances of knowing and expertise, bolstering the activists' impression that their movement comprised people with a deep and detailed knowledge of the issues in hand.

In addition, for many of the people I knew, the experience of learning had in itself been one of the pleasurable aspects of EDL activism. There is gratification in the process of learning and feeling that you know more about the world around you than you did previously and more than people around you do currently. Although much of what they learned may have provoked in them fear and anger, they spoke with excitement about websites that had 'opened their eyes' and, particularly among the football lads, the swerveys and the converts, their tales were thick with moments of revelation. As I started to describe in Chapter 2, this excitement about learning often translated into pride. Like Bev, many activists described a trajectory from relative ignorance to meeting people who 'genned them up' on EDL issues to starting to 'do my own research' to a point at which they occupied a position of de facto in-house expert, sharing information with and advising other activists. Initially this might have been very small-scale, sharing information with just a handful of new recruits in their local division or with family and friends. But over time, they, like Graham (above) and Phil (Chapter 2) might take a growing number of people 'under their wing'. I return to the social structures of these processes of learning in the third section of this chapter.

It is important however to recognise that such processes of ideological engagement were also embedded in and reflected people's lived experiences as activists. I would argue that if we want to explain how most activists came to the intensity of belief in the EDL cause that enabled them to sustain commitment to the group we must also look at how, through their participation in EDL activism, people did in effect transform their lives into part of an imagined 'front line'[15] in a millennial struggle between (militant) Islam and the West.

The transformation of their lives into part of the front line of this imagined struggle took place through a number of mechanisms. It related to the way participation in EDL activism entailed becoming part of a community that was saturated with tales of victimhood and heroism relating to EDL issues. As I described in Chapter 2, relatively few activists were able to identify personal injustices or grievances that had led them towards EDL activism. Once involved in the EDL, however, new recruits met, listened to and formed affective ties with established activists – in particular with activists such as Tony, whose life history marked him out as a victim par excellence (Chapter 2) – and EDL issues quickly became personal issues.[16] It was no longer simply a soldier who had been killed, but 'my mate's son', not just any church that had had its cross vandalised by what was 'probably a Muslim gang',[17] but the church that Jane had been going to since she was a girl.

What also helped to transform their lives into part of this struggle was how as people became involved in the EDL their lives were increasingly characterised by encounters that activated the identities and emotions associated with the EDL's protest narrative. Demonstrations in particular provided a space in which the activists' struggle was enacted and brought to life – encountering rows of 'lefties' screaming 'SCUM!' into their faces, having a shouting match with people (MAC supporters) who were openly calling for the abolition of democracy, or finding themselves surrounded by ranks of police officers, many in full riot gear. Every activist I knew had a story to tell about the physical and emotional injuries they had experienced – Terry had been struck on the head by a police baton at a demonstration in Walsall and had a photograph of his face covered in blood on his Facebook homepage; in Brighton, Steve had been spat on and hit by horse faeces thrown at an March for England (MFE) parade by anti-fascist campaigners; Susan had suffered the indignity of wetting herself when arrested with other activists in Whitehall on 11th November 2011 because she had been unable to undo her trousers while handcuffed; Jeff, along with another EDL activist, had been stabbed in the side during a scuffle with a group of young Muslim men after a protest and counter-protest outside the American Embassy on 11th September 2011; and Bev had visited Jeff in hospital, which clearly left her shaken – talking about the event almost three months later she disintegrated into tears. All of these incidents not only became personal grievances, but also 'collective representations' (Durkheim 1915) for the wider activist community: symbols laden with shared cognitive and emotional meanings, which were then frequently invoked during conversations among activists.

The activists also enacted their struggle and activated its attendant identities and emotions in the course of their everyday lives, beyond demonstrations and other official EDL events – a process akin to what Taylor and Whittier (1992) refer to as the 'politicization of everyday life'.[18] They would come into contact and argue with various opponents online; most reported visiting the websites, blogs and social media outputs of their opponents, including the online spaces of some of the most extreme and anti-Western Islamist groups. Waiting for transport to demonstrations, I often chatted with bleary-eyed activists who told me they had been up half the night arguing with 'lefties', 'trolls' or 'muzzies'. Offline, too, there was a sense that once a person became an EDL activist, he or she was never entirely off duty or out of role. Like Bev, most of the activists had spoken at length with family members about the EDL and EDL issues,[19] and while some were concerned that their participation in the EDL might jeopardise their job and therefore tended not to speak with colleagues about what they did on the weekends, others reported speaking with colleagues about EDL issues. Eddie described how he would 'wind up' some of his 'lefty' colleagues; Mark, a taxi driver, apparently spent much of his time guiding conversations with clients towards issues of militant Islam and always tried to ensure that he was working in the vicinity of any MAC activities that he knew of; Susan, a shopkeeper, also reported chatting with customers about EDL issues whenever the opportunity arose and Phil told me about how a black colleague calls him 'my favourite racist friend', adding quickly, 'as a joke, but clearly I'm not [racist]'. Phil was also one of several activists who used EDL-branded merchandise, in his case a very distinctive EDL trench coat,[20] to engage members of the public in conversations about the EDL and EDL issues (although the activists were by and large selective about where they had their EDL merchandise on display: some places, such as neighbourhoods with large South Asian- or Somali-origin communities were usually seen as too high risk):

> I used to wear it out and about wherever I go, I used to wear it up at the pub and – I had a few arguments over it, didn't get any fights over it, but people, some people didn't like it. People used to come up to me and go 'Oh I don't like it', or people used to say 'Oh what's it about?' and all that, so I used to talk to people about it and then I'd end up putting them onto the division page.
>
> (Phil)

Most of the activists also made a conscious effort not to eat halal food;[21] two older activists had written letters to newspapers, although neither had had their letter published, and one had called in to a radio talk-show; most core activists had at least one story about being stopped by the police at some point when not on EDL business and some described altercations with Muslims or 'lefties'. Graham, for example, described how

> I actually fronted a couple in Lakeside [shopping centre] last year, walked up to them and said 'I think you're a disgrace letting her dress like that',[22] and they said 'What, what?' and I said 'You heard me, you heard me', and I just walked away and I just felt so annoyed at it.
>
> (Graham)

It was also common for the activists to believe that being involved in the EDL made them particularly susceptible to attacks by Islamist extremists:

> They will attack you. They will follow you. When we leave a demo, you have to make sure you're not followed because the other week, on the 9/11 [counter-demonstration against Islamist protestors outside the US embassy], there was me, Daz, a few others. When we were going back to the car, just as them guys[23] were getting stabbed, when we went back to the car, there was a car full of Muslim extremists. And they were waiting on the nod from another geezer. We see him give it. We missed the stabbing by two minutes. If we hadn't popped back to the car, it could have quite easily been any one of us. They take your photo and then they target you at a later date. If you're seen there standing up against radical Islam, they will deliberately take your

photo and share it amongst themselves. So if you are by yourself, you will be attacked. If they find out where you live, they will come and attack your house.

(Tom)

These fears had led activists in Essex to set up an emergency number that they could call should they be under threat.

We've got, in Essex, we've got an emergency number. If any Essex member is threatened, they phone 999 for the police and they phone the emergency number for Essex. And there's many members so we can get there, get there and that is 24/7, no matter what time.

(Tom)

A failed plot by a radical Islamist cell to bomb an EDL demonstration in Dewsbury on 30th June 2012[24] suggests that such fears were not entirely without foundation.

As the activists swapped, circulated and embellished these stories, they created and became part of a narrative that permeated and transformed their lives – two police cars passing by became state surveillance, a new halal takeaway opening on the high-street became part of an imagined global zakat[25] network that activists believed to be financing terrorism. As well as generating a vast store of shared memories, anecdotes and grievances, they also created narrative structures – in effect a series of modular vignettes on which all the activists were able to draw on and elaborate.[26] I heard multiple versions, for example, of a story of somebody being asked to take down their St. George's flag.[27] Sometimes it was one flag to be taken down, sometimes it was many; sometimes it was a couple of weeks ago at a community fun day, sometimes a couple of decades ago in a sleepy Kentish village. What was consistent was that it was usually a Muslim or a 'lefty' who asked for the flag to be taken down and the sense of injury to the person asked to take it down and the moral tone of indignation. One of the most symbolically rich versions of this story was told to me by Susan: not only had a Pakistani made the request, but it had happened 'on St. George's day of all days!' [28]

I was asked to take my St. George's Cross off my house by a neighbour who is Pakistani. He came out of his house and he said to me, 'Can you take your flag out of your window?' I went, 'Why?' Now this was on St George's day of all days! I went, 'Why?' He said, 'Where it's flapping in the wind, it's keeping my kids awake of a night'. Now he lives two doors away. I said, 'Excuse me?' I said, 'My bed is – that flag is right under my bed, it doesn't keep me awake'. I said, 'Besides, your kids' – and you can hear his kids two doors up at three o'clock in the morning screaming, shouting and running around. He went, 'Alright then, it offends me'. I went, 'My flag, my St. George's Cross flag offends you?' He went, 'Yeah!' So I went,

'Do yourself a favour', I went, 'what's coming out of your mouth is offending me'. I said, 'All it smells of is bullshit', like that. I said, 'I live in England, I was born in England', I said, 'so do yourself a favour, put your Reeboks on and do one because I'm not taking it lying down'.

(Susan)

There were several other modular vignettes such as a story about applications for a St. George's Day parade being turned down; a story about a conversation where an activist discovered that their child/grandchild or friend's child had been learning all about Islam and slavery but not about English heritage and Christianity; a story about a police officer – usually an 'old-school police officer' or a 'cherry-nosed copper' showing visible signs of distress about the fact that the 'powers that be' had ordained that he had to facilitate the right of (militant) Muslims to protest against Britain and Western democracy. It is of course impossible to know how much truth there is in such stories. What matters however is that they function as truths for activists and provide them with tools[29] with which to spin their lives into much wider narratives of injustice.

It is important to situate activists' processes of ideological engagement within their lived experiences. If we do not, it is difficult to explain why they found some of the arguments that they encountered through, for example, the counter-jihad literature so persuasive. Furthermore, as well as strengthening their belief in and sense of connection to the EDL cause, their experiences as activists also shaped how they interpreted and framed their cause. While most of the EDL leaders were keen to maintain their focus primarily on (militant) Islam, the fact that the main opposition to the EDL tended to come from overtly left-wing groups such as UAF or Antifa meant that some EDL activists' focus shifted increasingly towards the left as clashes with these opponents gave rise to personal grievances and resentments. I return to this issue in Chapter 5. Similarly, clashes with state authorities intimidated some activists, but also deepened most activists' convictions that the state was in the thrall of the Left and led some to argue that the EDL should adopt more radical tactics.[30] Again, I return to this in Chapter 5.

From Gates of Vienna to the *Daily Mail* and . . . Christopher Hitchens?

I've just finished reading Robert Spencer's *The Complete Infidel's Guide to the Koran* where he quotes the Koran and compares it with similar quotations from the Bible. The difference between Christianity and the political dogma of Islam. Um, and I think I suggested to you that you might check out Christopher Hitchens: one of the most eloquent speakers you'll ever come across. I don't agree with everything he says, but I think when it comes to religion, in particular Islam, he's got it absolutely right, and I often find myself quoting him . . . Sometimes you hear somebody speak, or you read something and you think, that's absolutely 100% what I agree with. People like Christopher Hitchens and Sam Harris, I know his books;

[Richard] Dawkins too. When you start reading and listening to huge intellectuals such as these and realise that you independently have stumbled across the same idea about a particular thing as those great men, it inspires you to press on and study further.

(Terry)

Two things stand out about the range of materials that the activists engaged with through their research. The first is the almost complete absence of reference to materials from the traditional far right. In conversations on Facebook or at demonstrations, there were occasionally references to things that people had read on white South African or US nationalist sites – one activist in particular posted links to stories about 'white genocide' in South Africa – but this mainly occurred on personal Facebook pages rather than official EDL sites. From time to time, I also came across signs and symbols associated with the more traditional far right; for example most of the people selling EDL pin badges at demonstrations also had badges with various harder far right symbols available for purchase. However, such symbols were rarely worn openly during demonstrations or other EDL events, including meetings, and with the exception of Jim, Nick and Dave, who had been active in several far right groups and groupuscules, I rarely if ever heard people make reference to publications associated with far right groups. I never came across discussions about or recommendations to read racial nationalist magazines such as *Heritage and Destiny* or cult classic novels such as *The Turner Diaries* or any of H.A. Covington's titles.

One reason for this relative absence of references to far right literature, especially on EDL divisional pages, during the official proceedings of EDL meetings and at demonstrations, might be censorship. All the group admins I knew monitored divisional Facebook pages, and most reported that they had at some point removed posts and comments that were overtly racist or referred favourably to traditional far right groups. Some were adamant that a large proportion of these were posted by 'trolls' or 'lefties' with the intention of making the EDL look bad, although they were never able to present me with persuasive evidence to support such claims. It is also of course possible that the activists were particularly careful about what they said when they knew they were being observed by a researcher, although I believe that after I had followed the group around for several weeks and become part of the furniture, so to speak, my presence probably had little impact on the general pattern of conversations within my earshot. It is also likely, however, that at least part of the explanation for this general absence of more traditional far right material from discussions within the EDL activist scene is that most activists either did not engage with this kind of material or were conscious that it was not considered appropriate in the context of the EDL. I return to this issue in Chapter 4.

The second thing that stands out is that while, as might be expected, the activists did make frequent references to fairly esoteric authors associated with the counter-jihad network, their reference points as they did their research and developed their arguments and ideas also extended well beyond this niche literature into what might be considered 'mainstream'. When I first started attending EDL demonstrations and meetings, I was advised by senior activists that if I really wanted to understand why they were taking to the streets I should visit online sites such as Gates of Vienna, Pamela Geller's Atlas Shrugs, Robert Spencer's Jihad Watch, Ali Sina's faithfreedom.org and the chat rooms on Alan Lake's Four Freedoms site. I was also recommended to read various books including works such as Robert Spencer's *The Complete Infidel's Guide to the Koran* and *The Truth About Muhammed: Founder of the World's Most Intolerant Religion*, and Bruce Bawer's *While Europe Slept: How Radical Islam Is Destroying the West from Within*. Alongside these, several activists recommended that I look into the New English Review, a website which, while not specifically associated with the counter-jihad network, tended to cover cognate and sometimes overlapping themes about the supposed failings of contemporary Western liberalism and cultural loss and was only a couple of mouse-clicks away from the more prominent counter-jihad sites. It also had a contributor, Esmerelda Weatherwax, who wrote frequent and broadly sympathetic accounts of EDL demonstrations and campaigns in and around the London area.

These materials played an important role in the activists' ideological development. The websites and forums in particular provided a steady supply of stories which fuelled their anxieties about (militant) Islam and often helped the activists to imagine their activities as part of a much wider global struggle. It was here, for example, that they came into contact with stories about no-go areas for non-Muslims in various European cities, about Muslims raping and abusing European women, and arguments about how the deviant behaviours of which Muslims were accused of being the primary perpetrators (mainly terrorism, child sexual abuse and domestic violence) were somehow grounded in Islam itself. The dense patterns of cross-referencing between counter-jihad authors (Chipev et al. 2013), the fact that many of those writing on counter-jihad forums are published authors, and the academic style in which they were written helped to lend these sources gravitas and credibility.

While doing their research, however, the activists also cast their nets far wider. At least on the London and Essex Facebook pages the references and links to counter-jihad sites were heavily outnumbered by ones to news stories and commentaries in the mainstream media. Most popular were the right-of-centre newspapers such as the *Daily Mail*, the *Daily Express* and *The Telegraph*, whose reporting on issues such as immigration, security, integration and political correctness resonated with the activists not only in terms of their subject matter and vocabulary but also with their emotional repertoire of fear, outrage and moral shock. The activists posted links to articles such as 'Immigration soared by 20% last year – making a mockery of Government pledge to bring it DOWN';[31] 'Another three terrorists to dodge deportation by using Human Rights Act to stay in Britain',[32] and 'Islamic radicals "infiltrate" the Labour Party',[33] which broadly resonated with their emergent worldview and, once posted, quickly prompted a flurry of suitably irate comments from co-activists.

A number of prominent and what might be considered fairly mainstream intellectuals and commentators were also popular with at least some of the activists, mainly those who were interested in the more intellectual aspects of EDL activism. Predictably, several of them were broadly associated with the right of the political spectrum and have a reputation as vituperative critics of (militant) Islam, the perceived failure of liberal Western states to respond to the more authoritarian and anti-democratic impulses of certain strands of Islam and, in some cases, multiculturalism more generally – people such as Melanie Phillips, author of *Londonistan,* long-time columnist for newspapers such as *The Times* and the *Daily Mail* and a regular contributor to current affairs programmes in the broadcast media; Douglas Murray, a regular contributor to British and US current affairs broadcasts and to publications such as *The Spectator*, who has been highly critical of Islam and what he describes as the West's problem of 'cultural relativism' (see Murray 2006); Andrew Gilligan, who has worked for the BBC, *The Spectator* magazine, the *London Evening Standard, The Telegraph* and Channel 4's *Dispatches* programme, and has been a particularly vocal and persistent critic of Lutfur Rahman, the (now former) Muslim mayor of Tower Hamlets and more recently of the Faith Matters programme Tell MAMA;[34] Sam Harris, renowned atheist and author of books such as *The End of Faith: Religion, Terror and the Future of Reason*; and Pat Condell, a comedian popular in the 1990s who has subsequently become something of a YouTube sensation with a series of monologues criticising religion and in particular Islam.

Perhaps less predictably, some activists also referred to avowedly left-of-centre intellectuals and commentators such as Christopher Hitchens, a polemicist, journalist and author who, while he publicly called on Western states to deal with what he described as 'fascism with an Islamic face'[35] continued to publicly identify as a Marxist; and Nick Cohen, who, while he has been scathing about the Left's apparent unwillingness to critique authoritarian forms of Islam (see Cohen 2007) is also a columnist in *The Guardian*, a left-of-centre newspaper whose readership was often derided by EDL activists.

This range of intellectual references, stretching from the counter-jihad network into more mainstream political debate, highlights an important point about *how* claims-making in the EDL worked. To some extent the structures of belief developed by EDL activists took the form of what Barkun (1998, 61) describes as 'stigmatised knowledge' – 'claims to truth that the claimants regard as empirically verified despite the marginalization of those claims by the institutions that conventionally distinguish between knowledge and falsehood – universities, communities of scientific researchers and the like'. Like other radical political groups on the left and the right, the EDL activists claimed knowledge and insights based on a niche literature, in their case primarily the counter-jihad literature, which they also used to critique more mainstream political discourses about Islam and multiculturalism. The fact that these sources were often heavily criticised by more mainstream actors in fact served to reinforce the activists' narratives about the ignorance of the liberal elite and the creeping influence of things such as 'cultural Marxism'. Criticism from the mainstream, especially from the left, acted as a form of cultural capital for intellectuals associated with the counter-jihad, transforming them in EDL activists' discourse into heroic figures willing to speak truth to power. Yet at the same time, their structures of belief were also grounded in and drew upon mainstream political discourses.

In recent years, there has been considerable interest in academic and policy circles in the idea that radical and sometimes violent forms of political action are emerging through what have been described as 'echo-chambers' (Briggs 2012, Stevens and Neumann 2009, Von Behr et al. 2013) – environments 'where opinions that are not socially acceptable in mainstream society become the norm' (Hirvonen 2013, 81), because in these spaces activists find themselves either exchanging ideas and opinions with like-minded individuals[36] or locked in heated confrontation with their opponents. The expansion of online activism has been posited as particularly conducive to the construction of such spaces. To a certain extent this idea can be applied to the activism at the grassroots of the EDL. The activists did generate both offline and online spaces in which opinions, ideas and phrases that would normally be unacceptable or likely to attract social sanction were in fact praised and reinforced – where for example terms such as 'Muzzies' or 'Muzzrats' could be used without the censure that most of society believe they deserve, and where hostile exchanges with extreme Islamist or anti-fascist and anti-racist activists served to both validate the activists' ideas about the evil that they believed themselves to be struggling against and amplify their feelings of anger, hate, fear and pride.

It would be a mistake, however, to think of EDL activists' ideological development somehow taking place adrift from mainstream political discourses. As Christian Smith notes in his essay on human nature and belief,

> for any one person to assume and believe some assumptions and beliefs means that some larger cultural community of which they are a part, some historical tradition, some 'web of interlocutors'[37] shares these assumptions and beliefs together. For sustaining such sets of assumptions and beliefs requires a community, a 'plausibility structure'[38] to suppose, affirm, and communicate them.
>
> (Smith 2003, 49)

In some cult-like groups these webs of interlocutors may be severely truncated, with plausibility structures that are overwhelmingly internally referential (Barkun 1997, McCauley and Moskalenko 2011, 141–144). This was not the case among the EDL activists that I knew, whose plausibility structures extended deep into mainstream discourses, even if their reading of these discourses may have been somewhat idiosyncratic.

Social structures of learning

There is absolutely no brainwashing in the English Defence League at all. People can express any opinion they like. And no one's told, 'That's not in keeping with our ideas and beliefs', apart from fascists and racists, who we just won't tolerate. But that aside, there is no proclamation from leadership about how we must be and what books you must read, things you must say. There's none of that. The organisation is completely open, and anyone can express their opinion whenever they want to without fear of being politically incorrect or against the code of principles of the movement. You know, you can disagree with anybody. You can agree with anybody. Nobody's going to criticise you for your own personal point of view.

(Terry)

As in most social movement groups, activists were keen to share and promote their ideas, and considerable time went into doing this. As I have described, most of the core activists were enthusiastically involved in circulating what they considered to be relevant information to the rest of the activist community and beyond. Some local and regional coordinators estimated that they spent in excess of 15 hours per week 'try[ing] to find educational pieces for people, things that, you know, explain to you about different kinds of Islamic sects and explained about Muslims Against Crusades' and 'try[ing] to find stuff that new members could read and understand a bit more about what we were doing and our aims' (Andy). As I have mentioned above, most senior activists also made an effort to manage the parameters of activists' discussions during official EDL events and on the group's Facebook pages, primarily by encouraging fellow activists not to use, or in the case of Facebook sometimes deleting, overtly racist language or favourable references to traditional far right groups.

Yet in general learning about EDL issues was an overwhelmingly informal process and there was fairly scant official production of didactic materials. There was of course the EDL website and the official Twitter feed, which most of the activists I knew kept a close eye on,[39] but these were primarily used for information about forthcoming events, organisational developments and so forth, or as a way of linking to relevant news stories. They were not generally described by activists as a primary reference point for opinion formation and were rarely cited in conversation about (militant) Islam or cognate issues. There were none of the magazines or ideological pamphlets nor the study groups or camps often used by radical political groups on both the left and the right to promote ideological learning among their supporters (see Husain 2007, Macklin Forthcoming). In the spring of 2011, two of the regional organisers in London attempted to deliver some training to divisional leaders, primarily about the practicalities of running a division rather than ideological training per se, but this soon fell by the wayside. Similarly, while local organisers and activists encouraged their co-activists to read certain blogs or news stories, there was never any sense among those I knew of being *expected* or *required* to read such materials – something that had come as a surprise to activists such as Tony, Jim and Terry, who had previously been involved in established far right or radical left-wing politics. Neither were there any proscribed reading materials – there were things that, as was made clear, were unwelcome on EDL Facebook pages, namely identifiably far right material, but as far as I was able to identify, there was no attempt to impose more general proscriptions on participants.

What was also noticeable about the structures through which ideological learning took place was how diffuse ideological leadership was within the movement. While people such as Tommy Robinson and Kevin Carroll were recognised as national spokespersons for the movement, they were not seen as ideological leaders. The speeches they gave played an important role in motivating the activists and shaping the focus of the group – especially their continued assertion that the EDL was neither a racist nor a far right organisation. They were also generally admired both for what was seen as the personal sacrifices that they had made for the cause and for how they had become increasingly adept as public speakers.[40] They were however seen very much as organisational leaders rather than intellectual leaders; in fact part of their appeal was precisely that they were 'just normal lads'.

Tellingly, when people made suggestions to me about the people I should speak to if I wanted to gain a deeper understanding of the issues that the EDL campaigns about, rather than Robinson and Carroll, I was pointed in the direction of a handful of fairly local activists who had come to be identified as being 'not, you know, experts, but they know a lot about this stuff'.[41] These people were 'cognitively central' (Kerr and Tindale 2004) to their local activist scene. They were usually among the more prolific contributors to offline and online discussions, were the people who, like Graham, tended to take new recruits under their wing and other activists often referred to them in conversation about EDL issues. Their credibility among their co-activists had a number of bases: they were always among the more articulate activists; most had a fairly strong command of the counter-jihad literature and were able to weave references to this into discussions about the cause; like Graham, all were adept at bringing in multiple historical references to their discussions, whether to the crusades, to the expansion of the Moors' political and military power in the Middle Ages or to more recent Middle Eastern history; and some sprinkled their comments with various Arabic terms such as *kuffar* (non-Muslims), *dawah* (preaching) and *dhimmi* (the non-Muslim residents of an Islamic state), and even references to passages from the Koran, giving an impression of learnedness.

Some of these individuals had come to the EDL having already been involved in the counter-jihad network, such as Kinana Nadir, an occasional presence at EDL demonstrations, one of the main contributors to the Four Freedoms website and author of some of the EDL leaders' early demonstration speeches; and Roberta Moore, a friend of Pamela Geller who led the EDL Jewish Division for a while until a series of acrimonious fallings-out in early 2011 with various people in the EDL whom she accused of being Nazis.[42] But there were also people such as Eddie, who had only become involved in this type of activism in 2009 but was known to be an avid reader and had quickly 'become famous for his monologues'[43] within the local activist scene. These people elicited a certain amount of respect and even deference from their co-activists, at least until they started falling out with one another. They were usually afforded more time than other activists to speak during meetings and their opinions were actively sought, particularly by newer recruits. However they were neither described as, nor in my experience described themselves as 'leaders', and were neither considered to be, nor as far as I could see considered themselves to be, in a position to exercise ideological authority over their co-activists.

Multiple factors contributed to the evolution of this rather laissez-faire approach to activists' ideological development and the diffuse nature of ideological leadership within the movement.[44] It is likely partly to reflect the highly decentralised and often rather chaotic command structures within the EDL (see Chapter 1). It probably also reflects the fact that the EDL was a fairly young movement with scant financial or human resources for the development of a more systematic process of ideological socialisation. And, at least in the London area, it may also reflect the fact that a more co-ordinated programme of online and seminar-based learning about the counter-jihad was already being offered by Four Freedoms.[45]

Whatever the explanation, it had a number of implications for the experiences of EDL activists and the evolution of the EDL and wider anti-Muslim protest movement. Some of these were broadly 'positive' – they enhanced EDL activism as a project of collective world-making. First, these loose and non-hierarchical structures of ideological learning contributed to a sense among most activists that 'anybody can bring their ideas and you won't be told 'No, that's wrong, what do you know?' (Terry). Eventually, there would be calls for stronger leadership, particularly as the EDL started to unravel (see Chapter 5), but most of the time this feeling of being able to express one's opinions was one of the satisfactions of EDL activism (see Chapter 2). As Sutherland and colleagues observe, one of the things that activists often value in grassroots and relatively non-hierarchical social movement groups is that they provide, or at least give the impression of providing, every member with 'the opportunity to engage in meaning-making' (Sutherland, Land and Böhm 2013, 12). The fact that there was very little sense within the EDL of striving for ideological purity meant that activists rarely felt that they were being judged for their ideas by their co-activists,[46] at least until intra-movement framing debates became infused with personal resentments and power struggles as they increasingly did as 2011 wore on (see Chapter 5).

Second, the relative absence of prescription and proscription acquired symbolic value. One of the activists' most frequently used lines of attack against their 'lefty' opponents was to dismiss and disparage them as institutionally 'brainwashed':

> I seen a lot of young misguided people that went to university, joined the Anti-Nazi group or Unite Against Fascism. I bet it [being part of the Anti-Nazi group] is part of the curriculum, I'd go as far as to say. They don't know why they're going there.

(Jim)

The fact that 'anybody can bring their ideas and you won't be told "No, that's wrong, what do you know?"' helped to make them the antithesis of their opponents – they were able to imagine themselves as independently minded, as free thinkers searching out the facts for themselves. However, the diffuse nature of the structures of ideological authority, and of authority more generally, within the movement would eventually pose a challenge for the movement's leaders as intra-movement ideological tension began to surface in 2011. I return to this point in Chapter 5.

Notes

1 As Benford and Snow (2000, 616) explain, 'Since social movements seek to remedy or alter some problematic situation or issue, it follows that directed action is contingent on identification of the source(s) of causality, blame, and/or culpable agents'. Attributing blame also enables activists to define common enemies, thereby makes it easier to forge and sustain the collective identities on which movements depend (Gamson 1997, Sanders 2002, Taylor and Whittier 1992). When activists are unable to identify who to blame, or when it is evident that it is circumstance rather than the out-group that is to blame, instead of feelings of anger and pride activists are more likely to experience frustration; an emotion far less well-suited to encouraging mobilisation (van Troost, van Stekelenberg and Klandermans 2013, 195).

2 Graham was one of the activists who quite consistently spoke about Islam and Muslims in general rather than about militant Islam and Muslim extremists, telling me one day 'they all read the same book'.

3 See 'Muslims Against Crusades banned by Theresa May', Dominic Casciani, BBC, 10th November 2011, www.bbc.com/news/uk-15678275

4 The fact that one of the people who had apparently posted inflammatory statements about going to St. Paul's was a senior figure in the movement was a source of considerable irritation to some of the activists who were caught up in these events, that is, blame for these events was not only directed at the police and the influence of the liberal elite (the blame for what activists saw as discriminatory action by the police was usually attributed to its leaders rather than frontline officers), but also at those who had made what were seen by most activists to be highly irresponsible Facebook posts.

5 See 'Police arrest EDL members to 'avert planned attack' in London', Sandra Laville, *The Guardian*, 11th November 2011, www.theguardian.com/uk/2011/nov/11/edl-arrests-london-occupy-armistice-day

6 An expression used by two of his friends when expressing to me their disbelief about his charges.

7 There were in fact some people outside the EDL who raised concerns about these events, among them Patrick Hayes ('Who's afraid of the EDL 'clicktivists'?', *The Independent*, 16th November 2011, http://blogs.independent.co.uk/2011/11/17/who%E2%80%99s-afraid-of-the-edl-%E2%80%98clicktivists%E2%80%99/#disqus_thread), Brendan O'Neil ('Occupy London in cahoots with coppers', Spiked Online, 15th November 2011, www.spiked-online.com/newsite/article/11558#.VVzVFflViko) and human rights campaigner Peter Tatchell.

8 As research on issue framing has highlighted, a basic requisite for frames to gain traction is that they are grounded in a series of empirical referents (Benford and Snow 2000). The relationship between these empirical referents and the claims does not of course need to be verifiable, in fact, the empirical referents themselves need not even be objectively 'real': they need only seem credible to participants and broadly consistent with the claims being made when viewed from the perspective of those participants.

9 A long-established theme in backlash politics (Hewitt 2005, Rhodes 2009).

10 For an account of how this concept has travelled through various parts of contemporary radical right networks, see Jarmin (2014). Richardson (2015) explores the concept in transnational context.

11 Stands for 'for fuck's sake'.

12 Stands for 'no fucking surrender ever'.

13 This became self-reinforcing behaviour. An activist would post a story; co-activists would react with suitable expressions of outrage; the first activist would feel satisfaction at these responses and a sense of pride at having contributed to the group's discussions, and would be more likely to do so again in the future. (This observation is based on a discussion with two activists on the bus to a demonstration in Luton, about their first experiences as admins on duty.)

14 Citing Hovland and Weiss (1951) and Aronson and Golden (1962), Benford and Snow (2000, 620–621) observe 'It is a well-established fact in the social psychology of communication that speakers who are regarded as more credible are generally more persuasive'.

15 This metaphor was used both in the everyday conversations of the activists and during speeches and written communications by the national and regional leaders.

16 One of the characteristics of becoming part of a community of activists is a blurring of identity boundaries between the self, fellow activists and the activist community as a collective (Calhoun 1994, 267, Casquete 2006, 284). By creating new identity structures and self-categorisations people can be 'connected to others in such a way that they are likely to experience emotions even though they themselves are not directly confronted with the triggering situation' (Yzerbyt et al. 2010, 535)

17 A story that was widespread among local activists around February 2012. A small group of activists had spoken with the church curate about erecting a new cross but had not told them that they were associated with the EDL, due to concern about the controversy that this would cause.

18 Passy and Giugni (2000, 122) observe that the more frequently a particular set of identities are activated the more likely they are to become important in a person's life and therefore the more likely they are to generate sustained participation in the movement.

19 This was also captured in a documentary about women in the EDL titled *EDL Girls: Don't Call Me Racist* (Baker 2014)

20 Terry used an EDL key ring to strike up conversations; getting this out when buying drinks in pubs or when at the checkout of his local supermarket.

21 One of the more bizarre episodes of my fieldwork was on the way back from a demonstration in Birmingham on 29th October 2011. Some of the activists had asked if there was somewhere they could stop to get food that wasn't a service station because service stations were 'a rip off'. We pulled into a pub/truck stop, the activists all clad in their EDL hoodies, only to find that it was run by a Muslim family. There was much debate about whether or not to order food. One activist opined that he preferred not to because he suspected that they would spit in the food, another argued that people shouldn't buy food from them because it was 'like giving money to the enemy', but most people, keen to eat something to soak up the alcohol, ignored them both and got stuck into an assortment of burgers.

22 The woman in question was wearing a burka.

23 Two EDL activists.

24 See 'Six admit planning to bomb English Defence League rally', BBC, 30th April 2013, www.bbc.com/news/uk-22344054

25 Zakat is a form of obligatory alms-giving in Islam.

26 Citing work by Swidler and Arditi (1994, 308–310) and by Franzosi (2004), della Porta and Diani (2006, 108) note that it is quite normal for people, particularly groups

of people with overlapping identities to 'reappropriate social experiences and history, manipulating them and transforming them creatively, forging new myths and institutions'.

27 Flags, as Hewitt (2005, 127) notes, are particularly potent symbols and 'often do extra symbolic work when "ways of life" are thought to be under threat'.

28 Through sharing stories, the activists became attuned to the kind of themes and rhetorical flourishes which elicited the emotional feedback that they were, more or less consciously, looking for.

29 The idea of culture providing tools for actors derives from Swidler's (1986) now classic analysis of the relationship between culture and 'strategies of action'.

30 Interactions with public authorities can provide a particularly rich source of feelings of injustice (Gamson, Fireman and Rytina 1982). Activists expect their opponents to criticise and attack them, but what is taken as 'repression' by public authorities generates 'a sense of betrayal' among activists because 'one's own government, [is] the same agent that is supposed to protect citizens and process complaints' (Jasper 2014, 211). There is a considerable literature on the possible 'backfire effects' (Hess and Martin 2006) of forms of state repression, whereby repression can under certain circumstances fuel commitment and encourage tactical radicalisation (della Porta 1988, 1995, 2008). In della Porta's (1995) account of violence in Germany and Italy, she argues that the relationship between repression and radicalisation is curvilinear: heavy protest policing deters people at the more moderate fringes of movements but radicalises those who are already at the more tactically radical fringe. This finding is supported by Caiani and Borri (2013, 570).

31 www.dailymail.co.uk/news/article-2029948/575-000-come-UK-year-despite-Government-pledge-curb-immigration-cash-strapped-Britons-abandon-dreams-retirement-abroad.html#ixzz2ujPwOEGc cited on EDL London Division Facebook page 25th August 2011.

32 www.dailymail.co.uk/news/article-2042198/Another-3-terrorists-dodge-deportation-using-Human-Rights-Act.html#ixzz2ujQWuNLg cited on EDL London Division Facebook page 27th September 2011

33 www.telegraph.co.uk/news/politics/labour/7333420/Islamic-radicals-infiltrate-the-Labour-Party.html cited on the EDL London Division Facebook page 5th August 2011

34 See '"Tell Mama" did exaggerate anti-Muslim attacks: PCC rejects all Fiyaz Mughal's complaints against us', http://blogs.telegraph.co.uk/news/andrewgilligan/100266808/tell-mama-did-exaggerate-anti-muslim-attacks-pcc-rejects-all-fiyaz-mughals-complaints-against-us/

35 See Hitchens polemic titled 'Defending Islamofascism: It's a valid term. Here's why', www.slate.com/articles/news_and_politics/fighting_words/2007/10/defending_islamofascism.html

36 Social movement researchers have for some years spoken about how social movements can provide 'free spaces' where activists can develop ideas, arguments and identities relatively free from the pressure of dominant or elite discourses (Futrell and Simi 2004, Polletta 1999). I suspect that the current ascendency of talk of 'echo-chambers' in the context of security and terrorism research is partly due to the fact that it sounds somehow more sinister and, unlike the term 'free spaces', hints at delusion and distorted truths rather than discovery and innovation.

37 Here, Smith is referring to Charles Taylor (1989).

38 Ibid.

39 Kim and colleagues' (Kim et al. 2013) analysis of online activity within the EDL activist scene highlights the organisational centrality and importance of the EDL's official Twitter feed, at least within EDL activists' Twitter communication.

40 This was even the case among those who, in the autumn of 2011, became increasingly critical of the national leadership.

41 Notes from a conversation with Gary, an event organiser at my first demonstration on 12th March 2011.
42 Nadir and Moore both not only gained celebrity status among elements of the activist community but also became figures of notoriety in the eyes of the EDL's various opponents, attracting attention on anti-EDL sites such as EDL News, Loonwatch, Islamophobia Watch and Hope Not Hate.
43 A comment by one of the London organisers (Mark) when discussing what he saw as the range of different talents within the London leadership during the spring of 2011.
44 Such social practices of learning are not uncommon in social movements. As Barker and colleagues (Barker, Johnson and Lavalette 2001, 12) note, much of the training that happens in social movements takes place through 'informal watching, listening, talking and participation, where "learning" is as unplanned yet effective as the methods by which children acquire language'.
45 As in other organizational fields, within social movements, it is common for forms of task specialization to develop whereby different organizations develop different specializations (Zald and McCarthy 1987).
46 One of the effects of striving for ideological purity can be the emergence of particularly vicious ideological debates that can be upsetting and demoralising for activists. Ryan (1989) for example describes the strain caused on activists in the women's movement in the United States in the late 1960s and early 1970s at being constantly 'trashed' by other people within their movement, while Klatch (2004, 494–495) describes how experiences of being judged and constantly criticised by fellow activists undermined intra-movement relationships in one of the leading new left organisations of the 1960s.

References

Aronson, E., and B. Golden. 1962. "The Effect of Relevant and Irrelevant Aspects of Communicator Credibility on Opinion Change." *Journal of Personality* 30 (2):135–146.
Baker, F. 2014. EDL Girls: Don't Call Me Racist. BBC Three.
Barker, C., A. Johnson and M. Lavalette. 2001. "Leadership Matters: An Introduction." In *Leadership and Social Movements*, edited by C. Barker, A. Johnson and M. Lavalette, 1–23. Manchester: Manchester University Press.
Barkun, M. 1997. "Foreword." In *Radical Religion in America: Millenarian Movements from the Far Right to the Children of Noah*, edited by J. Kaplan, vii–x. New York: Syracuse University Press.
Barkun, M. 1998. "Conspiracy Theories as Stigmatized Knowledge: The Basis for a New Age Racism?" In *Nation and Race: The Developing Euro-American Racist Subculture*, edited by J. Kaplan and T. Bjørgo, 58–72. Boston: Northeastern University Press.
Benford, R.D., and D.A. Snow. 2000. "Framing Processes and Social Movements: An Overview and Assessment." *Annual Review of Sociology* 26:611–639.
Briggs, R. 2012. *Discussion Paper: The Changing Face of Al Qaeda.* London: Institute for Strategic Dialogue.
Caiani, M., and R. Borri. 2013. "The Extreme Right, Violence and Other Action Repertoires: An Empirical Study on Two European Countries." *Perspectives on European Politics and Society* 14 (4):562–581.
Calhoun, C. 1994. *Neither Gods Nor Emperors: Students and the Struggle for Democracy in China.* Berkeley: University of California Press.
Casquete, J. 2006. "Protest Rituals and Uncivil Communities." *Totalitarian Movements and Political Religions* 7 (3):283–301.

Chipev, B., P. Gulian, V. Dinga, R. Zimerman and I. Enache. 2013. *Counter-Jihadist Literature: A Network of Radical Authors and Their Influence Online.* Amsterdam: Digital Methods Initiative, University of Amsterdam.

Cohen, N. 2007. *What's Left: How the Left Lost Its Way.* London: Fourth Estate.

della Porta, D. 1988. "Recruitment Processes in Clandestine Political Organizations: Italian Left-Wing Terrorism." *International Social Movement Research* 1:155–169.

della Porta, D. 1995. *Social Movements, Political Violence, and the State: A Comparative Analysis of Italy and Germany.* Cambridge: Cambridge University Press.

della Porta, D. 2008. "Research on Social Movements and Political Violence." *Qualitative Sociology* 31 (3):221–230.

della Porta, D., and M. Diani. 2006. *Social Movements: An Introduction.* Oxford: Blackwell.

Durkheim, E. 1915. *The Elementary Forms of the Religious Life.* Translated by J. Ward Swain. London: Allen and Unwin.

Franzosi, R. 2004. *From Words to Numbers: Narrative, Data, and Social Science.* Cambridge: Cambridge University Press.

Futrell, R., and P. Simi. 2004. "Free Spaces, Collective Identity, and the Persistence of US White Power Activism." *Social Problems* 51 (1):16–42.

Gamson, J. 1997. "Messages of Exclusion: Gender, Movements, and Symbolic Boundaries." *Gender and Society* 11 (2):178–199.

Gamson, W.A. 1992. *Talking Politics.* Cambridge: Cambridge University Press.

Gamson, W.A., B. Fireman and S. Rytina. 1982. *Encounters with Unjust Authority.* Homewood: Dorsey.

Goodwin, J., J.M. Jasper and F. Polletta. 2001. "Introduction: Why Emotions Matter." In *Passionate Politics: Emotions and Social Movements*, edited by J. Goodwin, J.M. Jasper and F. Polletta, 1–24. Chicago: University of Chicago Press.

Hess, D., and B. Martin. 2006. "Repression, Backfire, and the Theory of Transformative Events." *Mobilization* 11 (2):249–267.

Hewitt, R. 2005. *White Backlash and the Politics of Multiculturalism.* Cambridge: Cambridge University Press.

Hirvonen, K. 2013. "Sweden: When Hate Becomes the Norm." *Race and Class* 55 (1):78–86.

Hovland, C., and W. Weiss. 1951. "The Influence of Source Credibility on Communication Effectiveness." *Public Opinion Quarterly* 15 (4):635–650.

Husain, E. 2007. *The Islamist.* London: Penguin.

Jarmin, J. 2014. "Cultural Marxism and the Radical Right." In *The Post-War Anglo-American Far Right*, edited by P. Jackson and A. Shekhovstov, 84–103. London: Palgrave Macmillan.

Jasper, J.M. 2014. "Constructing Indignation: Anger Dynamics in Protest Movements." *Emotion Review* 6 (3):208–213.

Kerr, N.L., and R.S. Tindale. 2004. "Group Performance and Decision Making." *Annual Review of Psychology* 55:623–655.

Kim, G.J., J. Rademakers, M. Sanchez and W. van Vucht. 2013. *Online Activity of the English Defence League.* Amsterdam: Digitial Methods Initiative.

Klatch, R.E. 2004. "The Underside of Social Movements: The Effects of Destructive Affective Ties." *Qualitative Sociology* 27 (4):487–509.

Macklin, G. Forthcoming. *White Racial Nationalism in Britain.* Abingdon: Routledge.

McCauley, C., and S. Moskalenko. 2011. *Friction: How Radicalization Happens to Them and Us.* Oxford: Oxford University Press.

Murray, D. 2006. *Neoconservatism: Why We Need It*. New York: Encounter Books.

Passy, F., and M. Giugni. 2000. "Life-Spheres, Networks, and Sustained Participation in Social Movements: A Phenomenological Approach to Political Commitment." *Sociological Forum* 15 (1):117–144.

Polletta, F. 1999. ""Free Spaces" in Collective Action." *Theory and Society* 28 (1):1–38.

Rhodes, James. 2009. "The political breakthrough of the BNP: The case of Burnley." *British Politics* 4 (1):22–46.

Richardson, J. E. 2015. "'Cultural Marxism' and the British National Party: A Transnational Discourse." In *Cultures of Post-War British Fascism*, edited by N. Copsey and J. E. Richardson, 202–226. Abingdon: Routledge.

Ryan, B. 1989. "Ideological Purity and Feminism: The U.S. Women's Movement from 1966 to 1975." *Gender & Society* 3 (2):239–257.

Sanders, J. 2002. "Ethnic Boundaries and Identity in Plural Societies." *Annual Review of Sociology* 28:327–357.

Smith, C. 2003. *Moral, Believing Animals: Human Personhood and Culture*. Oxford: Oxford University Press.

Stevens, T., and P. Neumann. 2009. *Countering Online Radicalisation: A Strategy for Action*. London: International Centre for the Study of Radicalisation and Political Violence.

Sutherland, N., C. Land and S. Böhm. 2013. "Anti-leaders(hip) in Social Movement Organizations: The Case of Autonomous Grassroots Groups." Organization Online First Version: 1–23. http://org.sagepub.com/content/early/2013/06/03/1350508413480254

Swidler, A. 1986. "Culture in Action: Symbols and Strategies." *American Sociological Review* 51 (2):273–286.

Swidler, A., and J. Arditi. 1994. "The New Sociology of Knowledge." *Annual Review of Sociology* 20:305–329.

Taylor, C. 1989. *Sources of the Self*. Cambridge: Harvard University Press.

Taylor, V., and N. E. Whittier. 1992. "Collective Identity in Social Movement Communities: Lesbian Feminist Mobilization." In *Frontiers in Social Movement Theory*, edited by A. D. Morris and C. M. Mueller, 104–129. New Haven: Yale University Press.

van Troost, D., J. van Stekelenberg and B. Klandermans. 2013. "Emotions of Protest." In *Emotions in Politics: The Affect Dimension in Political Tension*, edited by N. Demertzis, 186–203. Basingstoke: Palgrave Macmillan.

Von Behr, I., A. Reding, C. Edwards and L. Gribbon. 2013. *Radicalisation in the Digital Era: The Use of the Internet in 15 Cases of Terrorism and Extremism*. Brussels: RAND.

Yzerbyt, V., M. Dumont, D. Wigboldus and E. Gordijn. 2010. "I Feel For Us: The Impact of Categorization and Identification on Emotions and Action Tendencies." *British Journal of Social Psychology* 42 (4):533–549.

Zald, M. N., and J. D. McCarthy. 1987. "Social Movement Industries: Competition and Conflict Among SMOs." In *Social Movements in an Organizational Society*, edited by M. N. Zald and J. D. McCarthy, 161–181. New Brunswick: Transaction.

4   Trying to be not-racist and not-far-right

> Don't demonise everyone in the English Defence League as extreme or far right because I certainly am not that, I don't class myself as that. If others do, that's up to them, but I am not that.
>
> (Tony)

> What I should say – what it is about the English Defence League that I find more attractive than other groups that I might have joined – one of the things, well, I'll start by saying I'm not a racist. And so I would not have been part of any racist organisation.
>
> (Terry)

In the first couple of months that I spent with English Defence League (EDL) activists, almost every conversation I had with a new contact began in a similar fashion. One of the activists who knew me would present me to other activist(s), telling them that I was 'alright'; I would explain that I was a sociologist interested in understanding more about the EDL as a social movement group and how it managed to keep going in spite of the obvious challenges it faced, how being an EDL activist had affected their lives, and so forth; they would then launch into a short speech about the EDL not being a racist or far right group. In most cases, this also included a declaration of how they themselves were not racist and would not have considered becoming involved in a racist group.

To some extent, the activists' attempts to challenge and resist these labels were undoubtedly bound up with strategic considerations. These are terms that carry a particularly stubborn stigma and the activists were well aware of how damaging they were to the group's efforts to build public support. Yet among the activists I knew, the resistance to these labels was not just about attempting to develop a 'reputational shield' (Ivarsflaten 2006) for the organisation: most quite genuinely did not self-identify in this way and resisting such labels had become an important part of their sense of who they were – of their 'projects of the self' (Giddens 1991). Most people wish to see themselves as moral actors. Indeed, being able to conceive of ourselves as moral actors somehow contributing to securing and sustaining moral order is a basic tenet of most human lives

(Kleinman 2006, Smith 2003, 7–44).[1] For the overwhelming majority of the EDL activists that I knew, being not-racist and not-far-right had become part of this narrative of their moral selves, and being able to resist the attribution of these labels was important if they were to avoid or at least mitigate issues of identity dissonance or 'cognitive dissonance' (Festinger 1957, Wallace and Fogelson 1965). Identities, as Berezin (2001, 84) observes, tend to be 'multiple but not schizophrenic.[2]

If we are to understand how EDL activism worked as a project of collective world-making (see Chapter 1), it is therefore necessary to explore how activists managed these unwanted identity attributions. In the first section of this chapter, I outline a series of discursive moves[3] that the activists used to do this. In the second section, I discuss the consequences of these strategies for the EDL's emergent movement culture.

Discursive moves used by activists to resist and counter the 'racist' and 'far right' labels

The activists' response to these unwanted labels was built around a series of discursive moves that they acquired, developed and honed during the course of their journey through EDL activism and their interactions both with other EDL activists and with their opponents.[4] In their everyday discourse, the moves often intersected with and became difficult to disentangle from one another. For the purposes of describing and analysing these moves, and thereby understanding how EDL activists were by and large so able to fend off attacks along these lines, it is however useful to tease them apart.

Claiming social proximity to people not of white British backgrounds

Perhaps the most basic move comprised claiming social proximity to people who were not of white British heritage. At the group level this took the form of drawing attention to the participation of people from black and minority ethnic backgrounds in EDL events. Since the EDL emerged, its activists have sought to make political capital out of the fact that the group contains people from such backgrounds (Copsey 2010, Jackson 2011). As I described in Chapter 1, early communications from the EDL such as the video of EDL leaders burning a swastika tended to emphasise the 'black-and-white-unite' theme. The EDL also had small but high-profile Sikh and Jewish contingents, and there was even a Muslim activist, Abdul Rafiq, a fan of Glasgow Rangers, who became something of a celebrity within the activist community. These activists were often given special prominence at demonstrations.

Similarly, friends and family members who were not from white British backgrounds operated as a key part of most activists' non-racist credentials: 'My daughter is black, the love of my life is a Sikh woman, how can I be racist?!' (Terry); 'Even now I'm in the EDL, I've still got Muslim mates in college and all that' (Pete); 'Yeah, I won't be at the demonstration this weekend cos I'm at my Muslim neighbour's wedding – I'm a proper racist, me!' (Mark); 'Me being a racist with my black grand-daughter' (Laura, caption on a photograph of her with a young black girl on Facebook); 'They call us racists, but if you look at my friends, I've got friends from Lebanon, Egypt, Sri Lanka – I've got a son-in-law from Sri Lanka' (John). Several activists were also keen to point out that they themselves were the children of immigrants – in most cases Irish, although the Essex RO at the time, Paul Pitt, is of Greek descent. In a variation of the 'We've-got-all-sorts-of-people-in-the-movement' argument, Paul Pitt used his Greek heritage as evidence that the EDL was not racist:

> I'm running Essex, Kent and Sussex, and if it was a racist organisation, I would not be allowed to do that; I would never have been allowed to get that far. I can go to people anywhere in the country and I'm welcomed with open arms. So the racial issue is rubbish.

As with most of the activists' discursive moves, as well as operating defensively to protect them from and rebut the claims of their opponents they were also used offensively to restate their claims about the problem of (militant) Islam and the liberal elite's supposed failure to address this threat. The fact that somebody's parents were immigrants was used not only as evidence that they were not xenophobic, but also to ask why, if their own immigrant family has integrated with mainstream English/British culture, others cannot do the same. Mark, for example, argued:

> My family history is Irish Republican and they don't make any excuses for that, you know. That's their business. I was born and brought up over here, I pass the Norman Tebbit cricket test[5] and all I know is being English, you know. Although my parents, sometimes they'll make me out to be too English: that's how they wanted their kids brought up in this country, to integrate, and that's how I think everyone should be.

Activists also used stories about their proximity to people not of white British background to reinforce claims about the particular threat of (militant) Islam and (extremist) Muslims as opposed to other minority ethnic groups. Anecdotes were often shared about how they had found common cause in their animosity towards Muslims in conversation with Sikhs, Buddhists, Hindus and black people.

> My boy was playing with his friends on Xbox. His friend went to him, 'Don't you think it's a load of bollocks that you're not allowed to say Happy Christmas no more, you've got to say Happy Holidays?' So my boy shouted out to me, 'Mum, what's this?' I went, 'That's politically correct because they don't want to offend Muslims'. It's not offending Sikhs, Hindus, Buddhists or anything else, it's that they don't want to offend Muslims. Because all the Sikhs, Buddhists and Hindus that I know, and I know a few of them

through where I work, right, they hate – the woman I work with, she's a Buddhist, she hates Muslims.

(Susan)

Challenging the conceptual categories used by critics of the EDL

You know, there are white Muslims, black Muslims, brown Muslims. . .

(Eddie)

A second type of discursive move involved challenging the conceptual categories used by their critics – a strategy that broadly maps on to what McCaffrey and Keys (2000) call 'frame debunking'. They challenged the application of the racist epithet with the straightforward argument that 'Islam is not a race' (see also Pilkington 2014).[6] This logic was extended into claims that their definition of what it meant to be a 'patriot' was explicitly not defined by race, but only by whether or not somebody 'had St. George in their hearts'[7] (Tom).

This move echoes a framing strategy evident in much contemporary anti-minority politics whereby frames grounded in concepts of racial superiority/inferiority have largely been replaced by those that invoke ideas about cultural or religious incompatibilities. This move is often associated with the European 'new right' movements (Bar-On 2007) and, as many have argued, has also permeated mainstream political debates (Barker 1981). This 'new'[8] politics of us and them has been much critiqued by anti-racism campaigners and academics, many of whom argue that it is simply a new form of racism which, if anything, is more insidious because of its veiled nature (Balibar 2007, Barker 1981). However, the popular support achieved by a number of far- and radical-right groups using these types of cultural frames, such as the *Front National* in France, the Freedom Party (*Partij voor de Vrijheid* [PVV]) in the Netherlands and the Swedish Democrats (*Sverigedemokraterna*)[9] are testament to the fact that such critiques have gained only limited traction with the general public, a point I return to below.

Activists also sought to debunk their critics' use of the conceptual category 'far right' to describe the EDL in two main ways. The first of these is reminiscent of what Berbrier (2002, 560), in his discussion of stigma transformation, describes as 'distance claims' based on 'indexical dissociation'; that is, saying 'look at those people (whose status in that space is presumed and black-boxed); we are not at all like them'. The activists set up a definition of the far right as swastika-toting, Jew-hating Nazis and then pointed out that they did not fit in this category because they had a Jewish division in their movement, and people had been forcibly removed from their demonstrations for giving the Nazi salute. This was usually buttressed with tales of animosity between themselves and organised far right groups. A particularly popular anecdote among London activists, for example, was about an EDL London meeting in 2010 when Richard Barnbrooke, for some time one of the leading lights of the British National Party (BNP), attended the meeting only to be told by EDL activists that they wanted nothing to do with him or the BNP.[10]

What activists also used to debunk their critics' use of the category 'far right' was their identification of the EDL as a 'single-issue group, not a political group'. This definition was intended to put further distance between themselves and established far right political groups such as the BNP and the NF, and more generally to situate themselves outside the politics of left and right.[11] When I first started conducting fieldwork, I was repeatedly pulled up by activists if I said that my research was about political movements.

This positioning of themselves as 'a single-issue group, not a political group' had two further advantages. First, it enabled activists to play on a wider populist mood of 'anti-politics' (Weltman and Billig 2015), in which being 'political' has come to signify being at best partisan and at worst self-interested and corrupt – a mood by no means restricted to those at the political margins (see Bailey 2009, Hay 2007). Second, it helped the movement to accommodate the range of interests described in Chapter 3. Being a single-issue group reduced the pressure to achieve general ideological consistency across the activist community because all that really mattered to activists was that they were in agreement about the single issue around which the EDL was mobilising. This was particularly valuable to activists who did not associate with the far right, as it provided them with an explanation along the lines of 'I may not agree with their politics, but we agree on this specific issue'[12] when challenged about marching alongside people who, as they knew full well, did hold racist views and affiliations with established far right groups.

Arguments from equivalence

Susan: Someone said to me the other day about racism. If I stand here and say I'm white, I'm English and I'm proud I'm classed as a racist, but if there was a West Indian, Hindu, Sikh, standing there saying like, 'I'm black, I'm West Indian and I'm proud – '

Bev: No one would bat an eyelid.

Susan: But I take my hat off to that person, because if you're black and proud of your heritage good luck to you, it shows you've got a heart, you're patriotic to your own country and your own heritage. But why can't we say it?

Years ago when [Ken] Livingstone was mayor [of London] – he was asked by the Irish community 'Could we have some money for a St Patrick's Day parade?' 'Yes, of course'. They suddenly found this bag of money that they gave to them, thousands. And then someone asked, 'Can we have some money for a St George's event?' and they were kind of waved away . . .

(Eddie)

A third move involved claims that they were only trying to do what other culturally defined groups such as Muslims, Afro-Caribbeans and the Irish are often encouraged to do: celebrate their culture. Again, this replicates a move by many European new-right groups which use a form of multiculturalist discourse to emphasise difference and claim the right to protect their cultural heritage – what Spektorowski (2012) describes as a 'recognition/exclusion' framework of multiculturalism.

For the EDL activists, this argument worked on two levels. It was used to negate accusations of prejudice by developing their claims within a universalistic rather than a particularistic frame, thereby 'translating their particular injustices into the more universal language of civil injustice' (Alexander 2006, 277): how could they be doing something morally reprehensible if they were doing exactly the same as other groups who, in mainstream discourse, receive a positive evaluation? It was also used to reassert claims of injustice by linking back to the 'two-tier system' theme so prominent in the activists' claim-making (see Chapter 3, see also Harris, Busher and Macklin 2015, Pilkington 2014).

Claims of left-wing fascism

A fourth move comprised what could be called a strategy of 'inversion' (Durrheim et al. 2005, van Dijk 1992), with activists claiming that their 'lefty' opponents were the 'real fascists'. There were three elements to this move. The first was attributing the characteristics of fascists to the left. Activists pointed to campaigns to ban EDL demonstrations, coordinated by groups such as Unite Against Fascism (UAF), as evidence of a dangerous authoritarian impulse that ran contrary to the principles of free speech. They also told one another, and anyone else who would listen, stories about 'left-wing thugs'. After almost every demonstration the activists circulated tales about groups of 'lefties' attacking or threatening lone EDL activists or precipitating violent clashes between the EDL and their opponents. Incidents in which 'women and children' had been the victims of these left-wing thugs received particular narrative attention.[13]

The second element comprised positioning the left as apologists for 'Islamo-fascism', and therefore complicit in its diffusion.

> I just remember the total hand-wringing reaction of this little ginger bastard [a 'left-wing' colleague] when I had confronted these Islamists [at work]. He said [adopting a whining tone of voice] 'You were so rude to him, you were so rude to poor Usman'. I said 'I wasn't rude to the guy at all', I said, 'challenge extremism wherever you find it'. I said 'If I was making pro-Nazi statements or something like that, you wouldn't hesitate to be in my face about it, but with them you just sit there and smile!'
>
> (Eddie)

The third element of this move involved repeated references to a comment supposedly made by Winston Churchill that 'the fascists of the future will be called anti-fascists' – a quote for which, it should be pointed out, there is no historical record.

Being 'ordinary English people'

Susan: A lot of people are scared to be bothered. I think a lot of people have got that fear, 'What about my family? Am I putting myself on the frontline, getting a hiding or – No, you're not unless – if you go silly then yeah you are. We're just average working – I'm a working single mum, you're [addressing Bev] married with two kids, do you know what I mean? But when we go out petitioning, like the mosque in Dagenham, the one at Green Lanes, we done a lot of petitioning for that, we were out on the streets for days and the general public; they loved it.

Bev: It was for the mosque wasn't it; it was for the planning of the mosque. We were on the street for days and days, we got thousands and thousands of signatures. It was fun, you find with the local – with the locals it was like, 'Excuse me can you sign a petition?' They go, 'What's it for?' As soon as you said 'the mosque', they'll go, 'Yeah, come here, give us it', and we'd hand them a leaflet, they'd read it and go, 'Oh yeah, nice one', and that was quite interesting. We got a lot of response from petitioning around this way.

A fifth move used by the activists comprised attempting to position themselves as part of a different and less stigmatised category: 'ordinary English people'.[14] As I discussed in Chapter 2, to some extent, the activists did construct heroic identities for themselves that marked them out as being somehow special, noble and worthy – they were the people willing to take a stand and endure considerable hardship in order to secure a future for their children and their grandchildren. As in most social movements, the activists used various signs and symbols through which to mark themselves as belonging to this particular community – their EDL-branded hoodies and hats, EDL- or patriotism-themed tattoos, and expressions that they picked up and used such as 'Morning infidels!', NFSE (meaning 'No Fucking Surrender Ever') and so forth. Activists also frequently expressed frustration at how so many people, often people they knew, seemed uninterested in their cause:

> I really can't understand people who actually think that everything is rosy, you know, or people that just don't care, you know, that are actually quite selfish. I mean I've got quite a few friends who, really, they couldn't give a shit, I've tried to get them . . . I've said to them, 'You really should be doing more, the way the country is going and all that'. They've said, 'I don't give a shit, I'm alright, I've got enough money, you know'. I say, 'What about future generations?!' 'Don't you worry about them?!'
>
> (Mark)

Yet the activists also identified as belonging to the category of 'ordinary English people'. They developed this identity in a number of ways. In part, they did it by emphasising the apparent 'ordinariness' of the people in the EDL activist community. They would point out, for example, that far from only hooligans, skinheads and committed political activists, many of the people that attended EDL events were women, children and people with little or no political experience. For example,[15] describing the first EDL demonstration that he went to observe, Tony described how:

> I looked at the English Defence League and I saw all different people there. I was quite surprised that they wasn't all nationalist [BNP or NF] voters. That's the reason why it was different. I've been on BNP meetings and it's 99% men. So when I went to the EDL, the one in Dagenham, I see ranges of ages, and families. Now, I'm not saying BNP don't have families because they do, ordinary families like myself, but in the meetings it's predominantly men, and that struck a chord.

They also developed their identity as ordinary English people through claims about wider public support or at least sympathy for their cause. These claims were grounded in a variety of empirical referents. Activists made much of the size of their Facebook membership which, as mentioned in Chapter 1, had at several points been in the region of 100,000 people. They also pointed out that they were far from the only people in the public sphere expressing anxieties about (militant) Islam (see Chapter 3)[16] or for that matter organising campaigns against the building of new mosques.

> I just laughed, it was one of the biggest campaigns [against a mosque], but it wasn't EDL, it was these local people against this mosque in Camberley [an affluent area]. These people don't give a shit whether there's a big mosque going up in Dudley – but as soon as you put one in a white middle-class area, you know, 'not in my back yard', suddenly there are people out in the street.
>
> (Andy)

The activists also nourished this belief about wider public support with a diet of corroborating anecdotes about supposedly favourable public reaction to EDL demonstrations or petitions – 'It was great: we marched around the town, we had the people of Newcastle line the streets and they clapped and cheered as we went round . . . ' (Andy); accounts of conversations with people in pubs who started off thinking that the EDL 'were just a bunch of racists' but then came to realise that they were 'not like that at all' (Phil); or tales of police officers who had told them, 'off the record', at demonstrations that many members of the police force supported what the EDL was doing (see Busher 2013). There was of course a degree of exaggeration and even pure invention in these stories – I went on several demonstrations where supposedly 'the people of [town] had lined the streets' when in fact little more than half a dozen households had offered them any form of encouragement. But what mattered was that these stories circulated within the activist community as truths.

As with the activists' other discursive moves, this served not only to challenge claims that they were racist and far right[17] but also to develop their counter-narrative. Their self-identification as ordinary English people was used to develop the kind of anti-elite theme prominent in the rhetoric of many far right and populist political movements[18]– a theme that activists often then used to attack their critics, whether these were politicians accused of being out of touch and uninterested in the lives of ordinary English people, or their anti-fascist opponents whom they lampooned as middle-class or upper-middle-class kids intent on carrying out their own form of class oppression:

> [Politicians] are not – they're not interested. You try and engage with Margaret Hodge.[19] You [as if he were addressing Margaret Hodge directly] don't live in the London Borough of Barking & Dagenham, you know, because at the end of the day, Margaret, no disrespect, but you could say 'Right, I'm leaving office' and you can – you can fuck off with your fat pension and ill-gotten gains. It's not affecting you. But we're looking out for our children.
>
> (Tony)

TARQUINS & TALULAHS
UNITE & FIGHT

Smash the filthy white
working/lower-middle class scum!

I doubt any of them even quality for the 50p tax rate!

**Infact, I bet my Daddy earns more in a week
than any of these ghastly creatures do in a year!**

Figure 4.1 A spoof poster for an anti-racist counter-mobilisation circulated among EDL activists, summer 2012

The bulwark argument

A sixth move comprised what I call the bulwark argument. Even the activists who most vehemently insisted that they were not-racist and not-far-right acknowledged that the EDL had attracted some people with racist or far right views. They argued, however, that without groups such as the EDL, these people would form or become involved in more radical and dangerous groups[20] and that the EDL had in fact even helped to move some people away from more extreme views and violent orientations. These claims were supported with reference to stories such as that of Phil, who I introduced in Chapter 3. Prior to becoming involved in the EDL, he had been arrested for racially aggravated offences, but he claimed that he had revised his racist views and amended his behaviour since becoming involved in the EDL.[21]

> I did actually have, I wasn't completely racist before I started, but I had a lot more right-wing views. I grew up with mixed in school, I had loads of trouble from black kids and bits and pieces and I ended up hating some of them . . . But then once I started with EDL, I turned that all around and to this day like I've got black friends that I talk to in work and get on with and have a laugh with and that, and I've actually completely turned things around and now I'm just standing against one thing, and that's the one thing that we see as a problem.

In developing this line of argument, EDL activists discursively turned themselves into part of the solution to the problem of far right activism rather than part of the problem, once again providing those activists who did not identify with the far right another useful justificatory narrative about why they were marching alongside people who quite clearly did.

This argument came particularly to the fore after Anders Breivik killed 77 people in Norway on 22nd July 2011. As news emerged of the killings and as investigators pawed over Breivik's rambling manifesto and personal effects for clues of what had led him to undertake his murderous spree, it became clear that there were not only some resonances between his worldview and that articulated by most EDL activists, but also that he had made contact with some people associated with the EDL. In the days after the killings, the EDL found itself in the glare of deeply negative publicity. The activists I spoke with at the time expressed concern that, in spite of their protestations that their organisation categorically did not support such actions, this was likely to harm their ability to attract new supporters.[22]

> Most people that I know that are involved in the EDL hold Breivik in absolute fucking contempt, they think he's an absolute cretin. He has set the counter-jihad movement back in Scandinavia and Europe fucking years, years and years. It was getting off to a reasonably good start with the awareness growing, but it's in disarray now, because if you've got anything to do with the counter-jihad you have people saying you are a potential Anders Breivik in the making.
>
> (Eddie)

These events did not however undermine the commitment of those already involved in the organisation. Indeed, news coverage that linked Breivik in some way to the EDL – stories about EDL activists being Facebook friends with him, rumours that he had attended an EDL demonstration[23] or posts of encouragement by Breivik on EDL online forums – were held up as a further example of left-wing critics using any means they could to damage the reputation of the EDL regardless of the evidence they had at their disposal.[24]

———————

As might be expected, EDL activists' attempts to resist and counter being described as a racist or far right group have mostly been rejected by opposition groups, and politicians and the mainstream media have also continued on the whole to refer to the EDL as 'a far right group', at least publicly. Survey evidence about public perceptions of the group, however, indicates that some of the EDL's arguments may have achieved limited traction beyond the parameters of its activist community and declared support base (i.e. those who support the EDL online but do not participate in demonstrations or other activities). In 2012, a survey of a nationally representative sample of 1,682 British adults by the Extremis Project and YouGov (YouGov/Extremis 2012) found that while 74% of the 548 respondents who 'had heard of the EDL and know what they stand for' described it as 'a racist organisation', 17% stated that they did not view the EDL as a racist organisation and 9% said that they did not know whether or not they were a racist organisation. In a study of public attitudes to integration and cohesion in predominantly white neighbourhoods in West Yorkshire in 2013 (Busher et al. 2014, Thomas et al. 2014), my colleagues and I asked a more open question than whether or not the EDL is a racist organisation. We presented respondents with a series of 20 words with positive, negative or neutral signification and asked them to select all of the words from the list that they associated with the EDL.[25] Across the 459 respondents,[26] the most frequently chosen descriptors were overwhelmingly negative, with the top five including 'racist' (selected by 39% of respondents), 'extremist' (28%), 'hooligans' (25%) and 'violent' (23%). The most frequently selected response was however 'anti-Muslim' (55%). This finding indicates that, at least for our respondents, being anti-Muslim is not necessarily equated with being racist. Furthermore, whereas words such as 'racist' and 'hooligan' clustered together with other negative signifiers, 'anti-Muslim' was associated both with positive and negative signifiers. 'Right-wing' (20%) was the joint-sixth most frequently selected descriptor, along with 'dangerous'.

What is important in the context of understanding the world-making of activists themselves is that the development of this range of discursive moves and countermoves meant that, once involved with the EDL and familiar with these arguments, the activists found it quite easy to rebut claims that they were racists or right-wing extremists. In fact they turned these labels into discursive opportunities – undertaking a form of what McCauley (2006) calls 'jujitsu politics', whereby an actor uses the strength and intensity of the opposition or repression that they face to their own advantage. Their opponents' use of these labels was transformed into a sign of their own intellectual superiority: 'The fact you [an imaginary accuser] call me a racist is the last refuge, it's the last hiding place of someone who's lost the argument well and truly' (Eddie), and was also used as an opportunity to resuscitate and amplify feelings of injustice and righteous anger:

> *Bev:*   When we were leafleting the other month at Heathway, and we give
> out leaflets to all sorts of people, not just white people, we do – .
>
> *Susan:*   It's majority African up that way, isn't it.
>
> *Bev:*   It is, it's mainly African, so we give our leaflets to everyone and we
> approach people nicely – 'Excuse me sir, excuse me madam', because
> if you just go and shove a leaflet in people's face they don't take it.
> You've got to be polite – 'Hello, excuse me, would you like to have
> a read of this?' and most people go 'Yeah, alright', and they take it. I
> was just coming up to the crossing and there was a couple of young
> white girls with their buggies and everything, so I went and gave them,
> I went 'Excuse me girls, can you have a read of this? Blah, blah, it's
> for your children's future, it's what we do, blah, blah, blah'. Then there
> was a black girl standing right next to them and before I could even
> turn around and give her a leaflet, she went to me, 'I don't suppose
> you want to give me one of them'. I said, 'I wouldn't go that far, I
> was just coming to you next', and she went, 'Well, I don't think you
> was'. I went to her [raising her voice], 'I tell you what, I know where
> you're going with this, don't pull that racist one on me, love', I said,
> 'because I'm not racist and I was about to come to you next'. She
> went to me, 'Fuck off', and walked off. That's . . . I hadn't done noth-
> ing, she obviously knew what we were giving out, but I was going to
> her next, but she started pulling that racist card even before I'd opened
> my mouth, do you know what I mean, that's what we get as well. It
> really annoyed me and I was like, I went to Laura 'Did you see that?'
> and she went 'Yeah, fuck her'. It annoys me, totally.

Such stories were told and retold at meetings, demonstrations, in the pub
and on Facebook; each telling recharging activists' emotional batteries. In
Stein's (2001) account of the Christian Right in the United States, she observes
that when worked into a narrative of victimhood and exclusion, experiences
of being vilified served to energise the people she was interviewing.[27] A similar
idea could be applied to grassroots EDL activists. The activists were well
aware that labelling them racist and far right was intended to ostracise them
and provoke feelings of social shame. By dwelling on these stories they continually set off what Scheff (1994) calls 'shame-anger sequences' in which
the experience of shame, or in this case the experience of somebody attempting
to make them experience shame,[28] produces feelings of resentment and hostility.[29] Part of what gave these shame-anger sequences such intensity was that
they were situated within much longer sub-political struggles and resentments
related to perceptions that those with a public voice – politicians, the media,
academics and the like – often spoke about 'people like us' as if they were,
if not already racist, teetering on the brink of racism (see Collins 2004a,
Hewitt 2005, 35–55).[30] One activist from Eltham, for example, an area that
attracted a great deal of national media attention in 1993 after a group of

white youths killed Stephen Lawrence, a black teenager, there, often returned to the theme of how this 'one incident' had 'given this area such a bad name' and his indignation that the area had been labelled by some 'the racist capital of England' (Steve).

One of the clearest examples of the activists' use of the application of such labels to generate anger and indignation came in the summer of 2011. On the evenings of 9th and 10th August, at the height of the London riots, a handful[31] of EDL activists participated in much larger vigilante groups that emerged in Eltham in south London and Enfield in north London. Speaking in the House of Commons on 11th August 2011, Clive Efford, Liberal Democrat MP for Eltham, asked the Prime Minister,

> For the last two nights in my constituency, I've had a very, very heavy police presence due to right wing extremist groups focusing on Eltham and trying to create unrest and bad-feeling between different racial groups. Whilst we want to support people who are public spirited and coming out to defend their community, like some of my constituents have done, would the Prime Minister join me in saying to those people, 'don't be diverted from your efforts by the extremists seeking to exploit this situation?'

David Cameron responded,

> I think the honourable gentleman speaks not only for his constituents but frankly for the whole house in deprecating the EDL and all they stand for and their attempt to somehow say that they are going to help restore order is: I've described some parts of our society as sick; and there are none sicker than the EDL.

His comments provoked outrage among the EDL activists. After four days of rioting that had seen millions of pounds worth of damage to property and three young men killed in Birmingham, how could he claim that the EDL were the sickest of the sick? And why were they the ones being criticised when Kurdish and Sikh communities in London had also mobilised against the rioters? Why wasn't Cameron calling them sick?[32] On 8th October 2011, EDL Angels led a march to Downing Street under the slogan 'Mr. Cameron, we are not sick', and the phrase has continued to be used by activists as a symbol of a liberal elite interested only in stigmatising them.

The activists' ability to sustain their resistance to accusations of being racist and far right was however contingent on their own and their fellow activists' behaviour. To return to a point made in Chapter 3, for identity claims to be persuasive, they require a basic degree of coherence with observable facts; activists' framings of themselves are liable to collapse where their claims are incongruous with their own actions (Benford and Snow 2000). It is to this issue that I now turn.

The consequences of activists' not-racist and not-far-right identities

> Well I think, when I was being accused of being a fascist and a racist, I thought there's only one way to defend yourself and that is to obviously back up your theory that you are not by what you do; try to show what you do stand for.
>
> (John)

While it is possible to criticise and challenge the discursive moves that the EDL activists deployed, and while there might even be grounds for scepticism about the extent to which such arguments were made in good faith,[33] these were not *just* rhetorical strategies. Activists' identification of the EDL and, in most cases, of themselves as not-racist and not-far-right had a significant bearing on the evolution of this wave of anti-Muslim protest. First, as I discussed in Chapter 2, the assertion of these identities affected patterns of participation. The EDL attracted people who would probably not have participated had they believed it to be a racist or far right group. These identities also shaped the development of the emergent culture of the group and what, in Eliasoph's (1999) terms, we might call the basic 'ground rules for interaction' in the context of online and offline spaces associated with the EDL. They shaped what the activists actually did and the meaning they gave to what they did. This can be seen if we look at how they talked about and framed EDL issues, and at their action repertoire and protest rituals.

There can be little doubt that many activists' interests and concerns extended beyond (militant) Islam and the Islamification of Britain. In Bartlett and Littler's (2011, 21) study, when asked what they thought were the most significant problems facing the United Kingdom, only 31% of 804 respondents placed radical Islam in their top two. The other top five issues included immigration (42%), lack of jobs (26%), terrorism (19%)[34] and the financial crisis (14%). The cognitive and emotional resonance of the EDL narrative was partly achieved by the way it worked on and enabled activists to refer to such a range of other fears and anxieties. While the activists claimed that their focus did not extend to more general immigration issues, their commentaries on the threat of Islamification often did make symbolic linkages to discourses about immigration and to Malthusian anxieties about resource scarcity that have long dominated public debate about immigration in the United Kingdom. I rarely attended an EDL event or meeting without being reminded at some point that 'we are only an island', and conversation was thick with references to demographic change and anxieties about being 'outbred' by Muslims.

> *Bev:*   They have 6 and 7 children to our 2.5.
> *Susan:* They're outbreeding us, that's what they're doing.
> *Bev:*   They're not allowed no contraception.

As various cases of child sexual exploitation by networks of men from Muslim backgrounds have come to public prominence,[35] EDL activists and activists from several cognate groups[36] have also worked on one of the great British moral panics: paedophiles.[37]

> *Susan:* To me in their holy book allowing men, grown men to marry a nine-year-old girl and have sex with her – to me, that's giving every single paedophile in this country or in the world the right to go out and do what they want.
>
> *Bev:* I find that's where those converts [to Islam], that's what gets me about these converts. Why would you want to convert to Islam, right, and I think that must be a big part of it, there's something wrong in their brain somewhere . . .
>
> *Susan:* I think paedophilia comes into it, definitely, because why would you want to convert to something that says you can marry children?

More generally, activists' conversations were usually woven around and into a broad narrative of decline that has long been not only a theme of more or less extreme reactionary movements (Klandermans and Mayer 2006, 271) but also a fairly constant fixture in the mainstream right and centre-right media where, apart from the price of its houses, Britain is often portrayed as being in a state of almost inexorable decline,[38] a historical narrative that has gained particular traction in low income communities where middle-class images of history as a 'progressive unfolding' are often challenged by a 'more pessimistic counter-current . . . that sees limits or expects collapse' (Jasper 2007, 12). Activists' discussions, whether in the pub, on the coach to a demonstration or online, were permeated by a sighing and gloomy nostalgia which manifested in memories of a glorious past – the blitz spirit, Winston Churchill, chirpy neighbourhood police constables and the warm and welcoming local pub, blended with Enoch Powellesque[39] premonitions of an ignoble and apocalyptic future, a mood exemplified by one of Graham's Facebook posts:

> had the doom well and truly earlier and its still lingering, went for a stroll today around a town in east london called barking, its where the east end starts on its way to the city, it was a nice place 40 years ago where i met my missus, done all the courting bit around the many pubs and bars around the area. married at st margarets across the road from the pub i last took a drink in as a single man, the bull, now sadley closed as is the red lion, the hope, the harrow, . . . other pubs gone are the Westbury arms, captain cook, the stag. why you may ask, well decades of successive governments have moved all the dreggs of the 3rd world into the area all the way up to tower hamlets and sadly they have brought their primitive cultures with them, instead of making them assimilate they are left to destroy a once vibrant area, you can buy a bag of cows feet but you cant buy a traditional pie and mash, cant buy a nice bit of fresh meat unless its halal, and im talking ASDA here as well as the filthy shops in east street and station parade, even the chinese takeaway

across from the station is halal, i observed the few indigenous east enders sat huddled in the few cafes that remain, you can buy fancy shite from rumanian and polak shops but nothing at all for the few locals i observed on my walk, shops where i used to buy all the latest clobber turned into halal fast food outlets and gaming rooms. . . another area fucked over by multi-culturism, if only the pricks we vote into power knew how we realy felt about having all these un-invited aliens into our country perhaps they may understand why myself and many other folk turn to nationalism as a way of making the bastards listen . . . barking, oh my poor barking. . . ;

(Graham, Facebook Post, Jan 2012)

Yet there was little if any move within the activist community towards the elaboration of a wider ideological programme for the EDL. Even almost six years after its emergence, the EDL and its activists continue to identify overwhelmingly as a single-issue group.[40] This partly came from the EDL's national and local leadership. In media appearances and public speeches, the national leaders repeatedly stated that the EDL was a single-issue group and resisted being drawn on wider topics. At the local and regional level, besides monitoring Facebook pages and taking down what they deemed racist content, local and regional organisers led sometimes extensive discussions at meetings about what comprised EDL issues and what its activists should or should not therefore be campaigning about.

The idea that the EDL was a non-racist single-issue group also permeated everyday interactions at the grassroots of the movement. This did not mean that activists did not talk about other issues: the scope of their conversations constantly expanded and contracted. Particularly as they hit their rhetorical stride, some activists would segue from the stock repertoire of complaints ostensibly focused on (militant) Islam to a far more general lament ranging across themes that could include issues such as immigration, overcrowded social housing, benefit fraud (perhaps by Muslims, but also by other perceived serial offenders such as Romanians, Bulgarians and 'chavs'), Africans bringing their 'primitive cultures and AIDS' to the United Kingdom, how 'black culture' supposedly lay at the heart of the rioting and looting that broke out in London and elsewhere across the country in August 2011, local government corruption and a perceived general collapse of law and order. Yet they would usually work their way back to the core EDL themes, and as they did so would make clear that where they had strayed from the core EDL themes 'those are just my opinions, that is not the position of the EDL'.[41] Furthermore, while activists' interests ranged across multiple topics, especially in more formal interactions, such as meetings, their conversations tended to focus around the core EDL themes of (militant) Islam and the left, and it was comments about these topics that would elicit the most positive and unequivocal emotional feedback from their co-activists – heartfelt rounds of applause, pats on the back, and affirmations of what they had just said.

As Collins (2004b) argues, emotional energy is best generated when people become mutually entrained with one another. In the context of social spaces associated with the EDL, it was when activists' focused their comments and conversations on the core EDL themes that they tended to achieve mutual entrainment and generated and experienced the greatest emotional energy. As discussions in the activist community centred on, emphasised and emotionally rewarded comments on the core EDL themes, over time, the activists' interests, reading habits and even ideas also aligned with these issues. Some activists such as Phil (above) may indeed have developed less overtly racist views as a result of their participation in the EDL.

EDL activists' attempts to resist being labelled racist or far right also shaped the evolution of their action repertoire.[42] Early EDL demonstrations were characterised by significant public disorder as supporters clashed with assorted anti-racists and anti-fascists or, on other occasions, with groups of local (mainly Muslim) men (Copsey 2010, Jackson 2011, 69–73). To some extent, public disorder and physical violence have continued to be a feature of EDL demonstrations (see Chapter 5 for a more detailed discussion). There has however been a general decline in public disorder at EDL demonstrations, particularly after the summer of 2010 (Treadwell 2014). Some of this may be attributable to a combination of the development of more effective demonstration management strategies by the police and local authorities and the adoption of less confrontational strategies by those opposing the EDL (Bujra 2012, Harris, Busher, and Macklin 2015, Treadwell 2014, van der Wal 2011).

The relatively limited amount of public disorder at demonstrations after late 2010 is also, however, to some extent due to the efforts of some EDL activists, and particularly the organisers, to avoid looking 'like a load of fucking thugs chanting songs' (Phil). At least in London and Essex, hours were spent discussing ways of reducing the number of public order incidents at demonstrations. At meetings that I attended activists discussed options such as increasing the number of event stewards, banning known troublemakers and even banning alcohol or finding ways of reducing the pre-demonstration drinking time.[43] The stewards at all of the demonstrations I attended took their role seriously, seeking to ensure that the activists complied with police instructions, and on several occasions intervening to attempt to break up fights and reprimand people for racist chanting or the performance of a straight-arm Nazi salute. While activists often complained about how they were treated by the police (see Chapter 3), almost without fail, there were appeals to demonstrators by those giving speeches and by stewards to behave in accordance with the instructions of the police, and there were often comfortable and relaxed exchanges between police officers and EDL activists, with some activists building up quite a rapport over time with known police officers in the forward intelligence team.

These efforts to minimise public disorder can also be situated within a more general effort by a substantial proportion of the activist community to carry out protests that emphasised their respectability and their identity as '*ordinary*

English people'. While demonstrations were characterised by general drunkenness and outbursts of inflammatory and sometimes overtly racist chanting, at the same time, most activists sought to conform with a fairly standard contemporary protest repertoire – what Tilly (2004) describes as 'WUNC displays': displays of worthiness, unity, numbers and commitment. Where permitted, the demonstrations began with a march.[44] Most then proceeded in an orderly, if noisy, manner from the muster points to the demonstration site, shepherded by the event stewards in their fluorescent bibs. Activists sang popular songs and chants and many waved flags or carried banners and placards, some with the name of an EDL division, others with slogans such as 'Black and white unite against religious extremism' and 'Try appeasing the majority for a change'. Where the activists were not entirely contained within a police cordon, some would have responsibility for handing out flyers to passers-by. The speeches provided the main set pieces of the demonstrations. National or local leaders articulated their grievances and specified their claims – although as I observed in Chapter 2, there was considerable variation amongst the activists as to how much attention they paid to these speeches. There were sometimes other coordinated group rituals as well, the most common of which were collective acts of commemoration in the familiar form of a minute's silence, usually in remembrance of a recently-deceased 'patriot' (see Chapter 1), to remember people killed in 'terrorist attacks by Muslim extremists', the 'victims of Muslim grooming gangs', or for deceased British armed services personnel and their families.

As I described in Chapter 1, the symbolism deployed by activists was also often overtly not-far-right: gay pride flags, Israeli flags, speakers from black or minority ethnic backgrounds and so forth. Unlike the stylised militarism described in Virchow's (2007) account of extreme right-wing marches in Germany, at EDL demonstrations, there was no lining up or forming of ranks and the marching itself was more an amble or a jostle. At the smaller local or regional demonstrations that I attended, where the activists were not tightly cordoned off from the public, such as the one described in Chapter 1, some event stewards made a point of helping black and minority ethnic women and children through the EDL crowd – an act that invariably drew comments of approval from some fellow activists: 'good man, good man'.

The importance to EDL activists of these performances of respectability can be seen by their reactions when they did not play out as they had intended.[45] On 18th June 2011, ten weeks after the demonstration described at the beginning of Chapter 1, another demonstration about the same issue took place in the same area and with a similar number of activists (approximately 200). It started off like the previous three demonstrations with activists gathering, drinking and enjoying singing their songs. As before, there was only a limited police presence when the march set off from the pub (a solitary police community support officer). As before, the first port of call was the railway station, and as before, there was a meticulously observed minute of silence. Shortly after leaving the station, however, events took a quite different turn. Two young Muslim men crossed the path of the march, hostile words were exchanged with EDL activists at the front of the march, and suddenly a fight had broken out. As the two men tried to escape, some EDL activists punched one of the men and knocked the other to floor. Stewards and other activists sought to restrain them but by the time they had managed to do so the young Muslim man on the floor had had his jaw fractured.[46] As this happened, Kevin Carroll bellowed from the back of the procession at the EDL activists involved 'You're a disgrace! You're behaving like animals!' while Steve, one of the stewards and a mainstay of the local activist community, stormed away from the incident, grumbling 'it's a fucking waste of time' and, distraught, flung his cap to the ground. Later, during his speech, Carroll chastised the activists involved and event organisers made their anger and frustration clear. Some of the activists involved in the fracas were told they were not welcome at future demonstrations.

Attempts to assert not-racist and not-far-right identities also shaped wider tactical and strategic debates within the activist community. It was one of the reasons why most of the London leadership remained opposed to flash demonstrations, in spite of what they perceived to be the use of increasingly harsh policing tactics[47] and why so few of the core EDL activists in the London area had been in favour of the EDL formally participating in the formation of vigilante groups during the riots that took place in London and other English cities in the summer of 2011 (Busher 2012). It was also one of the reasons why most of the activists in London and Essex were sceptical about plans to forge a loose alliance with the British Freedom Party (BFP) which were announced by the national leadership in November 2011.

> I want to fight the cause but I don't want to be under BFP; it's too similar to BNP. They will be branded a racist party, they will be, that's what I believe. We've been spending three years trying to say we're not racists, we've got all different races, black, Asian, and all that in the English Defence League . . . I'm not doing BFP, no way. Three years telling people we're not like that. WE'RE NOT LIKE THAT! [faux shouting]
>
> (Susan)

As I discussed in Chapter 1, my intention in this book is not to enter into debate about whether the EDL is or is not a far right or racist group. What I do argue however is that if we want to understand how the EDL worked as a project of collective world-making, and if we want to understand the evolution of this particular wave of anti-minority protest more generally, we must take seriously their arguments about being not-racist and not-far-right as 'social facts' (Durkheim 2013 [1895]). This is because whether or not we subscribe to their arguments, they were causally significant. They shaped the activists' identities, their emotional reactions to different symbols, the types of strategic alliance that they were or were not willing to make, the way they performed their protests and even how they interpreted and thought about the world around them.

Notes

1 See for example Lamont's (2000) description of the construction of moral order among working class men in France and the United States.

2 The idea of the importance of a basic degree of narrative consistency can also be found in Giddens' (1991, 54) discussion of the construction of the self: 'A person's identity is not to be found in behaviour, nor – important though this is – in the reactions of others, but in the capacity to keep a particular narrative going. The individual's biography, if she is to maintain regular interaction with others in the day-to-day world, cannot be wholly fictive. It must continually integrate events which occur in the external world, and sort them into the ongoing "story" about the self'.

3 The idea of such moves draws on Goffman's (1967, 1969) work on the strategic interaction.

4 As Einwohner (2002) argues, processes of identity construction among activist groups usually happen both through their interactions with co-activists and with opponents and third parties.

5 In April 1990, in an interview with the *Los Angeles Times*, the Conservative politician Norman Tebbit contributed to the debate about integration with the comment that 'A large proportion of Britain's Asian population fail to pass the cricket test. Which side do they cheer for? It's an interesting test. Are you still harking back to where you came from or where you are?' His comments quickly gained notoriety and have been invoked in debates on immigration and integration ever since.

6 And EDL activists were quick to seize on the sheer apparent simplicity of their critics' 'error' in labelling them racist for opposing (militant) Islam as evidence of their opponents' general ignorance.

7 One of the EDL songs goes 'Keep St. George in my heart keep me English, Keep St. George in my heart I pray. . .' sung to the tune of the hymn 'Give me joy in my heart'.

8 While notions of cultural compatibility may have gained increasing prominence in anti-minority discourses in recent decades, the notion of cultural difference has long been part of more overtly racist ideologies (Cohen 1988, Macklin Forthcoming).

9 There are several books charting the rise to prominence of this wave of far and radical right parties, including works by Betz (1994), Kitschelt and McGann (1995) and Mudde (2007)

10 Brian, the organiser who had invited Barnbrooke to the meeting, reflected that it had been a strategic error on his part, one which he put down to *'seeing the dollar signs'* at a time when they were trying to generate resources to print flyers and produce other promotional materials.

11 It is interesting to note here a difference between processes of identity construction in the EDL and the BNP in this regard. Whereas being a single-issue group was seen as a positive attribute by EDL activists who used it help distinguish themselves from far right groups with wider platforms, such as the BNP; for the BNP, which was trying to develop its image as a credible political force, its activists were keen to counter portrayals of the group as a 'single-issue' movement because they believed this positioned them as extremists (see Goodwin 2008, 356). In seeking to situate themselves outside conventional right vs. left frames the activists reflect a wider adoption of a similar strategy by contemporary populist movements (see Kitschelt 2004).

12 My paraphrasing of this common line of argument, rather than a direct quote.

13 On the one hand activists made much of the idea that EDL women were equals with the men – an argument that was made as part of a strategy of playing on ideas about the subjugated and passive position of women in Muslim societies that have been prominent in culture clash narratives. On the other hand however male activists claimed the male protector role – in Brighton on 23rd April 2012 at the MFE St. George's Day parade, for example, in anticipation of an attack by opposition activists, event

organisers barked out a (broadly ignored) instruction to adopt a formation with 'women and children on the inside, men on the outside'. As such, when women or children were struck in the context of clashes, this was seen as particularly strong evidence of the moral baseness of their opponents.

14 There were a number of variations on this phrase such as 'average working people', 'just normal people' and so forth. Sometimes class identity was also included.

15 See also the quote by Andy in Chapter 2 about encountering some 'city guys' on his first EDL demonstration.

16 When I first started spending time with the group a number of activists made reference to the Daily Star poll suggesting that its readership largely supported the EDL (see Chapter 1).

17 As Billig (1995, 73) notes, the 'claim to exemplify, the values of the majority' is a common one among those who seek 'to create new movements of opinion toward a minority position'.

18 Goodwin, for example, describes precisely this kind of anti-elite discourse in the BNP's rhetoric in Barking & Dagenham (2008, 355) a few years earlier.

19 Margaret Hodge, Labour MP for Barking & Dagenham, lives in Highbury and Islington

20 A similar argument has been deployed by the BNP as it sought to gain respectability and public office (Goodman and Johnson 2013). There is some scientific basis for the logic of this argument. More ideologically and tactically radical challenger groups tend to occur when alternative opportunities to express anxieties, grievances and ideas are closed off or perceived to be closed off (della Porta 1995, Koopmans et al. 2005).

21 A similar story is told by one of Pilkington's (2014) respondents in the West Midlands.

22 There are not, as far as I am aware, data with which to reliably assess the impact of Anders Breivik's actions on public support for the EDL.

23 These rumours have never been verified. As one activist observed a couple of months after the killings, given that Breivik at an EDL demonstration would undoubtedly have been a 'money shot', all the freelance photo-journalists who covered EDL demonstrations would have been scouring their photographs for such an image, and if one had not been found by now, it was likely unlikely that any such image ever would be found.

24 Arguably, these events also gave Tommy Robinson a moment to shine, at least in the eyes of his fellow activists. Most of the activists in London and Essex were impressed with Tommy Robinson's performance on the BBC's *Newsnight* programme on 26th July, claiming that he had 'owned' Jeremy Paxman and cited this as further evidence of his growing stature as a public figure. Interestingly, their claims were also expressed by some of the EDL's staunchest critics, who complained that Paxman had given Robinson a 'softball' interview. See Andy Newman, Socialist Unity, 27th July 2011, http://socialistunity.com/jeremy-paxmans-shame/

25 The full list included (in alphabetical order): anti-Muslim, brave, dangerous, extremists, heroes, honest, hooligans, ill-informed, insignificant, a joke, a menace, misguided, misrepresented, a nuisance, patriots, peaceful, racist, right-wing, violent, well-informed. These were presented in a circular format so as to minimise list bias.

26 The total sample was 646. As with the Extremis/YouGov study, respondents who had not heard of the EDL were not asked this question. Unlike the Extremis/YouGov study, however, we did put this question to the 24% of respondents who agreed with the statement 'I have heard of them but am unsure what they stand for'.

27 A closer-to-home example of this dynamic is Millwall fans' famous 'No one likes us, we don't care' chant (Collins 2004a, Robson 2000). The idea that imposed identities can be used to cultivate an empowering 'oppositional consciousness' is discussed at length by Mansbridge (2001).

28 Whether or not the activists actually felt shame when confronted with these accusations is an interesting question, but not one that I am able to answer.

29 Gilligan (1997, 110) proposes that shame is the 'the primary or ultimate cause of all violence' (cited in Scheff 2013, 89). Turner (2009, 345) proposes that the reason shame is able to generate such sequences is that 'Shame is a painful emotion because it attacks the integrity and worth of self; and so it is not surprising that individuals employ defense mechanisms to protect themselves from this pain'.

30 Gillborn (2009, 22) is also critical both of portrayals of white working class children as 'race victims' and of 'TV series that present the white working class as alienated and inherently racist' because they 'rely on a partial and crude reading of data – often attaching sensationalist headlines to complex, sometimes unreliable, research'.

31 An activist calling himself 'Jack England' claimed in a television interview that there were about 50 EDL activists coordinating proceedings in Eltham. The accounts of all the other activists I knew and the social media threads involving people who participated in the events in Eltham contradicted England's version of events. The activists I knew estimated that there between eight and ten core EDL activists involved, and those who were there insisted that they were there as local residents rather than as EDL activists (Busher 2012). England was initially teased about his interview by other activists and then roundly criticised for it.

32 My paraphrasing of conversations with activists on the way to a demonstration in Telford on 13th August 2011.

33 For example, one activist who repeatedly asserted that he was neither racist nor far right occasionally posted stories from white nationalist South African websites on his Facebook page, often used blatantly racist language (words such as 'paki' and 'coon'), and as the EDL fragmented was not averse to attending events organised by the National Front (NF).

34 Arguably, this might be seen as being broadly equivalent to radical Islam, at least within the logic of most EDL activists.

35 A discussion of the media framing of and public discourse around child sexual exploitation cases extends beyond the scope of this discussion, but is explored by Miah (2015).

36 The EDL are far from being alone or the first to do this of course. Recently, the BNP, Casuals United, Britain First and the English Volunteer Force have all adopted similar strategies.

37 See Jenkins (1992) and Jewkes and Wykes (2012).

38 What Zúquete (2008) describes as a 'spirit of decadence'.

39 Enoch Powell was something of a hero among the activists. The frequent approving references to him reminded me of Collins' (2004a) observation of how the phrase 'Enoch was right' has somehow echoed down through the years within some parts of London's white working class communities.

40 On 19th July 2014, the EDL held a demonstration in Hexthorpe, South Yorkshire, about Roma immigrants, but other similar events have not followed (Harris, Busher and Macklin 2015).

41 This is not a direct quote, but a paraphrasing of a common comment. Particularly during initial conversations, new contacts were usually at pains to point out that the views they were providing were their personal views and were not necessarily representative of the group.

42 That activists' identities and identity struggles shape the choices they make about their protest repertoire is a fairly standard idea in the research on social movements (della Porta and Diani 2006, 181–185). As Snow and Benford (1992, 147) observe, 'the development or use of tactics that are inconsistent with the diagnostic and prognostic components of a movement's master frame as well as with constituency values is unlikely. If movement action is inconsistent with the values it espouses or with its constituents' values, it renders its framing efforts vulnerable to dismissal'.

43 In the next chapter, I discuss why most of these ideas were not implemented.
44 This was not possible where local police had made successful applications to the Home Secretary to ban the march, as was the case at Tower Hamlets on 3rd September 2011 and Telford on 13th August 2011. When this happened a 'static demonstration' could still be held, however, as banning orders do not cover such events.
45 As Garfinkel (1967) demonstrated with his 'breaching' experiments, we can learn a great deal about social norms and rules by studying what happens when they are violated.
46 See 'HOPE not hate secure EDL conviction', Sam King, *Hope not Hate*, 18th July 2012, www.hopenothate.org.uk//news/home/article/2364/hope-not-hate-secure-edl-conviction
47 The other main concern was about the safety of participants (see Chapter 5).

References

Alexander, J.C. 2006. *The Civil Sphere*. Oxford: Oxford University Press.
Bailey, G. 2009. "Citizenship For All: Including the BNP in the Neighbourhood Polity." 59th Political Studies Association Annual Conference: Challenges for Democracy in a Global Era, University of Manchester, 7th–9th April.
Balibar, E. 2007. "Is There a 'Neo-Racism'?" In *Race and Racialization: Essential Readings*, edited by T. Das Gupta, C.E. James, R.C.A. Maaka, G.-E. Galabuzi and C. Andersen, 83–88. Toronto: Canadian Scholars Press.
Bar-On, T. 2007. *Where Have All the Fascists Gone?* Aldershot: Ashgate.
Barker, M. 1981. *The New Racism: Conservatives and the Ideology of the Tribe*. Toronto: Junction Books.
Bartlett, J., and M. Littler. 2011. *Inside the EDL: Populist Politics in a Digital Age*. London: Demos.
Benford, R.D., and D.A. Snow. 2000. "Framing Processes and Social Movements: An Overview and Assessment." *Annual Review of Sociology* 26:611–639.
Berbrier, M. 2002. "Making Minorities: Cultural Space, Stigma Transformation Frames, and the Categorical Status Claims of Deaf, Gay, and White Supremacist Activists in Late Twentieth Century America." *Sociological Forum* 17 (4):553–591.
Berezin, M. 2001. "Emotions and Political Identity: Mobilizing Affection for the Polity." In *Passionate Politics: Emotions and Social Movements*, edited by J. Goodwin, J.M. Jasper and F. Polletta, 83–98. Chicago: University of Chicago Press.
Betz, H.G. 1994. *Radical Right Wing Populism in Western Europe*. Basingstoke: Macmillan.
Billig, M. 1995. "Rhetorical Psychology, Ideological Thinking, and Imagining Nationhood." In *Social Movements and Culture*, edited by H. Johnston and B. Klandermans, 64–81. London: UCL Press.
Bujra, J. 2012. "Grounding the Riots." *Radical Statistics* 106:53–56.
Busher, J. 2012. "'There are none sicker than the EDL': Narratives of Racialisation and Resentment from Whitehall and Eltham, London." In *The English Riots of 2011*, edited by D. Briggs, 237–256. Hook: Waterside.
Busher, J. 2013. "Grassroots Activism in the English Defence League: Discourse and Public (Dis)order." In *Extreme Right-Wing Political Violence and Terrorism*, edited by M. Taylor, P.M. Currie and D. Holbrook, 65–84. London: Bloomsbury.
Busher, J., K. Christmann, G. Macklin, M. Rogerson, and P. Thomas. 2014. *Understanding Concerns About Community Relations in Calderdale*. Huddersfield: The University of Huddersfield.

Cohen, P. 1988. "The Perversions of Inheritance: Studies in the Making of Multi-Racist Britain." In *Multi-Racist Britain*, edited by P. Cohen and H. S. Bains, 9–118. Basingstoke: Macmillan Education.

Collins, M. 2004a. *The Likes of Us: A Biography of the White Working Class*. London: Granta.

Collins, R. 2004b. *Interaction Ritual Chains*. Princeton: Princeton University Press.

Copsey, N. 2010. *The English Defence League: Challenging Our Country and Our Values of Social Inclusion, Fairness and Equality*. London: Faith Matters.

della Porta, D. 1995. *Social Movements, Political Violence, and the State: A Comparative Analysis of Italy and Germany*. Cambridge: Cambridge University Press.

della Porta, D., and M. Diani. 2006. *Social Movements: An Introduction*. Oxford: Blackwell.

Durkheim, E. 2013 [1895]. *The Rules of Sociological Method*. New York: Free Press.

Durrheim, K., M. Quayle, K. Whitehead and A. Kriel. 2005. "Denying Racism: Discursive Strategies Used by the South African Media." *Critical Arts* 19 (1–2):167–186.

Einwohner, R. L. 2002. "Bringing the Outsiders in: Opponents' Claims and the Construction of Animal Rights Activists' Identity." *Mobilization* 7 (3):253–268.

Eliasoph, N. 1999. "'Everyday Racism' in a Culture of Political Avoidance: Civil Society, Speech, and Taboo." *Social Problems* 46 (4):479–502.

Festinger, L. 1957. *The Theory of Cognitive Dissonance*. New York: Harper and Row.

Garfinkel, H. 1967. *Studies in Ethnomethodology*. Englewood Cliffs: Prentice-Hall.

Giddens, A. 1991. *Modernity and Self-Identity: Self and Society in the Late Modern Age*. Stanford: Stanford University Press.

Gillborn, D. 2009. "Education: The Numbers Game and the Construction of White Racial Victimhood." In *Who Cares About the White Working Class?*, edited by K. P. Sveinsson, 15–22. London: Runnymede Trust.

Gilligan, J. 1997. *Violence. Reflections on a National Epidemic*. New York: Vintage Books.

Goffman, E. 1967. *Interaction Ritual: Essays on Face-to-Face Behavior*. New York: Double Day Anchor.

Goffman, E. 1969. *Strategic Interaction*. Philadelphia: University of Pennsylvania Press.

Goodman, S., and A. J. Johnson. 2013. "Strategies Used by the Far Right to Counter Accusations of Racism." *Critical Approaches to Discourse Analysis Across Disciplines* 6 (2):97–113.

Goodwin, M. J. 2008. "Backlash in the 'Hood: Determinants of Support for the British National Party (BNP) at the Local Level." *Journal of Contemporary European Studies* 16 (3):347–361.

Harris, G., J. Busher, and G. Macklin. 2015. The Evolution of Anti-Muslim Protest in Two English Towns. Coventry: Coventry University/The University of Huddersfield.

Hay, C. 2007. *Why We Hate Politics*. Cambridge: Polity.

Hewitt, R. 2005. *White Backlash and the Politics of Multiculturalism*. Cambridge: Cambridge University Press.

Ivarsflaten, E. 2006. "Reputational Shields: Why Most Anti-Immigrant Parties Failed in Western Europe, 1980–2005." Annual Meeting of the American Political Science Association, Philadelphia.

Jackson, P. 2011. *The EDL: Britain's New 'Far-Right' Social Movement*. Northampton: Radicalism and New Media Group Publications.

Jasper, J. M. 2007. *The Art of Moral Protest: Culture, Biography, and Creativity in Social Movements*. Paperback Edition. London: University of Chicago Press.

Jenkins, P. 1992. *Intimate Enemies: Moral Panics in Contemporary Great Britain*. New York: Aldine de Gruyter.

Jewkes, Y., and M. Wykes. 2012. "Reconstructing the Sexual Abuse of Children:'Cyberpaeds', Panic and Power." *Sexualities* 15 (8):934–952.

Kitschelt, H. 2004. "Diversification and Reconfiguration of Party Systems in Postindustrial Democracies." *Friedrich Ebert Stiftung* (March):1–23.

Kitschelt, H., and A. McGann. 1995. *The Radical Right in Western Europe*. Ann Arbor: Michigan University Press.

Klandermans, B., and N. Mayer. 2006. "Through the Magnifying Glass: The World of Extreme Right Activists." In *Extreme Right Activists in Europe. Through the Magnifying Glass*, edited by B. Klandermans and N. Mayer, 269–276. London: Routledge.

Kleinman, A. 2006. *What Really Matters: Living a Moral Life Amidst Uncertainty and Danger*. Oxford: Oxford University Press.

Koopmans, R., P. Statham, M. Giugni and F. Passy. 2005. *Contested Citizenship: Immigration and Cultural Diversity in Europe*. Minneapolis: University of Minnesota Press.

Lamont, M. 2000. *The Dignity of Working Men: Morality and the Boundaries of Race, Class, and Immigration*. New York: Russell Sage Foundation.

Macklin, G. Forthcoming. *White Racial Nationalism in Britain*. Abingdon: Routledge.

Mansbridge, J. 2001. "The Making of Oppositional Consciousness." In *Oppositional Consciousness: The Subjective Roots of Social Protest*, edited by J. Mansbridge and A. Morris, 1–19. Chicago: University of Chicago Press.

McCaffrey, D., and J. Keys. 2000. "Competitive Framing Processes in the Abortion Debate: Polarization-Vilification, Frame Saving, and Frame Debunking." *Sociological Quarterly* 41 (1):41–61.

McCauley, C. 2006. "Jujitsu Politics: Terrorism and Responses to Terrorism." In *Collateral Damage: The Psychological Consequences of America's War on Terror*, edited by P.R. Kimmel and C.E. Stout, 45–65. Westport: Praeger.

Miah, S. 2015. "The Groomers and the Question of Race." *Identity Papers* 1 (1):54–66.

Mudde, C. 2007. *Populist Radical Right Parties in Europe*. Cambridge: Cambridge University Press.

Pilkington, H. 2014. 'Loud and Proud': Youth Activism in the English Defence League. Report on Work Package 7 of MYPLACE Project. www.fp7-myplace.eu.

Robson, G. 2000. *'No One Like Us, We Don't Care': The Myth and Reality of Millwall Fandom*. London: Bloomsbury.

Scheff, T. 2013. "Repression of Emotion: A Danger to Modern Societies." In *Emotions in Politics: The Affect Dimension in Political Tension*, edited by N. Demertzis, 84–92. Basingstoke: Palgrave Macmillan.

Scheff, T.J. 1994. *Bloody Revenge: Emotions, Nationalism, and War*. Boulder: Westview Press.

Smith, C. 2003. *Moral, Believing Animals: Human Personhood and Culture*. Oxford: Oxford University Press.

Snow, D.A., and R.D. Benford. 1992. "Master Frames and Cycles of Protest." In *Frontiers in Social Movement Theory*, edited by A.D. Morris and C. McClurg Mueller, 133–155. New Haven: Yale University Press.

Spektorowski, A. 2012. "The French New Right: Multiculturalism of the Right and the Recognition/Exclusionism Syndrome." *Journal of Global Ethics* 8 (1):41–61.

Stein, A. 2001. "Revenge of the Shamed: The Christian Right's Emotional Culture War." In *Passionate Politics: Emotions and Social Movements*, edited by J. Goodwin, J.M. Jasper and F. Polletta, 115–131. Chicago: University of Chicago Press.

Thomas, P., M. Rogerson, G. Macklin, K. Christmann and J. Busher. 2014. *Understanding Concerns About Community Relations in Kirklees*. Huddersfield: University of Huddersfield.

Tilly, C. 2004. *Social Movements, 1768–2004*. Boulder: Paradigm.

Treadwell, J. 2014. "Controlling the New Far Right on the Street: Policing the English Defence League in Policy and Praxis." In *Responding to Hate Crime: The Case for Connecting Policy and Research*, edited by N. Chakraborti and J. Garland, 127–140. Bristol: Policy Press.

Turner, J. H. 2009. "The Sociology of Emotions: Basic Theoretical Arguments." *Emotion Review* 1 (4):340–354.

van der Wal, R. 2011. "United Kingdom: Policing EDL Manifestations and Demonstrations Across England." In *Managing Collective Violence Around Public Events: An International Comparison*, edited by O. M. G. Adang, 119–152. Apeldoorn: Police Science and Research Programme.

van Dijk, T. A. 1992. "Discourse and the Denial of Racism." *Discourse & Society* 3 (1):87–118.

Virchow, F. 2007. "Performance, Emotion, and Ideology: On the Creation of 'Collectives of Emotion' and Worldview in the Contemporary German Far Right." *Journal of Contemporary Ethnography* 36 (2):147–164.

Wallace, A. F. C., and R. D. Fogelson. 1965. "The Identity Struggle." In *Intensive Family Therapy: Theoretical and Practical Aspects*, edited by I. Bozormenyi-Nagy and J. L. Framo. New York: Harper and Row.

Weltman, D., and M. Billig. 2015. "The Political Psychology of Contemporary Anti-Politics: A Discursive Approach to the End-of-Ideology Era." *Political Psychology* 22 (2):367–382.

YouGov/Extremis. 2012. *Under the Microscope: Public Attitudes Toward the English Defence League (EDL)*. London: YouGov.

Zúquete, J. P. 2008. "The European Extreme-Right and Islam: New Directions?" *Journal of Political Ideologies* 13 (3):321–344.

5   The unravelling of EDL activism

My biggest sadness would be if it all fell apart, because there would be nothing to fill the void, you know. It wouldn't give anyone any incentive to start up anything else and, you know – I can always remember, right at the very start, and it was Ryan [a police officer in the London Metropolitan Police's Forward Intelligence Team, who over the years became well known to EDL activists in the London area] initially who was giving me a history lesson on nationalist groups, actually groups in general, protest groups. He said what generally happens is they grow, they get to a certain critical level and then they start eating themselves: infighting, that's always what kills all organisations. He said everyone starts, you know, egos, petty grievances – although I think even he was surprised at how big the EDL got, before it started getting silly.

(Mark)

On the afternoon of 16th November 2011, Mark and I were sitting in a deserted and rather dingy University of East London canteen drinking coffee, with a selection of 1990s bubblegum pop music playing on the radio. A broad-shouldered man in his forties who usually had a spring in his step and a smile on his face, Mark was a popular figure with other English Defence League (EDL) activists in London and the southeast. He had been involved with the EDL since shortly after the group first emerged during the summer of 2009; he was articulate and witty, and had acquired a reputation for being brave, but also smart when faced with the opposition or the police. We had known each other for about nine months by the time of this meeting, and our conversations had become one of the elements of the field research that I most enjoyed. He could be a gifted and entertaining raconteur, and I found it easier to listen to him than to some of the others: although he expressed strong views about what he saw as the threat posed by militant Islam,[1] he was less prone than many of his fellow activists to sweeping generalizations about Muslims and, at least in my presence, never lapsed into the crude racist language that some activists adopted at times, particularly after a few drinks or in the heat of a demonstration.

For a little over two hours, Mark recounted his journey through EDL activism to me. In some regards, it was a story that I had heard before, in fragments, during our conversations at demonstrations or during EDL meetings: his first contact with the EDL through football casuals networks, some of his favourite run-ins with Muslims Against Crusades (MAC) activists, and various well-worn anecdotes about his encounters with certain police officers whom he had come to know quite well over the last two and a bit years. But there was something different about this particular telling of his story. In previous conversations, his narrative had been tilted towards the future of the movement. He would strike a defiant tone as he spoke about how the EDL would resist the efforts of opposition groups, the 'liberal elite' and the forces of 'cultural Marxism' to undermine and close down the group and enthuse about the expansion of the EDL's support base and the formation of new local divisions.[2] On this occasion, however, his narrative was drained of such optimism and his excitement about the EDL's future appeared largely to have given way to nostalgia for the heady days of its first mobilisations, when their activism was all raw energy, new-found friendships and countercultural swagger.

Mark was far from alone in talking in this tone in the autumn of 2011; it felt as though the whole activist community was shrouded in pessimism. In May and June, as activists made plans for a demonstration in Tower Hamlets later in the summer, there was earnest, if extravagantly optimistic, talk at meetings of getting up to 10,000 people out on the street for the event. By mid-October, as they prepared for a national demonstration in Birmingham at the end of the month, activists I spoke with thought they would be lucky to get more than 1,000 people and some expressed scepticism that there would even be 500 there. The lower estimate was closer to the mark, and every activist I knew considered the event to have been a resounding failure.

On 19th November, I attended a meeting of EDL organisers in West Bromwich. In the days before the meeting there had been considerable speculation within the activist community about what was going to be discussed. Some of the local organisers in the London area had been tantalising other activists with talk of 'a big announcement'. I drove up to West Bromwich with an activist from central London. There were about half a dozen cars going up from the London and Essex area. The exact location of the meeting was kept secret until the day to minimise the risk of it being disrupted by opposition groups. Even on the morning of the meeting as we drove up the motorway, we were still awaiting confirmation of the venue. When we got to the pub where the meeting was being held, there was the usual milling about and catching up with one another that I had become accustomed to. After about half an hour in the lounge bar, we were ushered through into a small function room, which was soon packed with people and the hum of conversation. For most, it was standing room only. At the front sat Tommy Robinson and Kevin Carroll alongside Tim Ablitt, one of the ROs who, as I mentioned in Chapter 1, would briefly take over the leadership of the organisation in the wake of Robinson and Carroll's departure in 2013. As the crowd settled, Tommy Robinson took the floor.

The purpose of the meeting was to discuss plans for the future of the movement – it was widely acknowledged that the last few months had not gone as most activists had hoped. The big announcement was a plan to forge an alliance with the British Freedom Party (BFP), a tiny (even by the standards of the British far right) and ultimately short-lived[3] political party led at the time by Paul Weston, a former UK Independence Party (UKIP) candidate for the Cities of London and Westminster, who in 2010 had aired concerns about what he saw as 'ethnic cleansing of the English' through mass immigration (Kim 2010). The discussion that followed was robust but respectful. As well as questions about the plan to forge the alliance with BFP, concerns were raised about other issues: what was seen as a widening north–south split within the organisation and declining support for EDL events, especially from the football casuals networks which had been so integral to the initial expansion of the movement. One of the comments that drew the most vocal chorus of approval from the floor was made by a woman who appealed for the EDL to 'get back to what it was about when we started all this' and expressed concern that 'we've lost our way'.

A few months later, on May 5th 2012, the London Division of the EDL managed to take just three-quarters of a busload of activists to Luton for a national demonstration; some way short of the two full buses that they had taken there in February 2011. As my main period of fieldwork drew to a close, several of the people I knew in London and Essex were speaking quite openly about either aligning themselves with other groups or 'taking a step back' from activism altogether.

Losing their way

'To me that is not an EDL issue'

The feeling among activists that the EDL was losing its way was grounded in three intersecting developments. The first of these concerned the way debates within the activist community about what it was that they were campaigning about became increasingly corrosive.

During the time that I spent with EDL activists, four issues in particular tended to divide opinion. The first of these, as discussed in Chapter 1, concerned the differentiation between Islam and militant Islam. On a day-to-day basis, most activists slipped in and out of the two terminologies, and it largely passed unnoticed. Where the distinction had more bearing and became the focus of attention was in the context of debates about the specific issues around which the organisation should or should not be mobilising. Several activists in the London area, mainly those who had become heavily ideologically engaged with the counter-jihad movement, expressed concern that by moving towards a more general anti-Muslim position the EDL risked diverting its attention from the most serious issues. They tried to encourage fellow activists to mobilise only against what they saw as the most dangerous forms of Islam – primarily the Salafist and Wahhabist branches of Islam – and argued that more time and energy should be invested in opposing events such as the 'hate conferences'[4] organised by groups like MAC and Hizb ut-Tahrir.

A second focal point for differences of opinion was the EDL's position vis-à-vis multiculturalism in general. On the one hand activists like Tommy Robinson and Kevin Carroll often stated that they did not have an issue with multiculturalism per se, and did not necessarily subscribe to the belief that 'multiculturalism has failed'.[5] On the other hand, there were activists who, while they tended to abide by the official line that the EDL was a single-issue group campaigning only about (militant) Islam – at least during official EDL activities or when asked about the group and what it stood for – tended to talk as much if not more about issues of multiculturalism, immigration and 'anti-white racism'[6] outside these more managed interactions. Those who shared a similar viewpoint to the EDL's national leaders, which at the time of my fieldwork included almost all of the London organisers, sought to smooth out this tension by making strategic arguments, claiming that the EDL's aim was to get

> more and more supporters, until we reach the point where politicians realise that listening to our concerns will win them more votes than ignoring them. Wholesale opposition to immigration and to multiculturalism would have the opposite effect – it would make politicians feel justified in ignoring our concerns.
>
> (official EDL webpost, cited in Richards 2013, 135)

However, there continued to be a groundswell of discontent within some sections of the activist community about the line being taken by the national leadership, and especially about the prominence given to some within the EDL who were of black and minority ethnic backgrounds (Blake 2011, 189–202). At a demonstration in Telford on 13th August shortly after the English riots of 2011, Kevin Carroll called for a minute's silence for three British Asian men killed during the rioting in nearby Birmingham and their families. This was studiously observed by most of the EDL activists present, but a handful loudly voiced their disapproval until they were forcefully removed by event stewards.

A third focus of differences of opinion was the prominence given by the national leadership to issues relating to Israel. Since the autumn of 2009, Israeli flags had been a prominent feature of EDL demonstrations; Roberta Moore, leader of the Jewish Division, had become a senior figure within the movement and was often photographed with Tommy Robinson; Robinson and Carroll had also forged increasingly strong links with high-profile pro-Israel campaigners such as Pamela Geller and Robert Spencer, and on 25th October 2010, Rabbi Nachum Shifren, an America conservative and staunch pro-Israel campaigner delivered a speech opposing the 'Islamification' of Britain to EDL activists outside the Israeli Embassy in London. While most activists recognised the value of the Israel connection as a symbol of their non-racist and non-far-right identity, as a way of forging ties with experienced and resource-rich counter-jihad activists in the United Kingdom and the United States and of 'winding up' their opponents, many also expressed misgivings about the emphasis given to this issue. Some argued that their misgivings were simply a matter of priorities:

> The Jewish division was always a big bugbear amongst a lot of members, you know. I mean even myself included. It wasn't the Jewish members, it was the support for Israel, which I thought was too much, you know. I can see the point of having Israeli flags as a wind-up, but when it started getting to the point where you've got the Rabbi Nachum Shifren coming over – I would go to these events, but only because all my mates were going: you only went to back each other up. I'd be more concerned with what goes on in this country. There's plenty of other groups out there if you're worried about foreign policy or Israel and Palestine, there's plenty of other groups you could join as well. English Defence League is what it says on the tin, that's what I was concerned about. Like I said at the start [of the interview], when I joined we were a one-trick pony, that's all I was worried about. I'm not interested in anything else, and that's still my overriding concern.
>
> (Mark)

Other activists, mainly those from the clique who had come to the EDL from the established far right, opposed the Israeli connection on more ideological grounds.

A fourth related issue that stoked up differences of opinion was about the extent to which they framed their cause as an international or national cause, and in particular whether or not the EDL should be investing its energies in supporting the activities of cognate groups elsewhere in Europe. On 30th October 2010, around 60 EDL activists went to Amsterdam in a show of support for Freedom Party leader Geert Wilders;[7] on 14th May 2011, Tommy Robinson, along with a handful of other EDL activists, went to Lyon to address a rally being held by *Bloc Identitaire,* and on 25th May 2011, about 30 EDL activists, mainly from London and the southeast of England, attended a demonstration against a mosque in Gothenburg organised by a group calling itself Sweden's Self-Defence Corps (*Försvarskåren Sveriges Självförsvar*).[8] Some activists, however, were sceptical about the value of these international forays. In a discussion about them at a London Division meeting on 18th May 2011, some (mainly those who had attended some of these events) emphasised the importance of the alliances that these events generated. Brian, a senior activist and staunch supporter of such internationalisation, argued that since the Islamists[9] were mobilising as an international movement the only hope for Europe and the West was to do the same. Others, however, countered this: Richard, an uncompromising man with a long history of participation in football violence and an appetite for confrontation, argued: 'We are the English Defence League, so let's get England right first. What I'm saying is if they have a problem in France or Sweden, that's for them to deal with.' His comments drew a murmur of approval from several others in the room but frustrated people like John, who was trying to encourage his fellow activists to mobilise around and organise petitions about the plight of

Coptic Christians in Egypt and the Middle East – 'they [some of the more parochially minded activists] don't see the bigger the picture', he told me repeatedly over a few drinks a few months later.

It is important to note that much of the time these differences of opinion did little to disrupt everyday activism at the grassroots of the movement. It is quite possible for a social movement or movement scene to accommodate different ideological positions, at least for a limited period of time (Fangen 1998, Gould 2009, Reger 2002). As Bailey (2009) illustrates in his fascinating account of the participation of British National Party (BNP) councillors in local democratic governance processes in Stoke, when people have joint tasks or projects to complete even those with vehemently opposing views can find ways of working together. The EDL activists I knew were all acutely aware that the success of the EDL, whatever that might look like, depended to a large extent on the number of people it was able to attract to its events, even if they did not always see eye to eye with one another on certain framing or ideological issues. During activists' day-to-day interactions conflicting viewpoints tended either to be 'hidden behind some basic assumptions to which everyone agrees'[10] or submerged beneath more emotionally rewarding conversations – usually movement gossip, football-related banter, discussions about the latest news story upsetting the activist community, or above all, regaling one another with tales of previous demonstrations. Avoiding difficult conversations was made easier by the activists' tendency to socialise primarily within intra-movement cliques characterised by similar views. Activists from the established far right, for example, tended to gravitate towards one another on demonstration days, sitting together on journeys to and from demonstrations, sitting around the same table for pre-demonstration drinks, often walking together during the demonstration itself and so forth, as was the case with those activists who were more intellectually engaged with the counter-jihad network or groups of football lads. As described in Chapters 3 and 4, activists also converted the fact that there were differences of opinion within the movement into a discursive opportunity, using it as a symbol of their commitment to free speech and the absence of 'brainwashing' within the movement: within the semiotic logic of the EDL, being willing to talk with people from far right groups could function as sign for open-mindedness and tolerance.

During the course of 2011 however a number of factors made these debates about what should or should not comprise an EDL issue increasingly toxic to intra-group relations. The first of these was that such discussions increasingly became infused with what Gould (2009, 328–394), in her discussion of conflict and fragmentation within AIDS activism in the United States, describes as a 'scarcity mentality'. Until sometime around mid-2011, the EDL had been expanding with the number of Facebook supporters increasing rapidly and attendance at EDL demonstrations generally following an upward trajectory. Activists discussed ever more ambitious plans for the group: their 'horizons of possibility' (Blee 2012, 32) were expanding. Once the number of Facebook members ceased to grow so consistently and attendance at demonstrations plateaued and then started to decline the mentality and mood of the group began to change. Activists began to feel more keenly the fact that the decision to invest energy in one activity meant that other activities would probably have to be neglected. They began talking far more than before about the opportunity costs associated with demonstrations, and whether or not certain issues warranted a national or a regional EDL demonstration.

Second, debates about what was or was not an EDL issue increasingly intersected with internal group politics, with intra-movement rivalries and a growing array of identity cleavages running through the movement (which I elaborate on further below). Criticism of Tommy Robinson's position vis-à-vis multiculturalism intersected with gripes about apparent influence within the movement being exercised by people from minority ethnic backgrounds such as Guramit Singh and Roberta Moore, and the internationalisation of the cause was cast by its critics as part of a vanity project on the part of the national leaders. Meanwhile there were incessant grumblings about which towns and regions were getting to host the national EDL demonstrations.

A third factor was the way the emotional mood of these debates became a lot pricklier: laced with accusations and slurs which, somewhat ironically, often were precisely the aggressive and intentionally stigmatising terms used in arguments between EDL activists and their left-wing opponents. People who opposed mobilising around Israeli issues and were critical of Roberta Moore's position within the movement found themselves labelled fascists and Nazis (see also Blake 2011, 189–202).[11] Meanwhile, some of those who were unhappy about the national leaders' unwillingness to criticise multiculturalism per se accused the national leaders and those who supported them of being swayed by precisely the political correctness – or 'PC' – agenda that they considered to be at the root of the liberal elite's failure to respond decisively to the problems of (militant) Islam and Islamification. They were accused of turning their back on ordinary English people or working class people and towards the 'middle class Pardonia' (Blake, 2011, 258). On all sides, criticism of one another's positions called into question not just people's ideas but also their moral character.

Towards a tactical impasse

It is hard to underestimate the importance of demonstrations to EDL activism.[12] In strategic terms, large-scale street demonstrations have been central to the EDL's ability to attract public, media and political attention, a fact that all the activists I knew were well aware of. As discussed in Chapter 3, demonstrations also played an important role in activists' political socialisation: as well as meeting and forging relationships with other activists, through their participation in these events new recruits also learned songs, symbols and phrases which helped to consolidate their belief in and feelings of commitment to the cause. Demonstrations also played an integral role in regulating the 'emotional rhythms' (Summers Effler 2010) of EDL activism and charging up activists' emotional batteries. Media coverage of groups like the EDL, and to some extent academic research on radical social movements more generally, tends to focus its gaze on the juicier bits of activism: the protest rituals, the speeches, the confrontations with opposition activists and so forth. Yet such incidents comprise only a fraction of the time that people spend engaged in activism, even if they are moments of particular symbolic and narrative importance. The day-to-day activities that occupy a far greater proportion of people's time – the phone calls to other activists to make sure they know where they are meeting, trawling the local newspaper for information about new planning applications, organising transport to the next demonstration, trying to encourage Joe and Jenny to talk to each other again – can be rather more mundane. Grassroots activism in most movements is, as Blee (2012, 9) describes, characterised by 'long periods of sagging energy, wearisome discussion, and irritating tedium as activists wait for meetings to start, events to come together, or something to happen'. Demonstrations provided a much-needed injection of emotional energy.[13]

Importantly, this meant generating and helping to sustain not only feelings of anger, injustice and indignation (Chapters 3 and 4), but also the positive emotions associated with EDL activism. Demonstrations were a rich source of feelings of solidarity and common purpose.[14] During the build-up to a demonstration, discussing and sharing information about why they were going to that particular town not only stirred up feelings of indignation and injustice but also helped to generate the 'shared focus of attention' (Collins 2001, 29) that is so valuable in forging in-group unity. On the day, activists had the chance to meet new people in the movement and refresh old acquaintances. The shared protest rituals – the chanting, flag-waving, marching and speeches – provided moments of 'collective effervescence' (Durkheim 1915) that transformed the activists into an 'emotional collective' (Virchow 2007)[15] making it easier for them to set aside, however fleetingly, whatever squabbles and arguments simmered beneath the surface and experience what I referred to in my fieldnotes as their 'that's what it's all about' moments – quite literally, the moments when one of the activists I knew would turn to me, pumped up with emotion, and say 'That's what it's all about!' There were also more personal experiences that provided activists with rich narrative material with which to strengthen their mutual affective bonds. The stories they told me about demonstrations were populated by characters who embodied the idea that the activists 'had each other's backs'[16] – the person with them in the police van when they were arrested, the person who helped patch them up when they had blood pouring down their face, the person who lent them £15 to get home when they had missed their train after being held in a police 'kettle'[17] for two hours, and so forth. These were fragments of shared life out of which the activists could construct collective identities and that would be revisited repeatedly in conversations with other activists in the months ahead.[18]

Demonstrations were also instrumental in charging up activists' feelings of possibility and pride. They provided them with little moments of victory that helped to nourish the feeling that the EDL was 'going somewhere' (see Chapter 2), whether due to a larger turnout than their opponents' or simply members of the public waving flags back at them or applauding them (see Chapters 1 and 4). Although some months prior to the Tower Hamlets demonstration on 3rd

September 2011, activists had been telling each other that it would be their larg-est event to date, in the end it only attracted in the region of 1,000–1,500 par-ticipants.[19] Yet that did not stop them claiming that the day had been a success. The fact that they had had any kind of demonstration was seen as a triumph. A week before the demonstration the Home Secretary, Theresa May, had granted a police request to ban marches in Tower Hamlets and four neighbouring London boroughs for 30 days. The EDL organisers, however, aware that such orders only apply to marches, had gone ahead with plans to hold a static demonstration,[20] with activists being ferried in to the demonstration site next to Aldgate East station on underground trains under heavy police supervision. Then there was the surprise guest appearance of Tommy Robinson, who at the time was under a banning order preventing him from attending any EDL-related activities. He arrived at the demonstration in disguise, dressed as a rabbi and accompanied by Roberta Moore, who beamed with delight as they strode past police lines towards the demonstration site. The icing on the cake was their exit from the demonstration site. With roads around Aldgate East and Tower Hamlets jammed with police vehicles and various groups of counterdemonstrators, the police decided to walk the EDL activists a mile and a half or so to cross to the south bank of the River Thames where their coaches were waiting, and from where they would be dispatched away from London. In doing so however they walked them across Tower Bridge, one of London's most iconic landmarks. The activists could not believe their luck: a march that had been banned turned into what felt to them like a glorious procession:

Susan: Tower Hamlets was good . . . Banned march?! We marched for five miles!
Bev: Banned march?! They took us around London and on that –
Susan: Tower Bridge.
Bev: On the bridge that was just nuts.
Susan: That was the best.
Bev: When everyone was knackered and they were like, 'Look at us, where are we?!' The whole of London – that was good that day.
Susan: We came, we conquered.
Bev: We did, that was our best march.

The problem for the activists was that while their demonstrations continued to be highly effective at generating negative and hostile emotional energy, they started to become less effective at generating positive emotional energies.[21] The activists I knew were unanimous in the view that EDL demonstrations no longer had the '*buzz*' (see Chapter 2) of the early days. This was partly because new policing strategies meant that EDL activists increasingly found themselves allocated to muster points and demonstration sites away from the busiest shopping areas, making them less likely to encounter onlookers, and now rarely caught more than a fleeting glimpse of their opponents, whose counter-demonstrations were usually located on the other side of town (see Treadwell 2014, van der Wal 2011).[22] It was also partly simply a case of 'demonstration fatigue' (see Casquete 2006, Pickvance 1998): the

novelty of these events had worn off and they had started to seem rather repeti-
tive. On 4th February 2012, waiting to use a portaloo[23] as snow-clouds loomed
over the carpark on the edge of Leicester town centre that had served as the
demonstration site for the day, one activist's explanation for the somewhat disap-
pointing turnout of this first national demonstration of the new year – police
estimate that there were about 800 participants – was straightforward and seemed
particularly apt: 'How many Saturday afternoons do people want to spend freez-
ing their nuts off in a car park?'

As well as losing some of their buzz, demonstrations also became far less
effective at generating feelings of intra-movement solidarity. This was partly the
result of confrontations between competing EDL factions. The highest-profile
incident took place at a demonstration in Blackburn on 2nd April 2011, when
activists aligned with the Northwest Infidels (NWI) and Northeast Infidels (NEI)
factions, at that time still part of the EDL, clashed with Tommy Robinson and
his closest supporters, leading to Robinson facing an assault charge for headbutting a fellow activist[24] and serving to consolidate a split in the movement
between the Luton-based leadership and activists loyal to the NWI and NEI
factions that had been gestating for several months. There were also scuffles
between rival divisions and factions at other demonstrations. During particularly
ugly scenes in Birmingham on 29th October 2011, some activists threw not
only punches but also glasses and, I am told,[25] fireworks at one another. Such
incidents took place against a backdrop of marginally more subtle, or at least
more legal, signs of intra-movement hostility such as the intentional breaking
of the minute's silence in Telford, and sections of the crowd heckling speakers
in Birmingham with chants of 'Who are ya? Who are ya?' During a service
station stop on the way back to Essex after the Birmingham demonstration a
group of activists told me that they had no intention of attending any more
demonstrations 'in the north.'[26]

What also undermined the EDL activists' feelings of solidarity were the obvious symbolic tensions in their protest performances. While organisers, stewards
and many of the event participants strived to prevent or at least minimise incidents
of violence or public disorder during demonstrations, these could not be elimi-
nated altogether. At all of the national demonstrations and most of the regional
demonstrations I attended I observed EDL activists throwing projectiles (usually
beer cans, stones or sometimes coins), issuing threats of physical harm to their
opponents, overtly racist chants, groups of individuals attempting to circumvent
police lines and attempts to recruit people to participate in physical confrontations at the end of the demonstration when there were usually more opportunities
to evade the police and come face to face with some kind of opposition.[27] A
situation developed in which nobody, it seemed, was happy. As Phil explained,

> As much as I'd love to go and kick off – and I would really fucking love
> it – but it's not going to get us anywhere. Putting our feet on the streets
> and doing the peaceful protesting is the best way we can do it, but you've
> got some people – the argument on this side going 'Well it's not enough,

it's not getting noticed', and you've got the argument on that side where they're going, 'Well kicking and shouting at people is not going to work either', so it's sort of an ongoing argument on both sides which – it's what sort of maybe split a lot of groups and a lot of people and why some people have backed away from it now, because it's not hard enough for them.

(Phil)

For those activists who were excited by and attracted to the prospect of physical or at the very least hostile verbal confrontations with their opponents, EDL demonstrations had become too anodyne and too easy for the media, the politicians and the public to ignore. Meanwhile, activists who had bought into the idea of the EDL as a peaceful protest movement were frustrated and often angry about incidents of 'ill-discipline'[28] during demonstrations. To some extent those activists who wanted to maintain claims about the EDL being a peaceful protest group were able to find ways of playing down or justifying incidents of violence or disorder,[29] usually attributing such incidents to 'a few bad apples' or deflecting blame onto their opponents or poor policing. The fighting at a protest in Dudley on 17th July 2010 was attributed to the fact that 'the local Muslim lads were spoiling for a fight, they were mobbing up in little gangs around the demo area and they've made an attempt twice to get over the barriers to get to us' (Andy); talking about how 'it kicked off at the train station towards the end' [of a demonstration in Luton on 5th May 2012], Phil explained 'to be honest with you the UAF start, they try and antagonise to get people to kick off, that's what they want because they think they're winning because we're getting a bad name for kicking off and retaliating' and, describing trouble at the end of a demonstration in Leicester on 9th October 2010, Steve reasoned:

People have got trains to catch and things like that – and people were just asking 'how long have we got to stay here'? 'When are you going to let us out'? And [the police officers] are just ignoring them. . . . Then if you pen people in like animals – Students do it, it's not just us. I mean you see all the students that get the hump because they can't go to the toilet, they can't get a drink and everything else and you treat people like that – I don't care who you are, you're going to retaliate, and that's what it was at Leicester.

(Steve)

Most activists were aware however that, even armed with such excuses and blame-deflection strategies, such incidents fuelled the public's association of the EDL with violence, drunkenness and public disorder and made it increasingly unlikely that they could attract the scale of public support to which some of them aspired. This generated both chronic feelings of frustration and the acute negative emotions I described in the final part of Chapter 4 where Steve stormed away from the march and flung his cap to the ground after fellow activists set upon a young Muslim man in Dagenham.

The decline in feelings of solidarity, common purpose and possibility that the demonstrations were able to generate was further exacerbated as attendance plateaued and then started to decline. Marching or chanting in a crowd of 300 people is simply not the same as doing so with a crowd of 2,000, and with each poorly attended demonstration different divisions traded criticism and recriminations about how they were letting the movement down.[30]

As the demonstrations became less emotionally rewarding many activists started to question what they were achieving through these events (see also Lowles 2012). As I have described above, there was a growing consensus among senior activists in both London and Essex that the kind of demonstrations being staged by the EDL were taking valuable resources away from other activities. Eddie, a London organiser, was one of several activists who were keen to see a reduction in the number of national and regional demonstrations and more small, targeted counter-demonstrations focused around 'hate conferences'. Similarly Andy, another London organiser, advocated limiting national demonstrations to about four per year and spending more time working with organisations like the Law and Freedom Foundation[31] to set up local campaigns to prevent the construction or expansion of Islamic buildings. As he explained:

> The more we concentrate on the demos and the more we ignore the local areas the less impact we're going to have. A prime example a couple of weeks ago: there was a planning application for a huge mosque in Ilford, which should have been opposed . . . and the EDL needs to be on top of that, we need to be tackling that, not standing in a car park, or sorry in a town centre in Birmingham shouting at people. 700[32] people all spent a day doing something not particularly constructive. So it's fair to say a working day is 8 hours; 700 times 8 – think of all those man-hours directed at local mosques, local authorities! That's what we need to be doing.
>
> (Andy)

From the end of the summer of 2011 onwards I had multiple conversations with organisers in London, Essex, Kent, Sussex and Hampshire about how the EDL had reached a point at which it must 'evolve or die'.[33] The problem was that shifting the emphasis to the other forms of collective action deployed by activists tended only to further highlight the different interests and tactical tastes within the activist community. Flash demonstrations (see Chapter 1) could be exciting: the planning, the communication through 'trusted only' networks, the stakeouts, the journey to the planned demonstration site looking out for signs that the police were on to them and so forth; they also provided particularly rich opportunities for people to develop their personal heroic narratives, and the fact that the activists were not tightly hemmed in by the police meant they also had more opportunity to engage with the public, whether this meant handing them EDL flyers[34] or assaulting them.[35] Operations to disrupt the activities of people they considered their opponents held a similar allure. Yet most of the organisers I knew also recognised the drawbacks of such activities. They expressed concern that they were likely to result in 'even more patriots getting nicked, you know, and more patriots getting hurt too' (Simon). There was also scepticism about what such activities were ultimately likely to achieve. As Tony opined, 'Now if I thought we would just kick down the doors of all the Mosques and that would be the end of it then we'd do it, but it's – it's not the way to do it.'

Similarly, most activists were, in principle, supportive of activities such as leafleting, organising petitions and undertaking legal challenges against proposed Islamic buildings. Like Andy, they recognised that 'the only way the EDL is going to get rid of this mindless, drunken football hooligan image, [is] if you go out and press the flesh and you talk to people and you prove that you're not idiots, because the only contact that people have with the EDL is what they see on the news. . . '. At every meeting I attended, there was enthusiasm for leafleting and sometimes frustration when leaflets were not available for distribution. In practice, however, it tended always to be the same handful of activists contributing to such activities. This in turn fed back into recriminations at meetings, resentment about how they were being left to shoulder the burden and an ever-diminishing sense of confidence in the movement and their fellow activists. As Andy lamented after a failed attempt to coordinate a campaign against a proposed Islamic building in Ilford, Essex:

> There was nine days between the details of the planning meeting going up and the meeting itself. The nine days included a weekend, and I was talking to the people that organised that area: 'Right, we need to be out on the street with a petition, you need to be in Romford, you need to be in Basildon, you need to be in Dagenham, you need to be in Ilford, you need to be doing a petition'. I mean, you can get 2,000 signatures a day. The petition needed to be given in to the planners so it could go to a formal open public planning meeting. And there wasn't the willingness or the manpower or the brainpower to organise it.

There was also considerable scepticism among activists about whether tactics that entailed engaging in dialogue and negotiation with public officials were available to them. Most activists had internalised their pariah status, fuelled by stories that circulated within the activist community about hostile encounters with councillors and MPs when they had tried to attend public meetings. Particularly present in the activists' discussions during late 2011 and early 2012 was the case of Blain Robin, a Conservative councillor in Southend-on-Sea, Essex, who, after attending an EDL meeting in order to find out more about the group and the concerns of its activists, was promptly suspended by his party.[36]

Grassroots activists found themselves at a tactical impasse, and Robinson and Carroll's announcement of the alliance with the BFP certainly did nothing to resolve the issue; if anything it made matters worse.[37] The activists I knew expressed a variety of reasons for opposing the move; as described in Chapter 4, some expressed concern that it would make it even harder than it already was to persuade the public that they were not a racist or far right group; others, particularly those who identified with and/or voted for established far right groups, were concerned that it would 'split the nationalist vote' – that is, it would take support away from other far right groups; and there was a more general feeling that it just did not fit with what they were as a movement:

> We're a street movement. We should stay a street movement; we shouldn't move into a political issue because the political side of things are there anyway.[38]
>
> (Tony)

Interestingly, part of the objection also related to how the decision had been taken and announced. Some activists resented the fact that the decision had come from the top without prior consultation: something that, to their minds, was out of keeping with the ethos of the EDL:[39]

> *Susan:* I feel like a lot of people I've asked about it – it's been sprung on us.
> *Bev:* My words were – my words were: 'We were all at Parliament the other day asking for a referendum on the EU, [40] you know, 'We should be asked, we should be asked as British citizens'. Sorry, but I know it's on a very small, a much smaller scale, but we should have been asked as foot soldiers, as, that's what they call us, 'foot soldiers' –
> *Susan:* Foot soldiers; we are the feet on the street, which you've probably heard before, and we're the ones who get things done.
> *Bev:* We should get the recognition, we don't get no recognition. We're the ones who actually get the job done.
> *Susan:* We get the job done, we've just been shoved aside. We should have been asked 'How do you feel about it, do you want to do it?' and I think 'No. They sprung it on us and there's a lot of people not happy about it'. I ain't going to be supporting the BFP, definitely.
> *Bev:* I ain't.

The only activists I knew who supported the move were some of the London organisers who were close to the national leadership. As I sat in a café in Barking in December 2011 with a group of activists from Essex discussing plans for a forthcoming demonstration, I listened to them being derided for being Tommy Robinson's 'arse-lickers'.

The growing salience of sub-group identities

The EDL activist community was crosscut with various sets of sub-group identities. Perhaps the most conspicuous of these were based on divisional affiliations and regional identities: activists in both London and Essex were often rather derisory about some of the northern activists, who they tended to stereotype as drunken and a bit racist,[41] although as with most stereotyping such sweeping generalisations were usually subsequently qualified. Intersecting with these regional and divisional identities however were several other sets of sub-group identities. There were identities relating to the range of social scenes that the 'formal' EDL structures had been grafted onto: the football violence scene, the patriotic networks, the counter-jihad networks and the established far right. For example, those who had come to the EDL from the football hooligan networks tended to identify themselves and be identified as 'football lads', and as described in Chapter 2, those who had come to the EDL from various patriotic or far right groups usually continued to identify with these groups as well as with the EDL. There were also sub-group identities that reflected the activists' different inter-pretations of the EDL cause: some activists such as John, Steve, Lucy and Eddie very much identified as part of the counter-jihad movement others were less prone to do so. Similarly, some activists such as Andy, Jim, Nick and Steve described themselves to me as 'nationalists', while others rejected this label insisting that they were 'patriots, not nationalists'.[42]

During the early phase of EDL mobilisations possible tensions arising from this patchwork of collective identities were usually circumvented by appeals to the overarching group identity offered by the EDL and the concept of all being 'patriots' together. As I have already described, the existing range of different identities was also turned into a discursive opportunity, the activists using it to narratively construct themselves as a diverse and therefore rather tolerant group of people (see Chapter 4 and above). However, some of these sub-group identi-ties did over time turn into sites of intra-movement conflict. In part this was a function of the growing perception among activists that the EDL might be losing momentum: as described above, each demonstration that did not attract as many participants as the organisers had hoped for or go as planned produced recrimi-nations; these recriminations usually activated sub-group identities, which in turn made it harder for the activists to achieve the rituals that successfully generated feelings of whole-group solidarity.[43] It was also a product of increasingly frac-tious relations between the national EDL leaders and some of the other prominent figures within the movement, at the centre of which were questions being raised about the role of Roberta Moore within the EDL and the influence of counter-jihad activists such as Pamela Geller and Alan Lake on decision-making within the group. These arguments came to dominate debates on the EDL online forum and permeated out through divisional and personal Facebook networks, eating away at activists' feelings of whole-group solidarity.

In London and Essex, from at least the summer of 2011 onwards there was protracted falling-out and sniping between some of the organisers in the two areas. Paul Pitt, the Essex Regional Organiser, and other members of the Essex leadership criticised some of the London leaders for failing to get themselves organised – why, for example, had they failed to arrange a coach to take London activists up to the Birmingham demonstration in October? And why were he and the Essex Division having to head up campaigns in London calling for the deportation of Abu Qatada to Jordan to face terrorism charges, when Qatada was living in London?[44] Meanwhile although Paul Pitt was acknowledged even by his critics in the movement to be highly committed to the cause, he was criticised for bullying and attempting to intimidate other people within the movement and for being one of the 'egos' that was creating disunity within the movement, a criticism that intensified in the autumn of 2011 when he was involved in a public falling-out with Hel Gower, Tommy Robinson's PA. As criticisms were thrown around, people found it hard not to take sides.

Similarly, some core activists who were not from a background in football violence made comments criticising the 'hooligan element', and there was even a rumour that football lads were no longer welcome on demonstrations. As might be expected, such comments were not well-received by individuals who identified with the football lads and resented having to defend or justify themselves. In turn, some of the football lads complained about people who were 'just drunken yobs' coming into the EDL and some experienced football lads complained to me that their local EDL divisions had been 'taken over by chavs'.

> They've said the football connection has outlived its usefulness, you know, and they say 'These kinds of people, we don't really want them around anymore', but the reality in my mind is most of the football boys know how to behave themselves. They're the ones that are actually getting the hump about all the idiots on the edge, the ones that turn up pissed, looking for trouble, knowing that there's going to be someone to bail them out if it goes wrong. Most of the football boys are very regimented and they won't get pissed. I don't ever drink before a football match; I'll have a couple of pints. If I know there's likely to be trouble at a football match there's no way I'm going to drink because you've got to keep your wits about you. You can't fight when you're pissed anyway, you know. Everyone who's anyone, they know that, you don't turn up acting the ass. So a lot of the real football lads, even the young ones, the youth boys which have all drifted away now, you know, and that's the reason because they didn't want to be seen to be tarnished by all of the drunks and idiots. No one's really taken any notice of that and they've not done what we've asked them to.
>
> (Mark)

Meanwhile, activists identifying with cognate groups such as Casuals United, English Nationalist Alliance (ENA), March for England (MFE) and Combined Ex-Forces (CXF) offered commentaries and criticisms of what was taking place within the EDL, thereby further stoking up intra-group arguments. Whether or not they did this intentionally is difficult to say. As events were called under different organisational banners, feelings of rivalry crept in. John encapsulated the sentiment of many of the activists I spoke with during the early autumn of 2011 when, reflecting on an argument between ENA organisers and EDL organisers earlier in the year (see Chapter 6) and the launch of a group called British Patriot Society (BPS) in June, he exclaimed 'I mean, how many fucking groups do we need?'

In London, feelings of disunity and the tendency towards the articulation and enactment of sub-group identities was accentuated by a protracted struggle for leadership in the area that was precipitated by the departure of six of the most senior activists over the summer of 2011 (for reasons that I discuss in the following chapter). During the remainder of the year various activists were put forward or put themselves forward as leaders, but none were able to generate the broad support that the previous group of admins had enjoyed. Even a vote among London admins to elect a leader did not succeed in ending the infighting, as activists complained that the outcome was rigged because those in the room happened to be mainly from one particular clique. With many rank and file members confused as to who was leading the EDL in London and through what mechanism, activists started looking for alternatives. Some affiliated themselves to Essex, where the leadership was more stable and better-established in spite of the spat between Paul Pitt and some of the national leaders; some spoke about aligning themselves with other groups such as MFE, the ENA or Casuals United who seemed to be hoovering-up some of the fallout from the EDL slump, while others simply drifted away from the activist scene altogether.

Running through all of this were various personal squabbles many of whose origins were difficult to uncover but at some point included accusations of financial wrongdoing involving EDL funds or personal debt, and/or of people having 'egos' and putting their own interests before those of the group. To cap it all, the infighting also became infused with sectarian identities. In the summer and autumn of 2011 stories emerged that Tommy Robinson and Kevin Carroll had attended the funeral of a friend associated with Sinn Fein. Rivals of Robinson and Carroll such as Paul 'Lionheart' Ray, the blogger involved in the initial mobilisation of the UPL (Chapter 1), had long sought to stoke up animosity towards them by playing on their Irish ancestry and the deep seam of sectarianism running through British football hooliganism.

> Then all of a sudden, you've got these people, they're turning the screws and saying, this proves they've got republican sympathies, they're IRA supporters, and all this, that and the other. Then of course now, all of a sudden you've got all these guys, these loyalists jumping up saying, 'They're IRA supporters, I'm off. I'm not having that, we're not having this'. They start referring to us as Fenians and Taigs and all this, which are derogatory terms, you know. I'm, to a degree now, I'm starting to get the hump with those now because I find it insulting to my family history that all of a sudden Irish people are deemed to be second-class citizens. I mean I don't turn around and say that anyone is second-class because of where they come from so I'm getting the hump about it a little bit. Even some of my friends, you know, I've had little spats with them. Over certain comments that they were making about Tommy and Kevin, as much a slur against, you know, sort of Irish in general.
>
> (Mark)

It was this infighting more than anything else that the activists spoke about when, as became increasingly common during the course of the autumn of 2011, the activists I knew expressed doubts about whether they would continue in the movement.[45] I return to this point in Chapter 6.

Five underlying tensions within EDL activism

These three developments made it increasingly difficult for the EDL and its activists to cope with the challenges that they faced: the pressure it was under as a pariah group, the limited financial and human resources at its disposal, and the problem of sustaining commitment in spite of the personal costs of activism (see Chapter 1). They also point to a series of underlying tensions within EDL activism as a project of collective world-making which can help us to think about the limitations and vulnerabilities of groups like the EDL.

The constraints of being a 'single-issue' group

Identifying as a single-issue group offered the EDL a number of advantages. As discussed in Chapter 4, it was central to the activists' attempts to distance themselves from the established far right and to reject accusations that theirs' was a racist movement. It also helped to mitigate possible ideological tensions within the activist community because, as a single-issue group ideological alignment among the activists was only required on a very limited number of points – that is, that they were opposed to (militant) Islam.

However, it did have a major drawback: in most activist groups, even where there is a defined idea about what comprises 'the problem', members 'rarely stay with this definition for long' (Blee 2012, 107). How they frame and conceptualise the problem changes over time as a function of tactical debate, encounters with their opponents and with the state, and other events that might cause activists to re-evaluate earlier positions. There may be a narrowing of focus as they become more realistic about what they can achieve – as their horizons of possibility shrink – or there may be a refocusing as new enemies are identified or activists start to perceive that the issues around which they initially mobilised are nested in a wider set of cognate issues (Blee 2012, 81–108).

In the case of the EDL, there were multiple impulses towards a broadening of the focus of their campaigning. The fact that the activists often found themselves confronted by left-wing anti-fascist groups meant that many became increasingly entrained on their left-wing opponents, their appetite for organising counter-demonstrations or attacks on such opponents fuelled at least partly by the prospect of revenge. There was also an appetite in some quarters of the movement for mobilising around the issue of 'anti-white racism', whether or not such incidents could be specifically linked to (militant) Islam, and more general anxieties about immigration. The identification of the EDL as a single-issue group made it difficult however to accommodate the shifting interests of the activists and prospective activists without at the same time undercutting a part of the group's identity that was important to some of its adherents.[46] Two former activists told me that part of their motivation for leaving the EDL had been that they were unwilling to participate in more general anti-Muslim activism and now preferred to challenge Islamist extremism through other channels. Similarly, when the EDL called a national demonstration in Leicester for February 2012 in response to what most EDL activists and some other commentators[47] saw as the unreasonably lenient sentence imposed on four women of Somali background who, while drunk, had assaulted a white woman and her partner shouting 'Kill the white slag!', not all the activists were convinced that the EDL should be 'leading on this issue' because, while they agreed that it was a terrible case of injustice, it was more about anti-white racism than about *militant* Islam.[48]

The violence paradox

On the one hand minimising public disorder and attempting to eradicate violent incidents from EDL events was integral both to the group's ability to recruit from beyond the fringes of the football hooligan networks and the established far right[49] and to activists' ability to sustain their narrative about being a peaceful single-issue protest group. On the other hand however, violence, or at least the threat of violence, has been integral to EDL activism.[50]

On a strategic level the activists were well aware that the threat of significant public disorder had helped them to attract media attention and unsettle and even intimidate public authorities:[51]

> As much as I disagree with [violence] – I don't necessarily think it's the right way to conduct yourself in a civilised society – maybe that kind of revolt and maybe that kind of protest shakes the authorities into thinking this is what 3,000 people can do, what happens when we put 30,000 or 300,000 disaffected, disenfranchised souls who, you know, aren't prepared to tolerate the country building its own funeral pyre?[52]
>
> (Eddie)

Physical confrontations with opponents, or at least the prospect of them, were also central to the emotional alchemy that lay at the heart of EDL activism. As well as the adrenaline that such confrontations produced, these incidents and activists' retelling of them were a rich source of feelings of solidarity, and 'kicking off' and 'fucking showing their anger' (Phil) provided an effective mechanism for converting feelings of anxiety, fear, shame or inferiority into pride and confidence.[53] Even if activists recognised the strategic advantages of allowing themselves to be shepherded along by the police, for many such protest performances did not offer anything like the same emotional rewards.

Furthermore, *appropriate* forms of violence could act as a source of cultural capital within the activist community. Physical violence was officially discouraged and participation in violent incidents could attract a considerable stigma even from within the activist community: the activists who attacked the young

Muslim men at one of the demonstrations in Dagenham (see Chapter 4) were shouted down for being 'fucking animals', and those who got involved in various other brawls were often criticised as 'idiots' or 'thugs'. Yet there were also cases where activists had gained considerable kudos among their peers for their part in physical confrontations. Perhaps the most obvious example of this is Tommy Robinson, whose leap over a crash barrier to confront Emdadur Choudhury, the 'poppy burner' did much to bolster his standing within the activist community.[54] There were however other activists whose position within the group also seemed to have been elevated by their involvement in confrontations with opponents and the subsequent entering of these deeds into EDL folklore. For example almost every time I met one activist, nicknamed 'Rambo', he and others were enjoying reliving an incident in which he had landed what was by all accounts a hefty punch on an opponent. I would propose that one of the differences between those who rose to the most high status positions within the EDL and those who remained at its margins was that the former were generally more skilled at identifying the moments for and modes of utilising violence that would elicit a generally positive response from their fellow activists, for example, when they could successfully frame their actions as self-defence and when there was a culturally suitable level of provocation.[55]

Becoming trapped by their own brand

Closely related to the violence paradox was a further issue. As intimated in the previous chapter, on 9th August 2011, a crowd of people gathered on the streets of Eltham, ostensibly to protect the area from the rioting that had shaken London for the previous two days. No more than about a dozen EDL activists were present, most of whom insisted that they were there as local residents rather than EDL activists (Busher 2012). Yet the news stories in the following days were of a group of agitators led by EDL thugs; stories that were fuelled at least partly by scenes of angry young white men chanting 'E-D-L' at, among other things, a bus carrying mainly black people.[56]

The EDL had become a well-known political brand. Wherever people used the group's name they were more or less assured of attracting media attention and 'EDL' was being used as a badge by primarily young white people across the country to express frustration and anger and to challenge a society in which they perceived people like themselves to be increasingly marginalised and ignored.[57] This has helped the group to continue to attract new recruits and the extent to which it has entered into the public's consciousness could itself be considered a form of success.[58]

The problem for the EDL, or at least for those activists who wanted to conceive of the group as a peaceful and respectable social movement, was that its public image as a highly aggressive and hostile group meant that it tended to attract people who wanted 'to fucking show their anger and kick off' (Phil), thereby further precluding attempts to build a larger movement that could achieve significant reach beyond the far right and football hooligan scenes.

The challenges associated with the EDL's loose and highly devolved mode of organising

The EDL's loose and highly devolved mode of organising offered the group a number of advantages. First the network structures and porous external group boundaries both facilitated the rapid expansion of the movement (Copsey 2010, Jackson 2011, see also Chapter 1) and enabled the activists to exaggerate the group's size,[59] thereby building momentum and promoting feelings of confidence. Second, affording autonomy to local groups of activists was an effective way of maximising the movement's scarce material and human resources, with local groups taking on much of the responsibility for identifying issues to mobilise around, promoting the EDL, organising promotional materials and so forth. Third, and related to this, the devolved structure helped to cultivate the activists' sense of ownership of the movement, which in turn reinforced feelings of commitment and pride (see Chapter 2).[60]

A fourth facet of these highly devolved structures was that they provided opportunities for almost all the activists to have some kind of official or quasi-official role, and to enjoy the status and deference that such roles entailed (see Chapter 2). Fifth, the tight-knit local groups played a crucial role in cultivating feelings of solidarity,[61] with local divisions described by several activists as being like a family. These feelings of solidarity could be converted into the feelings of duty to one's fellow activists that played a crucial role in sustaining participation in the EDL even when their enthusiasm for the cause or its protest events wavered.[62]

Sixth, the activists were able to use the porosity of the EDL's boundaries and the burgeoning array of sub-group identities to externalise blame for incidents with which they did not want to be associated, thereby negotiating unwanted identities and sustaining feelings of pride in themselves as activists and in the EDL as an organisation.[63] For example, after the debacle in Whitehall on 11th November 2011 (see Chapter 3), Mark was able to direct blame away from the EDL and towards CXF, a small group who at the time had an ambiguous relationship with the EDL[64] and whose organiser had been primarily responsible for spreading the rumour that the EDL intended to go to St. Paul's to attack Occupy protestors:

> Well thankfully Michael Rafferty [a prominent member of the CXF], to people in EDL they know that he's not part of the EDL and the EDL made a statement saying basically he's an idiot, disregard him. Then, to people outside the EDL they continue to make associations between Combined Ex-Forces, the EDL and the BNP, NWI; they don't seem to get the fact that these are all separate groups that actually have issues with each other.
>
> (Mark)

Similarly, after several demonstrations where there had been substantial public disorder some activists in London and Essex attributed this to some of the northern divisions, in particular those associated with the NEI and NWI factions.

Such strategies for externalising blame could also be used when cases emerged of serious criminal incidents involving people associated with the EDL, such as attacks on persons, criminal damage and the desecration of religious buildings.[65]

Seventh, the porosity of the internal boundaries between divisions and between different groups also meant that individuals were largely free to tailor their affiliations to suit their own interests and friendships. In London and the southeast, it was common for activists to identify themselves as members of more than one division, and several switched their divisional affiliations at one point or another for logistical reasons, because they thought another division was better organised and 'more active', or due to changing friendship patterns and fallings-out. Danny, for example, started spending a lot of time with a different division due to romantic interests. Terry recalled how when he was told that he could no longer be a divisional admin in London because he was 'not pulling his weight', he 'threw his toys out of the pram' and joined up with the Essex group. When he subsequently made his peace with his old division he simply attended the meetings of both. Phil meanwhile set up his own division when he felt that he was not getting sufficient support from either Kent or London:

> 'I wasn't really getting too much out of the Kent Division because they were Dover-based, I wasn't really getting too much out of London Division because they're London, you know, and we were basically on the borderline; so I went off by myself and opened up Bromley Division and started getting people in'.

Eighth, and finally, there was a symbolic consistency between these structures and activists' identification as 'ordinary English people' and as a 'single-issue street movement'. Social movement structures are not simply pragmatic or rational solutions to organisational problems[66] but are themselves symbols more or less consciously used by the activists to say something about themselves, about what they represent, and in some cases about their visions of what they are trying to achieve as a movement (Jasper 2007, Pearce 1980, Sutherland, Land and Böhm 2013). EDL activists identified themselves as 'the feet on the street', an authentic upsurge of widespread public anger; a rigidly hierarchical mode of organising would have jarred with this collective identity.

Yet the EDL's loose and highly devolved mode of organising also generated challenges. First, it made it difficult to arrest the tendency towards factionalism and arguably ultimately fuelled it. Social psychologists have demonstrated that group fragmentation, or 'fissioning' is most likely to occur where self-categorization becomes focused on sub-group rather than superordinate group identities (Hart and van Vugt 2006, Turner et al. 1987). The EDL's tight and largely self-organising local groups and the rivalries that bubbled up between them lent themselves to just such a focusing on sub-group identities, with these morphing over time into distinct group identities, as happened for example with the Southeast Alliance (SEA), the NWI, the NEI, or CXF.[67] The tight-knit local groups also made it easy for personal fallings-out between activists from different divisions or cliques to quickly escalate into inter(sub-)group fallings-out: a spat between two activists becoming a feud between two divisions or between the cliques that the two activists associated with.[68]

Second, the loose and highly devolved structures made it difficult for leaders to exercise leadership when leadership was required.[69] The porosity of the EDL's external and internal boundaries limited leaders' capacity to sanction activists – activists who fell out with divisional organisers could simply go to another division. The various alternative social structures through which they organised themselves – the informal friendship groups and other cognate groups and groupuscules whose membership overlapped with the EDL – also helped to ensure that any leader's authority was always circumscribed and circumscribable. Furthermore, as the EDL's loose and devolved mode of organising became socially embedded, it generated what could be described as a culture of anti-leadership reminiscent of some left-wing movements, by which I do not mean necessarily opposition to the actual leaders but generalised opposition to forms of top-down leadership (see Sutherland, Land and Böhm 2013).[70] Leaders were expected to act as spokespersons and to motivate their fellow activists, but decision-making was expected to take place through more collective processes, and there was a general resistance to activists, whoever they were, telling other activists what they could or could not do. As described above, it was partly the fact that the decision to form an alliance with the BFP breached this cultural norm that prompted most of the grassroots activists to resist the move. Grassroots activists had been similarly put-out by a top-down decision taken back in mid-March 2011 to replace the original EDL online forum with an in-house based platform on the grounds that this would enable them to exercise more control over the forum when necessary.

The limited capacity of organisers to exercise authority was particularly evident in relation to the efforts by some activists to turn demonstrations into more orderly affairs.[71] For example, the amount of alcohol consumed at demonstrations was a cause of considerable consternation among London and Essex organisers because of the association between drunkenness and public disorder. However, while organisers made several suggestions about what might be done to tackle the problem, these were not by and large followed through or enforced because leaders feared that it would lead to a drop in attendances and few wanted to be associated with such an unpopular decision. Eddie's comments were typical of the London and Essex organisers on this topic:

> I would like to see EDL demos where alcohol is banned, I really would. I mean I'm not a big drinker myself, it's a big fucking enemy that we've got, it really is – it's counterproductive. The press will always zoom in on people like that and it just gives us a bad look, a bad reputation. But once you start to try to impose alcohol-free [demonstrations] those people who see it as a day out or say 'I can do what I like, it's my freedom', or

'It's my choice, how dare you?', they'll move away from it, and that's probably the reason they haven't done it; it's because you'll haemorrhage members.

When the police told Essex organisers that their demonstration in Barking on 14th January 2012 would have to be alcohol-free, it came as something of a relief to Sarah, one of the organisers, as it allowed her and the other organisers to attribute what she knew would be an unpopular decision to the police. Even then, organisers were unable to prevent some activists swigging from beer cans during the march.

The failure to impose greater discipline itself in turn became a source of discontent among some of the activists. John grumbled that there were too many people in leadership positions who 'just want to be one of the lads' while Mark complained:

> If people can't behave themselves they shouldn't come. People that are seen to be drunk should be removed before the demo; it's up to their division leaders and ROs to take control and say to people, you know, 'You're an embarrassment, fuck off'. People that are known to only be looking for trouble, get rid of them.

As such, leaders at all levels found themselves on the horns of a dilemma, facing demands from some parts of the movement for stronger leadership while at the same time facing criticism for attempting to provide just that.

The downsides of mobilising via social media

> I'm very, very careful about what I write [on Facebook], you know. I can be quite damning against our own people for their behaviour and what they do but I mean I would never make a threat [via Facebook], I wouldn't dream of it. In my view I think [the EDL] should ditch Facebook completely.
>
> (Mark)

A fifth underlying tension within EDL activism related to the organisation's and activists' use of social media. One of the characteristics of the EDL has been its rather adept use of social media: particularly Facebook and also to some extent Twitter. As described in Chapter 1, as the EDL emerged, it quickly developed a substantial social media presence, with not only the organisation's main Facebook page and later Twitter account, but also with a rapid proliferation of divisional and regional pages. Their use of social media enabled the group to communicate its message more quickly and to a wider audience than would otherwise have been possible; provided an easy point of access to the group for members of the public interested in joining; helped the group to appear as though it enjoyed considerably more support than it probably ever did, thereby building activists' sense of momentum; created online space in which people of like mind could share ideas and interact; and provided a way of communicating within the activist community that was not only cheap and effective but also highly mobile – with smartphone technology activists could be in contact with one another via social media around the clock, almost regardless of where they were, sharing images, stories, ideas and emotions. These enabling qualities of social media to EDL and more generally contemporary anti-Muslim activism have been discussed at some length (Allen 2014, Bartlett and Littler 2011, Copsey 2010, Jackson 2011, Kim et al. 2013).[72]

As I described in Chapter 2, the fact that most activists had an online presence also facilitated the building of friendship networks during offline interactions, and vice versa. On several occasions during demonstrations I witnessed conversations in which two people from different parts of the country meeting each other for the first time suddenly realised that their paths had already crossed on Facebook, usually as a result of having mutual friends – 'oh, you're Micky Bexley!'; 'oh, you're Oxford Dave!' Similarly, conversations between new acquaintances during demonstrations and other events often ended with invitations to 'Facebook me'.

Activists' prolific use of Facebook also had its downsides, however. The first of these relates back to the issues of discipline within the movement. The nature of social media is such that it is difficult and enormously time-consuming for movement leaders to monitor and control this space. The sheer volume of traffic on these online forums meant that in spite of some leaders' efforts to minimise the amount of material posted on Facebook that expressed opinions that clearly contradicted EDL organisers' attempts to position the EDL as a non-racist and non-far-right group, they were not able to eradicate such material altogether. The fact that many of these posts were made either on public sites, or sites where it was very easy to gain access, meant such posts were readily available to the EDL's opponents who often used them to reinforce their claims about the character of the EDL (Davidson 2014).

The other problem related to the deterioration of relations within the activist community. Activists' prolific use of Facebook meant personal squabbles tended to occur in a very public place, and the open format of Facebook conversations (when not using the messenger service) meant other activists were also liable to pitch in. This contributed to the process described above whereby personal squabbles were transformed into factional or inter-clique arguments. Furthermore, the fact that these arguments were visible to other people not directly involved in the argument (to anybody who was a Facebook friend of one of the protagonists), meant that these arguments were broadcast across the movement, sapping activists' feelings of solidarity as they went. Many personal Facebook pages took on a rather Gollum-like quality, with activists getting stuck into their various enemies and rivals with all sorts of snipes and barbs one minute and the next appealing to their fellow activists for unity.

Social media, and Facebook in particular, were central to EDL activism but were also seen by most activists as one of the main vectors of the factionalism that was pulling the movement apart. There was some discussion at a meeting of local organisers in London and the Southeast in February 2012 about establishing a Facebook code of conduct to try to address the issue. The suggestions that gained most approval included banning people from using EDL Facebook pages after midnight and discouraging the use of Facebook when drunk, but as far as I am aware, nothing ever came of these proposals.

Notes

1 Here I use 'militant Islam' rather than '(militant) Islam' because Mark very rarely made generalisations about Islam or Muslims.
2 As Blee (2012, 70) notes, 'activist groups generally operate with an upbeat sense of themselves and their future even under difficult circumstances'.
3 The BFP was registered on 18th October 2010 and was deregistered by the Electoral Commission in December 2012 after it failed to return the required annual registration form.
4 Events at which the invited speakers included people known for their vehement anti-Western and usually anti-democratic, misogynistic and anti-Semitic rhetoric.
5 A reference and challenge to Prime Minister David Cameron's comments about the 'failure' of what he described as 'state multiculturalism' in his speech to a security conference in Munich, 5th February 2011.
6 Claims about 'anti-white racism' have long been part of the discourse of far right and more general backlash, with the concept often being used to invert accusations of racism levelled at them by their opponents (Goodman and Johnson 2013, 56–78, Hewitt 2005, Seidel 1987, van Dijk 1992).
7 Support that Wilders was apparently far from happy about; see 'Britons arrested at Amsterdam EDL protest', *The Independent*, 31st October 2010. www.independent.co.uk/news/world/europe/britons-arrested-at-amsterdam-edl-protest-2121551.html
8 The event was initially being organised by the Swedish Defence League. See 'EDL and Swedish Fascists', by Acker Bilk and Pete Norman, *EDL News,* 25th May 2011. http://edlnews.co.uk/2011/05/25/edl-and-swedish-fascists/
9 The term he used in his speech.
10 I have borrowed this phrase from Fangen's (1998, 208) description of the extreme right scene in Norway.
11 Tommy Robinson, while not adopting such strong language, also spoke out about what he claimed was the growing influence of right-wing extremists on the movement when he stepped down as leader in 2013. On 8th March 2015 via Twitter Robinson offered what appeared to be, if not a retraction, at least a softening of his earlier comments: 'I have to admit when I was wrong. I predicted when I left that EDL would be taken over by Nazi and racist elements. That has not happened'.
12 As Bartlett and Littler (2011, 18–19) point out, as of mid-2011 only around half of the EDL's online supporters had been on a demonstration and as few as 24% reported having travelled more than 100 km to attend a national demonstration. However, Bartlett's (2011) claim that the 'heart of the EDL army is online, not on the streets' misunderstands and underestimates the importance of demonstrations to EDL activism and to the experiences of EDL activists. I would argue that demonstrations were very much, to use Bartlett's metaphor, the beating heart that kept EDL activism alive.
13 For a similar observation see Virchow (2007, 155)
14 Using a similar metaphor, Casquete (2006) talks about the 'catalysing' of feelings of solidarity.
15 Berezin's (2001, 93) 'communities of feeling' conveys a similar idea.
16 A phrase much used in the activists' descriptions of what they valued about the EDL community.

17 A term popularly used to refer to the police tactic of containing or corralling protestors within a police cordon. For a critique of its application to EDL, and indeed other, demonstrations, see Pilkington (2012).

18 As Berezin (2001, 93) notes, public rituals not only help to produce 'communities of feeling' at the time but also generate the basis for a collective memory.

19 The demonstration was billed as a march 'into the lions' den', presumably on account of the Tower Hamlets local authority having one of the highest proportions of Muslim residents in the country.

20 As the name suggests, this is a demonstration held in one fixed place.

21 And as Jasper (2014, 209) notes, 'The good or bad moods created in interactions accompany us to our next interactions, affecting them in turn'.

22 At an event in Barking on 13th January 2012, the police, by accident or by design, managed to situate the EDL and their opponents at precisely the distance at which the activists were able to gain a good sense of the decibel levels of their opponents without being able to hear what they were shouting. The two sets of activists spent well over half an hour engaged in trying to out-noise one another, with only a brief hiatus for the usual minute's silence and a speech or two.

23 Given the quantities of alcohol consumed during demonstrations, locating and defining suitable toilet facilities became an important sub-plot of these events – a source at times of humour, but also of anxiety, rising desperation, irritation and sometimes anger.

24 He was convicted of common assault on 29th September 2011 ('EDL leader Stephen Lennon convicted of assault', BBC, 29th September 2011, www.bbc.com/news/uk-england-lancashire-15117961). On 3rd November, he was sentenced to a 12-week jail term suspended for 12 months. A request by the prosecution for an anti-social behaviour order was turned down ('EDL leader sentenced for headbutting fellow protester', *The Guardian*, 3rd November 2011, www.theguardian.com/uk/2011/nov/03/edl-leader-sentenced-headbutt)

25 I did not witness this personally; I heard about it on the bus back to Essex.

26 Birmingham is in the West Midlands but seems to qualify as 'in the north' to many people who have grown up in and around London.

27 One of the characteristics of the violence that occurred after demonstrations was that it often did not explicitly involve people who had attended counterdemonstrations.

28 These issues were usually discussed in terms of 'discipline' or the lack thereof.

29 Violence may be tolerated in the context of social movement activism even by those who profess to oppose it if it can be construed as an expression of anger, frustration and pain. As Yang (2000) describes, part of the nature of social movement activism, and especially of protests, is that people 'let their feelings overflow', often breaking with social conventions.

30 This vicious cycle of decline, mutual recrimination, negative emotional energy and further decline is also described by Jasper (2014, 209) in an overview of the production of indignation in the context of social movements, and by Owens (2009) in her study of Amsterdam squatters.

31 Previously called Mosquebusters, The Law and Freedom Foundation is run by Gavin Boby, a Bristol-based lawyer, with the aim of mounting legal challenges to plans to building Islamic buildings in the United Kingdom and elsewhere.

32 It was probably closer to 500 people.

33 This specific phrase was used by Mark and Andy, but other local and regional organisers expressed a similar idea.

34 This was the case, for example, with a fairly benign flash demonstration organised by EDL activists in Brentwood, Essex on 12th March 2012 to protest about the vandalism of a plaque commemorating members of the Royal Anglian Regiment who had been killed in Afghanistan.

35 'EDL supporters sentenced for offences on day of flash demonstrations', *Engage*, 27th June 2012, www.iengage.org.uk/news/1960-edl-supporters-sentenced-for-offences-on-day-of-flash-demonstrations

36 See 'Southend councillor suspended over link with English Defence League', *Echo*, 7th October 2011, www.echo-news.co.uk/news/local_news/9293470.Southend_councillor_suspended_over_link_with_English_Defence_League/l/. He was reinstated a month later. See 'Essex EDL meeting Tory member reinstated', *BBC News*, 5th November 2011, www.bbc.com/news/uk-england-essex-15606304

37 When it was announced in the spring of 2012 that Robinson was to be appointed deputy leader of the BFP it also upset some members of the BFP. See 'British Freedom Party fallout begins', Sonia Gable, *Searchlight*, 1st May 2012, www.searchlightmagazine.com/blogs/searchlight-blog/british-freedom-party-fallout-begins

38 By 'the political side of things,' Alex was referring to parties such as the BNP and UKIP, which were seen to be taking a strong line on cognate issues around immigration and multiculturalism.

39 Zald and Ash Gardner (1987, 122) note that the shift from more democratic or non-hierarchical structures to more oligarchic structures 'is typically evaluated as morally wrong and as a prelude to member apathy'. They and others have observed however that that most groups do eventually become more oligarchical in structure partly as they seek to meet the demands of mobilising, and partly as a function of the concentration of forms of capital accruing to those located at central or critical points within the group (Gitlin 1980, Michels 1962, Nepstad and Bob 2006).

40 Several activists had attended a UK referendum protest outside the Houses of Parliament on 24th October 2011 that was supported by a number of organisations including the BNP, UKIP and the European Alliance for Freedom.

41 A stereotype not altogether without foundation: the activists that went on to form the NWI and the NEI (and who do not, it should be noted, include all of the activists in these regions) have in general had far closer ties with established far right groups, have advocated more radical protest tactics and have been more prone to the use of explicitly racist issue frames than most of the activists who have aligned themselves with the Luton leadership and later that of Steve Eddowes (Harris, Busher and Macklin 2015, Pilkington 2014). Pilkington (2014) also notes that among the EDL activists she spoke with it was those with affiliations to the NWI that expressed more overtly racist attitudes. Having said that, it should be observed that several known EDL activists in the southeast of England have also participated in demonstrations in support of established far right groups such as the Neo-Nazi Greek party Golden Dawn (see Roberts 2015) and have openly marched alongside groups such as the National Front (NF) for example in Rotherham on 16th May 2015 (see 'Far-right protesters march through streets of Rotherham', Sam Jackson, The Star, 16th May 2015, www.thestar.co.uk/news/local/video-far-right-protesters-march-through-streets-of-rotherham-1-7263197).

42 For example, a lengthy conversation with Brian and Gary, two of the London organisers, at the end of a demonstration in Dagenham on March 12th 2011.

43 As Hopkins and colleagues (2015) describe, feelings of collective effervescence are best achieved when participants perceive themselves as sharing a common collective identity which they feel able to enact.

44 Comments made during a regional meeting held in London on 26th February 2012

45 A finding very much in keeping with the observations of Linden and Klandermans (Linden and Klandermans 2006).

46 This is a variation on Kitschelt's (2004, 20) observation that groups that mobilise around 'single, isolated issues' tend to be 'doomed to failure, since they cannot mobilize the population beyond this one issue and offer a holistic political alternative'. In this case, it is not so much about being able to mobilize the public as being able to mobilize their own activists, indeed, themselves.

47 See 'Girl gang who kicked woman in the head while yelling 'Kill the white slag' freed after judge hears 'They weren't used to drinking because they're Muslims'', Andy Dolan and Katherine Faulkner, *The Daily Mail*, 6th December 2011, www.

dailymail.co.uk/news/article-2070562/Muslim-girl-gang-kicked-Rhea-Page-head-yelling-kill-white-slag-FREED.html

48 Notes from a conversation with a group of London-based activists prior to a demonstration in Barking on 14th January 2012.

49 Public surveys repeatedly indicate that it is their association with violence, rather than the ideas that they espouse, that most damages their capacity to attract support (Busher et al. 2014, Thomas et al. 2014, YouGov/Extremis 2012)

50 As Blee (2007, 124) notes, there is a tension in '[m]any extremist groups' as they 'try to balance the extremist agendas necessary to retain their hard-core supporters and project an image of power with more temperate tactics that can appeal to a wider base of recruits and voters'. Citing work by Decker and Lauritson (1996) on gang membership, Bjørgo and Horgan (2009, 7) also draw attention to the sometimes ambivalent effects that violence can have on loyalty to the group: 'on the one hand, violence is a defining feature of gang life, forging the group together. On the other hand, members often want to leave the gang because of the high level of violence, especially when they themselves or close friends become victims'.

51 While disruptive protest may have a number of possible political, reputational, emotional and physical costs, under some circumstances it can be an effective means of acquiring new advantages (Gamson 1990, Piven and Cloward 1977).

52 A reference to Enoch Powell's now notorious 'Rivers of Blood' speech on April 20th 1968 to the General Meeting of the West Midlands Area Conservative Political Centre.

53 The use of anger to convert shame into pride is discussed by Britt and Heise (2000) and by Gould (2009).

54 See 'Right-winger charged with assault at Muslim poppy-burning protest', Justin Davenport, London Evening Standard, 12th November 2010, www.standard.co.uk/news/rightwinger-charged-with-assault-at-muslim-poppyburning-protest-6535648.html. As a police respondent in research by Harris et al. (Harris, Busher and Macklin 2015) observes, there were probably also a considerable number of people outside the movement who thought, 'Good for him for standing up for that'.

55 Of course, the more influential or respected they were within the activist community already, the easier it would be for them to impose their own interpretation on subsequent conversations about the events. How specific acts of violence become sources of honour or shame within activist communities like the EDL warrants further systematic analysis and might provide a useful extension to work on the micro-sociology of violence being undertaken by people such as Randall Collins (2008).

56 One of the participants at these events told me that in this instance 'EDL' stood for *Eltham* Defence League, but semiotically it was clearly a play on the English Defence League symbol. As described in Chapter 4, these stories were also fuelled by a television interview given by one activist calling himself 'Jack England', who claimed that there were about 50 EDL activists there coordinating proceedings.

57 A recurring theme in conversations with local authority and police officers in towns that have endured EDL demonstrations is the fact that the EDL label has been used at times by a small number of young people, particularly teenage boys and young men, as a way of threatening, provoking and asserting themselves against young Asian men (Busher et al. 2014, Harris et al. 2015, Thomas et al. 2014).

58 See Collins (2001) discussion of social movement activism as a competition for 'social attention space'.

59 In the absence of a defined membership activists often used Facebook membership as a measure of support, which enabled them to make the group appear far larger than it ever was. Ironically, some of the media coverage of the group did likewise.

60 As Barker and colleagues (Barker, Johnson and Lavalette 2001, 17–23) note, less authoritarian structures are conducive to a heightened sense of own commitment among participants and to the adoption of creative strategies to resolve problems.

61 The primary solidarity within activist groups is often local (della Porta and Diani 2006, 141–2, Gould 1995). As Gamson (1990, 175) notes, by building around small groups a social movement organisation 'uses naturally occurring social relationships and meets a variety of organisational and individual needs for emotional support, integration, sharing of sacrifice, and expression of shared identities'.

62 Feelings of duty may be closely linked to feelings of shame. Goodwin and Pfaff (2001) for example describe how people in the East German civil rights movement used notions of duty to invoke feelings of shame that in effect increased the emotional cost to individuals of not participating in protest events. When EDL activists spoke of having each another's backs, they were building feelings of duty to one another but also creating a store of potential shame should they fail to do so. I return to this point in Chapter 6.

63 Pride, as Jasper (2014, 211) notes, 'often depends on externalizing instead of internalizing anger and blame for a group's plight'.

64 On 1st August 2011 the national EDL leadership issued a statement urging 'all EDL supporters to distance themselves from the CXF group and its members and to remove yourselves from any groups that you inadvertently may be in that are CXF or run by Mike Rafferty [a prominent member of the group]', a statement prompted by an incident in Plymouth when a 'meet and greet' involving members of the EDL and the CXF group ended with some members of the group being involved in an attack at a kebab shop. This led to a series of heated exchanges between the national leadership and the CXF leadership, but CXF activists and CXF insignia continued to be visible at EDL events.

65 Primarily Islamic buildings, as might be expected. There has however been at least one attack on a Hindu temple (see 'Dudley EDL rally "wanted men" CCTV released by police' BBC, 23rd September 2010, www.bbc.com/news/uk-england-black-country-11401975) and a group of young people identifying with the EDL attacked a summer camp for Sikh children in Chigwell in August 2011 (see 'Sikh Summer Camp of 125 kids in Chigwell attacked by racist idiots', Lancaster Unity, 7th August 2011, http://lancasteruaf.blogspot.com.es/2011/08/sikh-summer-camp-of-125-kids-in.html). EDL organisers in the area told me that those involved were not part of the EDL but were just using the group's name.

66 This is also true of organisations in general (DiMaggio and Powell 1983, Meyer and Rowan 1977).

67 As Jasper (2004, 13) notes, movements face a 'band of brothers dilemma': if they emphasise affinity with sub-groups or cells they can generate tight-knit highly motivated units, but this may not transfer to the whole group.

68 A similar dynamic is described by Goodwin and Pfaff (2001, 288) in relation to the East German civil rights movement: 'While intimate ties and a strong sense of collective purpose and community helped to unite and encourage activists in the face of disappointment and adversity, this informal structure had the disadvantage of making personal conflicts simultaneously conflicts within and between groups'.

69 As Diani (2003, 106) notes, even where activists may by and large reject formal leadership roles, this 'does not automatically eradicate the problems leaders used to tackle, or the need for the functions they used to perform'. See also Melucci (1996, 344–347).

70 Although as far as I was able to ascertain, the anti-leadership culture within the EDL was not intellectualised to the extent that it has been in left-wing and anarchist movements, where such structures have formed part of activists' 'blueprints for social change' and have been used to articulate their visions of how society as a whole might be reorganised (Maeckelberg 2009, Sutherland, Land and Böhm 2013, 11)

71 Van der Wal (2011, 143) notes from a policing perspective that 'Another complication [with policing EDL demonstrations] is that the people police speak with don't necessarily speak for the entire organisation of the EDL or the UAF. Maybe the people

that seriously want to promote the EDL ideology want to comply but they don't have control over the bigger group, who want to cause violence.'

72 These studies and commentaries comprise part of a much wider and rapidly growing body of literature on how social media are creating new possibilities for and modalities of social movement activism (see Benkler 2006, Castells 2012, Joyce 2010).

References

Allen, C. 2014. "Anti-Social Networking: Pilot Study on Opposing Dudley Mosque Using Facebook Groups as Both Site and Method for Research." *Sage Open* 4 (1):1–12.

Bailey, G. 2009. "Citizenship For All: Including the BNP in the Neighbourhood Polity." 59th Political Studies Association Annual Conference: Challenges for Democracy in a Global Era, University of Manchester, 7th–9th April.

Barker, C., A. Johnson and M. Lavalette. 2001. "Leadership Matters: An Introduction." In *Leadership and Social Movements*, edited by C. Barker, A. Johnson and M. Lavalette, 1–23. Manchester: Manchester University Press.

Bartlett, J. 2011. "The Heart of the EDL Army is Online, Not on the Streets." *The Guardian*, 30th October. www.theguardian.com/commentisfree/2011/oct/30/edl-heart-facebook.

Bartlett, J., and M. Littler. 2011. *Inside the EDL: Populist Politics in a Digital Age*. London: Demos.

Benkler, Y. 2006. *The Wealth of Networks: How Social Production Transforms Markets and Freedom*. New Haven: Yale University Press.

Berezin, M. 2001. "Emotions and Political Identity: Mobilizing Affection for the Polity." In *Passionate Politics: Emotions and Social Movements*, edited by J. Goodwin, J.M. Jasper and F. Polletta, 83–98. Chicago: University of Chicago Press.

Bjørgo, T., and J. Horgan. 2009. "Introduction." In *Leaving Terrorism Behind: Individual and Collective Disengagement*, edited by T. Bjørgo and J. Horgan, 1–13. London: Routledge.

Blake, B. 2011. *EDL: Coming Down the Road*. Birmingham: VHC.

Blee, K.M. 2007. "Ethnographies of the Far Right." *Journal of Contemporary Ethnography* 36 (2):119–128.

Blee, K.M. 2012. *Democracy in the Making: How Activist Groups Form*. Oxford: Oxford University Press.

Britt, L., and D.R. Heise. 2000. "From Shame to Pride in Identity Politics." In *Self, Identity, and Social Movements*, edited by S. Stryker, T.J. Owens and R.W. White, 252–268. Minneapolis, MN: University of Minneapolis Press.

Busher, J. 2012. "'There are none sicker than the EDL': Narratives of Racialisation and Resentment from Whitehall and Eltham, London." In *The English Riots of 2011*, edited by D. Briggs, 237–256. Hook: Waterside.

Busher, J., K. Christmann, G. Macklin, M. Rogerson and P. Thomas. 2014. *Understanding Concerns About Community Relations in Calderdale*. Huddersfield: The University of Huddersfield.

Casquete, J. 2006. "Protest Rituals and Uncivil Communities." *Totalitarian Movements and Political Religions* 7 (3):283–301.

Castells, M. 2012. *Networks of Outrage and Hope: Social Movements in the Internet Age*. Cambridge: Polity Press.

Collins, R. 2001. "Social Movements and the Focus of Emotional Attention." In *Passionate Politics: Emotions and Social Movements*, edited by J. Goodwin, J.M. Jasper and F. Polletta, 27–44. Chicago: Chicago University Press.

Collins, R. 2008. *Violence: A Micro-Sociological Theory*. Princeton: Princeton University Press.

Copsey, N. 2010. *The English Defence League: Challenging Our Country and Our Values of Social Inclusion, Fairness and Equality*. London: Faith Matters.

Davidson, T. R. 2014. "The Paradox of (Anti)Social Media: A Qualitative Content Analysis of Conflictual Framing in a Far-Right Social Movement." Social Media and Social Movements, Higher School of Economics, St. Petersburg, Russia, 18th–19th September.

Decker, S. H., and J. L. Lauritsen. 1996. "Breaking the Bonds of Membership: Leaving the Gang." In *Gangs in America*, edited by C. R. Huff, 103–122. Thousand Oaks: Sage.

della Porta, D., and M. Diani. 2006. *Social Movements: An Introduction*. Oxford: Blackwell.

Diani, M. 2003. "'Leaders' of Brokers? Positions and Influence in Social Movement Networks." In *Social Movements and Network: Relational Approaches to Collective Action*, edited by M. Diani and D. McAdam, 105–122. Oxford: Oxford University Press.

DiMaggio, P. J., and W. W. Powell. 1983. "The Iron Cage Revisited: Institutional Isomorphism and Collective Rationality in Organizational Fields." *American Sociological Review* 48 (2):147–160.

Durkheim, E. 1915. *The Elementary Forms of the Religious Life*. Translated by J. Ward Swain. London: Allen and Unwin.

Fangen, K. 1998. "Living Out Our Ethnic Instincts: Ideological Beliefs Among Right-Wing Activists in Norway." In *Nation and Race: Developing Euro-American Racist Subculture*, edited by J. Kaplan and T. Bjørgo, 202–230. Boston: Northeastern University Press.

Gamson, W. A. 1990. *The Strategy of Social Protest*. Second ed. Belmont: Wadsworth.

Gitlin, T. 1980. *The Whole World is Watching: Mass Media in the Making & Unmaking of the New Left*. Berkley: University of California Press.

Goodman, S., and A. J. Johnson. 2013. "Strategies Used by the Far Right to Counter Accusations of Racism." *Critical Approaches to Discourse Analysis Across Disciplines* 6 (2):97–113.

Goodwin, J., and S. Pfaff. 2001. "Emotion Work in High-Risk Social Movements: Managing Fear in the U.S. and East German Civil Rights Movements." In *Passionate Politics: Emotions and Social Movements*, edited by J. Goodwin, J. M. Jasper and F. Polletta, 282–302. Chicago: University of Chicago Press.

Gould, D. B. 2009. *Moving Politics: Emotion and ACT UP's Fight Against AIDS*. London: University of Chicago Press.

Gould, R. V. 1995. *Insurgent Identities: Class, Community, and Protest in Paris from 1848 to the Commune*. Chicago: University of Chicago Press.

Harris, G., J. Busher and G. Macklin. 2015. *The Evolution of Anti-Muslim Protest in Two English Towns*. Coventry: Coventry University/The University of Huddersfield.

Hart, C. M., and M. van Vugt. 2006. "From Fault Line to Group Fission: Understanding Membership Changes in Small Groups." *Personality and Social Psychology Bulletin* 32 (3):392–404.

Hewitt, R. 2005. *White Backlash and the Politics of Multiculturalism*. Cambridge: Cambridge University Press.

Hopkins, N., S. D. Reicher, S. S. Khan, S. Tewari, N. Srinivasan and C. Stevenson. 2015. "Explaining Effervescence: Investigating the Relationship Between Shared Social Identity and Positive Experience in Crowds." *Cognition and Emotion* Early Release.

Jackson, P. 2011. *The EDL: Britain's New 'Far-Right' Social Movement.* Northampton: Radicalism and New Media Group Publications.

Jasper, J. M. 2004. "A Strategic Approach to Collective Action." *Mobilization* 9:1–16.

Jasper, J. M. 2007. *The Art of Moral Protest: Culture, Biography, and Creativity in Social Movements.* Paperback Edition. London: University of Chicago Press.

Jasper, J. M. 2014. "Constructing Indignation: Anger Dynamics in Protest Movements." *Emotion Review* 6 (3):208–213.

Joyce, M., ed. 2010. *Digital Activism Decoded: The New Mechanics of Change.* New York: International Debate Education Association.

Kim, G. J., J. Rademakers, M. Sanchez and W. van Vucht. 2013. *Online Activity of the English Defence League.* Amsterdam: Digitial Methods Intitiative.

Kim, M. 2010. "Interview: Paul Weston." *politics.co.uk,* 5/5/2010.

Kitschelt, H. 2004. "Diversification and Reconfiguration of Party Systems in Postindustrial Democracies." *Friedrich Ebert Stiftung* (March):1–23.

Linden, A., and B. Klandermans. 2006. "The Netherlands. Stigmatized Outsiders." In *Extreme Right Activists in Europe: Through the Magnifying Glass,* edited by B. Klandermans and N. Mayer, 172–203. London: Routledge.

Lowles, N. 2012. "Where Now for the British Far Right?" *Extremis Blog,* 21/9/2012. http://extremisproject.org/2012/09/where-now-for-the-british-far-right/

Maeckelberg, M. 2009. *The Will of the Many: How the Alterglobalisation Movement is Changing the Face of Democracy.* London: Pluto Press.

Melucci, A. 1996. *Challenging Codes: Collective Action in the Information Age.* Cambridge: Cambridge University Press.

Meyer, J. W., and B. Rowan. 1977. "Institutionalized Organizations: Formal Structure as Myth and Ceremony." *American Journal of Sociology* 83 (2):340–363.

Michels, R. 1962. *Political Parties: A Sociological Study of the Oligarchical Tendencies of Modern Democracy.* Translated by E. and C. Paul. New York: Free Press.

Nepstad, S. E., and C. Bob. 2006. "When do Leaders Matter? Hypotheses on Leadership Dynamics in Social Movements." *Mobilization* 11 (1):1–22.

Owens, L. 2009. *Cracking Under Pressure.* Amsterdam: Amsterdam University Press.

Pearce, J. L. 1980. "Apathy or Self-Interest? The Volunteer's Avoidance of Leadership Roles." *Journal of Voluntary Action Research* 9 (1):85–94.

Pickvance, K. 1998. "Democracy and Grassroots Opposition in Eastern Europe: Hungary and Russia Compared." *The Sociological Review* 46 (2):187–207.

Pilkington, H. 2012. "When is a Kettle not a Kettle? When it is on Slow Boil." *MYPLACE,* 12th September. https://myplacefp7.wordpress.com/2012/09/04/when-is-a-kettle-not-a-kettle-when-it-is-on-slow-boil/.

Pilkington, H. 2014. 'Loud and Proud': Youth Activism in the English Defence League. Report on Work Package 7 of MYPLACE Project. www.fp7-myplace.eu.

Piven, F. F., and R. A. Cloward. 1977. *Poor People's Movements: Why They Succeed, How They Fail.* New York: Vintage Books.

Reger, J. 2002. "More than One Feminism: Organizational Structure and the Construction of Collective Identity." In *Social Movements: Identity, Culture, and the State,* edited by D. S. Meyer, N. Whittier and B. Robnett, 171–184. Oxford: Oxford University Press.

Richards, B. 2013. "Extreme Nationalism and the Hatred of the Liberal State." In *Emotions in Politics: The Affect Dimension in Political Tension,* edited by N. Demertzis, 124–142. Basingstoke: Palgrave Macmillan.

Roberts, J. 2015. Angry, White and Proud. Channel 4.

Seidel, G. 1987. "The White Discursive Order: The British New Right's Discourse on Cultural Racism with Particular Reference to the Salisbury Review." In *Approaches to Discourse, Poetics and Psychiatry*, edited by I. M. Zavala, T. A. van Dijk and M. Díaz-Diocaretz, 39–66. Amsterdam: John Benjamins.

Summers Effler, E. 2010. *Laughing Saints and Righteous Heroes: Emotional Rhythms in Social Movement Groups*. London: University of Chicago Press.

Sutherland, N., C. Land and S. Böhm. 2013. "Anti-leaders(hip) in Social Movement Organizations: The Case of Autonomous Grassroots Groups." *Organization* Online First Version: 1–23. http://org.sagepub.com/content/early/2013/06/03/1350508413480254

Thomas, P., M. Rogerson, G. Macklin, K. Christmann and J. Busher. 2014. *Understanding Concerns About Community Relations in Kirklees*. Huddersfield: University of Huddersfield.

Treadwell, J. 2014. "Controlling the New Far Right on the Street: Policing the English Defence League in Policy and Praxis." In *Responding to Hate Crime: The Case for Connecting Policy and Research*, edited by N. Chakraborti and J Garland, 127–140. Bristol: Policy Press.

Turner, J., M. A. Hogg, P. J. Oakes, S. D. Reicher and M. S. Wetherell. 1987. *Rediscovering the Social Group: A Social Categorization Theory*. Oxford: Blackwell.

van der Wal, R. 2011. "United Kingdom: Policing EDL Manifestations and Demonstrations Across England." In *Managing Collective Violence Around Public Events: An International Comparison*, edited by O. M. G. Adang, 119–152. Apeldoorn: Police Science and Research Programme.

van Dijk, T. A. 1992. "Discourse and the Denial of Racism." *Discourse & Society* 3 (1):87–118.

Virchow, F. 2007. "Performance, Emotion, and Ideology: On the Creation of 'Collectives of Emotion' and Worldview in the Contemporary German Far Right." *Journal of Contemporary Ethnography* 36 (2):147–164.

Yang, G. 2000. "Achieving Emotions in Collective Action: Emotional Processes and Movement Mobilization in the 1989 Chinese Student Movement." *The Sociological Quarterly* 41 (4):593–614.

YouGov/Extremis. 2012. Under the Microscope: Public Attitudes Toward the English Defence League (EDL). London: YouGov.

Zald, M. N., and R. Ash Gardner. 1987. "Social movement organisations: Growth, decay, and change." In *Social Movements in an Organizational Society*, edited by M. N. Zald and J. D. McCarthy, 121–160. New Brunswick: Transaction.

6   The persistence of organised anti-Muslim activism

This [Facebook] status is gonna probably piss a few people off but to be honest I don't care if you think it's about you then it probably is. I have been EDL since about day one. I have made lots of friends and try not to tread on toes but this needs to be said as it shows how much things have changed over the years. It used to be about patriots from all over the country getting together as one voice so we could be heard, we went in done what had to be done and got out, yet now all I read from different divisions is 'we got the biggest flag', 'our division had most at the demo', 'we were the loudest', and if that wasn't bad enough you then get the boozed up few that think that every camera is there for them and so jump in front of it beer in one hand with either masked up face or angry face and one finger in the air (of course they want your pictures coz your showing all against us exactly what they want to see)

Come on everyone it's NOT all about you and your divisions it's about getting patriots from ALL OVER the country and having one voice,

Also one last thing where were the stewards yesterday when a loud group in the middle of our demo was shouting 'we hate pakis'? A steward's job is not just standing at the front of demo and holding the frontline it is about controlling the whole demo.

That's it rant over, sorry if I've touched a nerve but if the cap fits,

Now all enjoy the rest of your Sunday

Love you all

> (Facebook post by Laura, February 2015,
> after a demonstration in Dudley)

As Laura's post suggests, the issues that contributed to the unravelling of the English Defence League (EDL) – the tensions between different ways of framing the EDL cause, divergent ideas about what their protest performances should look like and the sub-group rivalries – did not go away. Neither, however, did the EDL or organised anti-Muslim activism. The anti-Muslim/minority[1] protest movement fragmented and lost momentum but did not collapse.

As described in Chapter 1, though it was by and large no longer able to attract the same level of support, the EDL continued to hold frequent demonstrations and could still muster enough people to close down a town centre, or at least a couple of streets, for an hour or two, and the group experienced sharp if fairly short-lived spikes in support after the killing of Drummer Lee Rigby on 22nd May 2013[2] and on the back of various scandals about systematic child sexual exploitation involving networks of Muslim men in towns such as Rochdale, Rotherham and Oxford.

Alongside this, there has been a veritable alphabet soup of other self-identifying patriotic protest groups, whose 'membership' has usually overlapped to some degree with that of the EDL, carrying out demonstrations and online campaigns: the Northwest Infidels (NWI), the Northeast Infidels (NEI), the Southeast Alliance (SEA), March for England (MFE),[3] Combined Ex-Forces (CXF), English Nationalist Alliance (ENA), the British Patriot Society (BPS), the English Volunteer Force (EVF), the New Patriot Alliance (NPA), the British Patriotic Alliance (BPA), the United British Patriots (UBP), the North West Frontline Firm (NWFF), Infidels of Britain (IOB) and no doubt several others.[4] More recently Britain First, a group established by former BNP activists,[5] has gained considerable public profile through a number of direct action campaigns including their 'Christian Patrols'[6] and their harassment of anti-UKIP activists in the run up to the 2015 general election.[7] In 2015, there were also attempts by PEGIDA UK,[8] a spin-off of the mass demonstrations organised by the eponymous group in Dresden in late 2014, to organise demonstrations in the United Kingdom, although their first attempt, in Newcastle, drew only about 400 supporters[9] and their subsequent demonstration in London less than half that number.[10]

In this penultimate chapter, I outline a number of factors that have contributed to the persistence of this wave of organised anti-Muslim activism even after it began to lose momentum during the course of 2011. To some extent, as already intimated above, the answer can be seen to lie in a number of external events such as the killing of Lee Rigby and the breaking child sexual exploitation scandals. These events have provided mobilisation opportunities for the EDL and cognate groups, enabling existing activists to recharge and refocus their feelings of outrage and righteous anger[11] and providing opportunities to reach out to and to attract new recruits to their offline activities and online spaces. Importantly, such events have also provided windows of opportunity for people across the anti-Muslim protest movement to re-find common purpose, appeal for unity, and patch up intra-movement relationships frayed by the niggles and gripes that had been accumulating and festering for the last couple of years.

Other political developments have also arguably provided a favourable backdrop for the movement. The rise to prominence of the Islamic State of Iraq and Syria (ISIS) and the growing number of young British Muslims who have gone to support ISIS lend themselves easily to the EDL narrative about the dangers posed by (militant) Islam and have served to keep the 'Islam-as-a-threat-to-European-security-and-values'[12] frame front and centre in media and public discourse and in the minds of those who might be attracted to groups like the EDL. The increasingly shrill debates about immigration have also been picked up and much discussed by EDL activists and supporters, particularly where discourse about immigration has intersected with discourse about the danger posed to the United Kingdom by foreign fighters returning from Syria and Iraq.

As well as these external events, however, there have also been a number of characteristics of EDL activism itself, and of activism in the wider anti-Muslim/minority protest movement, that have helped to sustain this wave of protests. It is these that I focus on here.

The lack of dependence on central EDL structures

The scale of support that the EDL was able to draw on as a genuinely *national* movement, the media profile that it generated and the feelings of possibility that it exuded were integral to the EDL's processes of recruitment and mobilisation. As discussed in Chapter 2, for many of the activists, part of the attraction of the EDL was that it felt like an organisation that was 'going somewhere'. It is also clear that Robinson in particular provided an effective figurehead for the movement. He became a widely recognised public figure, able to attract the attention of the media[13] and, seemingly, increasingly comfortable under the glare of publicity – as noted in Chapter 4, activists in London and Essex had been particularly impressed by his *Newsnight* interview with Jeremy Paxman after Anders Breivik's killings in Norway.

Activism at the grassroots of the EDL however largely operated independently of these national structures and their leaders. National leaders such as Robinson and Carroll played only a fairly minor role in the processes of belief formation among grassroots activists (see Chapter 3), and local EDL divisions had always acted with considerable autonomy; identifying which local issues to mobilise around, organising their own promotional materials and for the most part conducting their own liaison with public authorities over planned protest activities and so forth (see Chapter 1).

This highly devolved mode or organising did generate certain organisational challenges: making it difficult to maintain discipline and stem a rising tide of factionalism (Chapter 5). However, the lack of dependence on central leaders that this generated also helped grassroots anti-Muslim activism to persist even as the national movement fragmented and lost momentum. First, the fact that local EDL divisions had been largely self-organising meant activists at all levels of the movement developed skills and experiences that enabled them to organise, and to feel confident about organising, protest activities with or without the support of national organisational structures.[14] As I walked around Barking with activists on a pre-demonstration 'recce' in December 2011, they reflected on how much they had learned in the last year about how to go about making arrangements for a demonstration – they knew who to speak to in the police and at the council, the time frames for planning demonstrations and the legal context. It all seemed 'quite easy' now, but twelve months earlier they 'didn't really have a clue about most of this' (Sarah).

Second, the activists were already well used to operating largely through their own local and often informal networks. In fact, by mid-2012, a growing number of activists described themselves as having no attachment to any local division. While Jim, for example, would travel to demonstrations with other activists from his area, he hardly ever attended divisional meetings or visited the divisional Facebook pages, preferring instead to associate via personal networks that he had formed through years of activism, first with the NF and later with the BNP and various loyalist groups. Similarly, after bouncing from EDL division to EDL division, including setting up his own (see Chapter 5), Phil reached a point at which his personal networks meant that he saw little need to be part of the official structures:

> I'm not really linked to a division now – I'm still there, 100% supporting the cause, but I don't really need to be part of a division and nothing like that; I know my rules, and I know my regulations and I know what not to do and what to do, sort of thing. I can talk to everyone pretty much, so there's no need for me really to be in a division.
>
> (Phil)

While organisational badges provided valuable symbols for people to mobilise around, the social networks through which mobilisation took place were at least as much a constellation of personal networks as they were any kind of official organisational channels. As Killian (1984) describes in his account of mobilisation in the civil rights movement, even when there is no formal coordination across groups, coordination is still sometimes possible through informal networks.

The anti-Muslim protest scene had not become as fragmented as it looked from the outside

On 12th March 2011, at the second in the series of four demonstrations held in Dagenham, Bill Baker, the founder of the ENA, was very clearly a persona non grata. As the EDL activists gathered at their rendezvous point, I heard multiple comments about how 'he'd better not show his face', and throughout the morning, there were rumours about whether he would or would not appear at some point during the proceedings. Accused of generally disrupting the movement, he had recently been told by the national leaders that he was not welcome at any EDL event. Not only had he appeared on a television debate as a representative of the EDL without prior authorisation, he had also proceeded to make what the EDL leaders considered racist comments that were liable to further damage the group's reputation.[15] To make matters worse there was a widely held view among the activists that he was trying to take over the Dagenham protests – he had called his own protest about the same issue at the same location for the following Saturday.[16]

A few months later, on 30th July in Walthamstow, east London, however, as Baker staged a counterdemonstration against an MAC march that was calling for Sharia-controlled zones in London, a crowd of about 30 EDL activists stood side-by-side with him. The local EDL divisions had decided against organising their own counterdemonstration: there was a view among some organisers that they would simply bring more attention to MAC by turning out to oppose them, and in the wake of the Anders Breivik killings and with a planned march of their own in Tower Hamlets only five weeks away they were keen to avoid providing the police or local authorities with an excuse to ban it. Thus those who wanted to protest against the MAC march went and stood alongside Baker. John, one of the activists who chose to do so, told me that he thought 'it was quite brave of Bill' to go up there and organise the protest, given both the earlier animosity and the fact that he knew he would be heavily outnumbered by MAC on that occasion. Steve, another EDL activist who went to Walthamstow, commented 'You can say what you want about Bill, and he should not have done what he did, but he is there, you know, he is fighting the cause'.

The proliferation of 'patriot' groups made the organizational field of anti-Muslim protest increasingly complex, making it more difficult to coordinate across the whole movement[17] and creating more opportunities for inter-group/intra-movement conflicts. However, what has looked like a highly fragmented scene from the outside looks less fragmented from the inside.

First, even as organisational identities multiplied and recriminations were exchanged, activists were able to appeal to collective identities of being 'patriots' or 'proper patriots' that extended beyond their organisational identity; identities that not only encouraged recognition of common purpose in the present, but were also forged through earlier shared experience to which activists could cast back for affective bonds. As the anti-Muslim protest scene fragmented, it became almost *de rigueur* for speakers at demonstrations or those organising events under new organisational banners to appeal for unity and emphasise their desire to work with 'all patriots' or 'all patriotic groups', and the activists often circulated photographs from earlier demonstrations during more fraternal times.[18]

Second, and intersecting with these collective identities, the webs of personal networks spun out by activists during the course of demonstrations, Facebook conversations and so forth also remained largely intact. This was partly achieved by the fact that all of the groups and groupuscules in this scene had highly porous boundaries and most activists either claimed multiple affiliations or at the very least supported the events of other groups. As several studies of social movements and social movement scenes make clear, such patterns of overlapping memberships or ties across movement groups can generate social capital within these movements that extends across putative group boundaries (Diani 2003, Melucci 1996, Whittier 1995).

What also helped EDL activists to sustain these webs of personal networks was their use of social media. In Chapter 5, I drew attention to the downside of Facebook for EDL activism: the difficulties associated with trying to regulate social media content and the way arguments that played out on Facebook had the potential to do more damage more quickly to group solidarity than those that took place offline. Yet as the EDL fragmented, these online networks also helped to preserve social relations that might otherwise have withered. Even activists who no longer came into contact with one another offline did so online; sometimes intentionally but sometimes courtesy of the algorithms of Facebook. These online encounters gave activists a chance to re-find common purpose by doing things like commenting on news stories that had angered them or sharing photographs and memories from earlier demonstrations and events. Earlier in 2015 Gary, one of the former London leaders, passed away. News of his death and photographs that were circulated of him drew comments from many current and former activists, most of which comprised fond recollections of the man and invoked the earlier spirit of unity within the movement. While there has been considerable academic interest in how Facebook and other social media have facilitated the expansion of protest movements (see Chapter 5), such technologies also offer considerable potential as part of the structures that can sustain ideas and relationships during periods of decline or movement abeyance.

Zald and Ash Gardner (1987, 134) propose that inclusive organisations – those with 'looser criteria of affiliation and of doctrinal orthodoxy' – may be more 'split-resistant than the exclusivist organization'. The case of the contemporary anti-Muslim protest scene bears this out to some extent, although it might be more accurate to describe it as split-resilient than as split-resistant.

Even people who left the protest scene often retained personal ties with those who remained

In the same way that entering radical political or religious activism can be accompanied by processes of social bridge-burning (see Chapter 2), so too can exiting it. This might simply involve the truncation of friendship networks associated with that activist scene, or it might entail threats and even physical violence from former co-activists (Bjørgo 1998, 2002, 2009). As with bridge-burning on the way into activism, this process can serve to inhibit activists' impulses to leave the movement due to fear of reprisal or of losing their friendship network. However, just as I found scant evidence of intentional bridge-burning on the way in to EDL activism (Chapter 2), I also found little evidence of it on the way out. On leaving, some activists chose to sever personal ties that reached back into the movement, but at least among the core activists such cases were few and far between.[19] It was more common to continue to have a number of friends within the movement and even for former activists to reappear from time to time at a meeting, a social or memorial event, or even a demonstration by the EDL or a another similar group.[20]

There are a number of factors that contributed to this tendency for personal ties to outlive active involvement in protest activities. First, being a 'proper patriot' was a status that people could carry with them for some time after they had ceased to be actively involved in the group – something which may reflect the fact that most activists recognised how financially, socially and emotionally costly EDL activism could be and were therefore sympathetic to the idea that people sometimes needed to retire to recharge their batteries. There were several cases where, even after 'taking a step back', an activist who had been involved in the group for some time would still be spoken about in these terms.[21] Second, as discussed in Chapter 2, there was little if any attempt by movement organisers to control activists' personal relationships outside the context of EDL activities.

Third, and as with the previous point about the persistence of personal networks across the different groups and groupuscules, the persistence of these ties was also facilitated by the use of Facebook, with several activists who had 'taken a step back' continuing to be regular contributors to conversations online.

The persistence of these personal contacts has meant that former activists' cognitive and affective ties with the group and with group members have degraded more slowly than they probably otherwise would have done, making it easier to re-mobilise people, particularly in the context of the kinds of moral shock events referred to earlier in this chapter.

The persistence of belief in the core EDL narrative

The decision to leave activism,[22] like the decision to enter it, usually comprises many smaller steps and combines multiple considerations. These are likely to include both 'push' factors, such as a declining sense of faith in the group's cause, feeling uncomfortable with the group's tactics, dissatisfaction with its inner workings, or feelings of exhaustion and burnout, and 'pull' factors, such as wanting to have a 'normal' life, concern about the impact of their activism on their career prospects and those of their family, or wanting to forge a relationship with somebody outside the movement (Bjørgo 2002, 2009). As Klandermans (2004) argues, even where a specific event would appear to have precipitated the decision – an argument with a fellow activist, a sudden change in life circumstances, something that throws an individual's belief in the cause into doubt – the same event might not have had the same effect several months earlier when the same individual was finding activism more gratifying and felt a deeper sense of commitment to the group and the cause.

Conversations with EDL activists who were thinking about leaving or had recently left the group contained multiple themes. As mentioned in Chapter 5, these included without fail feelings of frustration and disillusionment about the infighting within the activist community, as well as references to growing doubts about what the group was actually achieving through its demonstration strategy. Other common themes included struggling to meet the financial costs associated with regular attendance at EDL demonstrations,[23] the behaviour of fellow activists during demonstrations[24] and, as mentioned in the previous chapter, a more general sense that demonstrations had lost their 'buzz'. There were usually also references made to changes in their life circumstances – to a decline in their 'biographical availability' (Jasper 2007, 152–180, McAdam 1986). The disintegration of the London leadership between July and September 2011 provides a particularly good illustration of this. Of the six prominent figures who took a more or less temporary step back during this period, one left the area to take up the offer of a work contract; one left the area at least partly for romantic reasons; one was apparently[25] experiencing serious health problems and was advised that he needed to avoid stress and travel; one's decision to take a step back was influenced by the fact that his son was unwell and was going to require considerable support over the coming months; one's decision to leave was influenced by his growing concern that his business might be failing, and one, Andy, stood down because the rest of the leadership team had gone, and he felt that he was having to take it all on himself:

> We picked up a lot of recruits and we picked up a lot of good people, but it's just the sustainability of this rolling recruitment thing[26] where we were out three nights a week in various parts of London . . . and it wasn't, they weren't local, it wasn't sort of Newham and Tower Hamlets, it was Hillingdon and Brent and you know, sort of places outside Bexley and out there. There was a lot of travelling involved and of course I work full time as well , so it was finish work, go out dealing with all that and then come home at midnight and then work next day, and then the next night we'd be in Enfield or Barnet . . . We had sufficient people, but as people drop out, people become unavailable, their personal circumstances change, it drops down from five of us running it, you know, to two, to one, and then when you get to the point where you're the sole admin person and there's no one else around, then the thing just basically fragments and you're in a situation where you can't do or organise anything.

References to loss of belief in the EDL cause were conspicuous by their absence.[27] Several activists, especially those who were most insistent that the EDL should only campaign about *militant* Islam, expressed concern about what they saw as a growing far right influence within the movement, as Tommy Robinson did in October 2013. But such concern was always framed in terms of the EDL losing its way rather than doubts about the EDL's underlying organising idea about the threat of (militant) Islam and the failure of the liberal elite to do something about it.[28] Even as some individuals drifted further away from activism, most of those with whom I remained in some form of contact continued to express anxiety and anger about (militant) Islam, the 'two-tier system', 'lefties', 'cultural Marxism' and so forth.

The persistence of these beliefs in the basic protest narrative made it easier to remobilise those activists who had been drifting away from the protest scene when there was a specific event around which to mobilise. Furthermore, the fact that people who had largely exited the activist scene continued to be broadly supportive of the cause and, as I discussed above, often shared these views online, helped to encourage those who remained not to give up their struggle.

'No surrender': EDL activists' emotional resilience to diminishing feelings of possibility

Driving home from the meeting in West Bromwich at which Tommy Robinson had made his ill-fated announcement about the planned alliance with the British Freedom Party (BFP), I was talking with Terry in the car. As was often the case, we found ourselves arguing – me asking him to explain how he could really believe in the clash of civilisations thesis, he telling me that he too had been a

Marxist as a young man and that I would grow out of it in time. As we crossed the North Circular and the end of our conversation loomed, he said, 'If they take over, if our green and pleasant land becomes part of a global caliphate, at least I will be able to look my daughter in the eye and say "'I tried'"'.

As well as the persistence of social ties and beliefs, and the activists' lack of dependence on national organisational structures, a further factor that has facilitated the persistence of EDL activism and the wider wave of anti-Muslim/minority protest relates to how the emotional batteries of EDL activism work.

In his *Social Movements in an Internet Age* Castells (2012, 14) draws attention to the importance of hope in achieving mobilisation. Hope, he tells us, 'is a fundamental ingredient in supporting goal-seeking action' because it counterbalances the anxiety and fear that might otherwise inhibit collective action. This broadly coincides with traditional theories of social movements in which mobilisation flows from belief among prospective activists that they have an opportunity to bring about change (Diani 1996, Gamson and Meyer 1996, McAdam 1982, 1986). Where this is the case, one would expect that declining perceptions of efficacy would undermine feelings of hope, which would in turn lead people to withdraw from activism.

In the context of grassroots EDL activism, such an argument is only partly born out. Feelings of efficacy and possibility were certainly prominent themes in most activists' accounts of their initial encounters with the EDL (see Chapter 2). As described in Chapter 5, as the EDL started to lose momentum feelings of efficacy and commitment to the group, even if not initially to the cause (see above), were eroded. Yet there have also been important emotional countercurrents within EDL activism that have given rise to an emotional dynamic of motivation quite different to that described by Castells.

Even as people were first recruited into EDL activism, the feelings of possibility and efficacy were attenuated by a strong undertow of pessimism – most activists remained deeply pessimistic about the world around them and the way it is changing.[29] What activists spoke about more than hope were feelings of defiance, and duty:[30] to the cause, to future generations of ordinary English people and to one another. As Treadwell and Garland (2011) observe, the stories that activists' told about themselves were to some extent heroic narratives. They were however narratives of heroic and noble defeat rather than of victory, and activists urged each other on with phrases such as 'no surrender' and 'Better to die on your feet than live on your knees'.[31] Where there was hope, it was by and large not hope associated with utopian visions of a better world, but hope that their children and grandchildren would recognise that 'at least they tried' and appreciate that 'their grandad was not just a racist' (Tony).[32]

I would argue that the motivating power of these feelings of defiance and duty lay in the way they intersected with feelings of actual and potential pride and shame – pride at standing up for their cause regardless of the odds, pride at 'having the backs' of their fellow activists, the shame of letting one's fellow activists down, pride in their refusal to be shamed into submission by their opponents (see Chapter 4) and so forth. The value of this particular emotional dynamic was that it was especially well-suited to mitigating the psychological impacts of the decline in the EDL's fortunes and enabled activists to generate motivation even out of apparent failures. A poorly attended demonstration could be transformed into an act of glorious if doomed resistance; a heroic last stand.

Notes

1 While some of the groups that emerged from or parallel to the EDL followed it in seeking to retain a narrow focus on (militant) Islam, others mobilised around a broader range of issues, anxieties and animosities. For example, some of the Facebook pages of NWI divisions carry multiple references to 'race mixing', the 14 word slogan ('We must secure the existence of our people and a future for White Children') used by white racial nationalist groups, and statements about their opposition to 'communism'. In 2013, activists associated with the NWI were charged with an assault on anti-fascist campaigners in London in 2012 (see 'Right-wing thugs locked up after Liverpool city centre attack', Gary Stewart, *Liverpool Echo*, 26th September 2013, www.liverpoolecho. co.uk/news/liverpool-news/right-wing-thugs-locked-up-after-6100974) and, along with activists from groups such as SEA and the SDL, have organised events in collaboration with the NF.
2 See Feldman and Littler (2014).
3 MFE's annual St. George's Day parade in Brighton became for a few years something of a ritualised clash between assorted 'patriots' and anti-fascist opposition. In 2015, MFE relocated their march to Blackpool.
4 It was difficult at times not to think of the People's Front of Judea and the Judean People's Front in Monty Python's *Life of Brian*.
5 Jim Dowson (a former BNP fundraiser in Northern Ireland), who left the group July 2014, Paul Golding (a former councillor in Sevenoaks, Kent representing the BNP and BNP Communications Officer), Andy McBride (former BNP South East regional organiser) and Kevin Edwards (a former BNP councillor in Wales)
6 Organised as a direct response to the Sharia patrols organised by extreme Islamist groups (see Chapter 1).
7 Among other activities Britain First also stood candidates, very unsuccessfully, in the 2014 European elections in Wales (gaining 0.9% of the votes cast) and Scotland (1.02% of votes cast) and in the Rochester and Stroud by-election of 20th November 2014 (0.14% of votes cast). For an introduction to the group see (Allen 2014)
8 PEGIDA is the acronym of *Patriotische Europäer gegen die Islamisierung des Abendlandes*, translated as Patriotic Europeans against the Islamification of the West
9 '"Anti-Islamisation" group Pegida UK holds Newcastle march', BBC, 28th February 2015, www.bbc.com/news/uk-england-tyne-31657167. The event was addressed by erstwhile BFP leader Paul Weston.
10 'Pegida in London: British supporters and anti-fascists clash at Downing Street protest', Lizze Dearden, *The Independent*, 5th April 2015, www.independent.co.uk/news/uk/home-news/pegida-in-london-british-supporters-and-antifascists-clash-at-downing-street-protest-10156674.html.
11 As Gould (2009) discusses, while the idea of moral shocks was initially applied in discussions about how people are initially mobilised into action (see Jasper and Poulsen 1995), they can also play an important role in sustaining commitment and adjusting the focus and emotional tone of activism.
12 Zúquete (2008), see Chapter 1.
13 Even after Robinson left the EDL, he continued to attract more public and media attention than the new leaders Tim Ablitt and later Steve Eddowes. For example, in

March 2015, Robinson rather than Eddowes was the main focus of news stories about a proposal by Afzal Amin, Conservative candidate for Dudley North, to call and then cancel an EDL demonstration in the town as part of a quite perverse strategy to position himself as somebody able to promote harmonious relations in the town. See 'Exposed: Star Tory candidate plotted with race thugs to stage fake EDL demo in cynical bid to win votes', Nick Craven and Ben Ellery, *Mail on Sunday*, 21st March 2015, www.dailymail.co.uk/news/article-3005845/Exposed-Star-Tory-candidate-plotted-race-thugs-stage-fake-EDL-demo-cynical-bid-win-votes.html. As discussed in Chapter 5, a common theme in the contemporary literature on the leadership of social movements is that the position and influence of leaders usually emerges through interactions with multiple actors both inside and outside the movement and consolidate their position at the centre of networks of power (Nepstad and Bob 2006).

14 Something that contributed to a mood of defiance among the remaining activists when Robinson and Carroll left the EDL in October 2013 (Baker 2014, Pilkington 2014).

15 A statement on the EDL website gives some sense of the depth of the animosity: 'For far too long this parasite of a man [Bill Baker] has dragged us down by claiming to speak as an authoritative member of the EDL, whilst actually being nothing of the sort. He has been attempting to exploit our success and our genuine intentions. He is an embarrassment not only to himself and his party, but also to those who don't see him for what he is: an opportunist. Some time ago he decided to engage in a televised debate with a Muslim convert that was then publicised all over the internet. This appearance was not sanctioned by the EDL leadership, it was a decision he made entirely on his own initiative. Although we'll acknowledge that he did make a few valid points, he ultimately made a complete fool of himself. We do not appreciate our name being blackened with racist connotations, so we always have to be wary of being judged guilty by association. So we want to make it clear: Bill Baker does not speak for us'. Recovered from 'The EDL and the JTF', *Gates of Vienna*, 1st March 2010, http://gatesofvienna.blogspot.co.uk/2011/03/edl-and-jtf.html

16 On 19th March, a handful of EDL supporters turned out to heckle Bill Baker and his meagre group of supporters. ' Far-right groups confront each other in Dagenham', John Phillips, *Barking and Dagenham Post*, 21st March 2010, www.barkinganddagenhampost.co.uk/news/politics/far_right_groups_confront_each_other_in_dagenham_1_836331

17 Since 2012, there have been ongoing meetings between representatives from the various groups as attempts have been made to forge alliances.

18 In situations where organisations have scant resources, they are less likely to emphasise difference or pursue factional politics (della Porta and Diani 2006, 130).

19 On two occasions when this did happen, it provoked suspicion among the remaining activists that the person concerned had been working for the police.

20 In October 2011, I started writing a conference paper about leaving EDL activism based on lengthy conversations with two activists who had been talking with me about leaving the group. Within three months, both had reappeared on the scene, one again involved in street activism, the other primarily focused on online activity.

21 This seemed especially to be the case when people had left for family reasons.

22 Here I am referring to voluntary rather than enforced desistance from activism. There were two forms of forced exit from the group. One of these was being forced to leave the group by other activists (e.g. the case of Bill Baker, above). The other, which became increasingly common from 2011 onwards, was of enforced desistance arising from receiving anti-social behaviour orders (ASBOs) and criminal anti-social behaviour orders (CRASBOs) prohibiting participation in any EDL activities for a defined period (see 'First CRASBO for EDL activists', Police Professional, 17th December 2010, www.policeprofessional.com/news.aspx?id=11730; EDL Criminals, http://edlcriminals.com/tag/crasbo/). The use of such banning orders has provoked some debate about whether or not such orders might infringe civil liberties. See for example the comments

of Patrick Hayes ('The right to protest is not exclusive to the left', *Spiked*, 11th May 2011, www.spiked-online.com/newsite/article/10504#.VWBvm09Vikp) and Bob Pitt (*Islamophobia Watch*, 12th May 2011, www.islamophobiawatch.co.uk/spiked-indignant-over-asbo-for-edl-thug/).

23 Even with group transport, trips to demonstrations outside the local area often cost close to or in excess of £100 once refreshments were factored in.

24 Sarah was one of several activists to complain about the general behaviour of some fellow activists during demonstrations – 'some of them, you know, are fucking disgusting: I've seen people pissing on buses', while John described some of the baiting and chanting at opponents as 'a bit childish'.

25 I was never able to verify this.

26 The 'meet and greets' being held by the new borough-level divisions (see Chapter 1).

27 The finding that decisions to leave were not reducible, were rarely preceded and only sometimes accompanied by ideological disengagement is broadly in keeping with other sociological and social psychological accounts of disengagement from radical political activism (Horgan 2009). It is also consistent with research on the biographical impacts of social movement activism more generally, with several studies drawing attention to the fact that activism can generate changes in people's identities and worldviews that often outlive direct participation (McAdam 1989, Polletta and Jasper 2001, Robnett 1997, Rupp and Taylor 1987, Whalen and Flacks 1989, Whittier 1997).

28 It is possible that this way of narrating their process of disengagement acted as a form of face-saving, thereby enabling activists to avert possible feelings of shame, that is if the group had 'had the right idea', but this had somehow been corrupted, then there was little reason to feel ashamed at having been involved in that group and marched alongside those people.

29 Interestingly, Bartlett and Littler (2011, 29, emphasis added) found that 'EDL *demonstrators* are significantly more likely than EDL *non-demonstrators* [i.e. those only active online] to feel pessimistic about the future. More than half (52 per cent) of them said they expected their lives to get worse over the next 12 months (n=231), compared with 39 per cent of non-demonstrators (n=144)'.

30 Pilkington (2014, 119–120) finds a similar dynamic among the activists she spoke with in the West Midlands.

31 A phrase which, curiously enough, is usually attributed to the decidedly leftist Mexican revolutionary Emiliano Zapata.

32 One of the reasons Tony accepted my offer to have a copy of the transcript of our formal interview was, he told me, that he wanted to gather information that would enable his grandchildren and great-grandchildren to better understand why he was involved in the EDL.

References

Allen, C. 2014. "Britain First: The 'Frontline Resistance' to the Islamification of Britain." *The Political Quarterly* 85 (3):354–361.

Baker, F. 2014. EDL Girls: Don't Call Me Racist. BBC Three.

Bartlett, J., and M. Littler. 2011. *Inside the EDL: Populist Politics in a Digital Age.* London: Demos.

Bjørgo, T. 1998. "Entry, Bridge-Burning and Exit Options: What Happens to Young People who Join Racist Groups and Want to Leave." In *Nation and Race: The Developing Euro-American Racist Subculture*, edited by J. Kaplan and T. Bjørgo, 231–258. Boston: Northeastern University Press.

Bjørgo, T. 2002. *Exit Neo-Nazism: Reducing Recruitment and Promoting Disengagement from Racist Groups.* Oslo: Norwegian Institute of International Affairs.

Bjørgo, T. 2009. "Processes of Disengagement from Violent Groups of the Extreme Right." In *Leaving Terrorism Behind: Individual and Collective Disengagement*, edited by T. Bjørgo and J. Horgan, 30–48. London: Routledge.

Castells, M. 2012. *Networks of Outrage and Hope: Social Movements in the Internet Age*. Cambridge: Polity Press.

della Porta, D., and M. Diani. 2006. *Social Movements: An Introduction*. Oxford: Blackwell.

Diani, M. 1996. "Linking Mobilization Frames and Political Opportunities: Insights from Regional Populism in Italy." *American Sociological Review* 61 (6):1053–1069.

Diani, M. 2003. "'Leaders' of Brokers? Positions and Influence in Social Movement Networks." In *Social Movements and Network: Relational Approaches to Collective Action*, edited by M. Diani and D. McAdam, 105–122. Oxford: Oxford University Press.

Feldman, M., and M. Littler. 2014. Tell MAMA Reporting 2013/14: Anti-Muslim Overview, Analysis and 'Cumulative Extremism'. Middlesborough: Teesside University.

Gamson, W. A., and D. S. Meyer. 1996. "The Framing of Political Opportunity." In *Comparative Perspectives on Social Movement Opportunities, Mobilizing structures, and Framing*, edited by D. McAdam, J. D. McCarthy and M. N. Zald, 275–290. Cambridge: Cambridge University Press.

Gould, D. B. 2009. *Moving Politics: Emotion and ACT UP's Fight Against AIDS*. London: University of Chicago Press.

Horgan, J. 2009. "Individual Disengagement: A Psychological Analysis." In *Leaving Terrorism Behind: Individual and Collective Disengagement*, edited by T. Bjørgo and J. Horgan, 17–30. London: Routledge.

Jasper, J. M. 2007. *The Art of Moral Protest: Culture, Biography, and Creativity in Social Movements*. Paperback Edition. London: University of Chicago Press.

Jasper, J. M., and J. D. Poulsen. 1995. "Recruiting Strangers and Friends: Moral Shocks and Social Networks in Animal Rights and Anti-Nuclear Protests." *Social Problems* 42 (4):493–512.

Killian, L. M. 1984. "Organization, Rationality and Spontaneity in the Civil Rights Movement." *American Sociological Review* 49 (6):770–783.

Klandermans, B. 2004. "The Demand and Supply of Participation: Social Psychological Correlates of Participation in a Social Movement." In *The Blackwell Companion to Social Movements*, edited by D. A. Snow, S. Soule and H. Kriesi, 360–379. Oxford: Blackwell.

McAdam, D. 1982. *Political Process and the Development of Black Insurgency, 1930–1970*. Chicago: University of Chicago Press.

McAdam, D. 1986. "Recruitment to High-Risk Activism: The Case of Freedom Summer." *American Journal of Sociology* 92 (1):64–90.

McAdam, D. 1989. "The Biographical Consequences of Activism." *American Sociological Review* 54 (5):744–760.

Melucci, A. 1996. *Challenging Codes: Collective Action in the Information Age*. Cambridge: Cambridge University Press.

Nepstad, S. E., and C. Bob. 2006. "When do Leaders Matter? Hypotheses on Leadership Dynamics in Social Movements." *Mobilization* 11 (1):1–22.

Pilkington, H. 2014. 'Loud and Proud': Youth Activism in the English Defence League. Report on Work Package 7 of MYPLACE Project. www.fp7-myplace.eu.

Polletta, F., and J. M. Jasper. 2001. "Collective Identity and Social Movements." *Annual Review of Sociology* 27:283–305.

Robnett, B. 1997. *How Long? How Long? African American Women in the Struggle for Civil Rights*. New York: Oxford University Press.

Rupp, L., and V. Taylor. 1987. *Survival in the Doldrums: The American Women's Rights Movement, 1945 to the 1960s*. Oxford: Oxford University Press.

Treadwell, J., and J. Garland. 2011. "Masculinity, Marginalization and Violence: A Case Study of the English Defence League." *British Journal of Criminology* 51 (4):621–634.

Whalen, J., and R. Flacks. 1989. *Beyond the Barricades: The Sixties Generation Grows Up*. Philadelphia: Temple University Press.

Whittier, N. 1995. *Feminist Generations: The Persistence of the Radical Women's Movement*. Philadelphia: Temple University Press.

Whittier, N. 1997. "Political Generations, Micro-Cohorts, and the Transformation of Social Movements." *American Sociological Review* 62 (5):760–778.

Zald, M. N., and R. Ash Gardner. 1987. "Social Movement Organisations: Growth, Decay, and Change." In *Social Movements in an Organizational Society*, edited by M. N. Zald and J. D. McCarthy, 121–141. New Brunswick: Transaction.

Zúquete, J. P. 2008. "The European Extreme-Right and Islam: New Directions?" *Journal of Political Ideologies* 13 (3):321–344.

7 Conclusions

Through the course of the preceding chapters, I have explored how English Defence League (EDL) activism has worked as a project of collective world-making[1] for those who have chosen to march under its banner. I have discussed how people became involved with the EDL, how they engaged with and forged commitment to the group's cause, the strategies through which they sought to counter their opponents' attempts to frame the EDL as a racist or far right organisation and the implications that their resistance to these labels had for activism at the grassroots of the organisation. I have also discussed how and why EDL activism began to unravel during the course of 2011, but did not do so entirely. I conclude with some observations organised around five broad themes: the heterogeneity of EDL activists' journeys into and through activism; the ideological structures around which they mobilised; their identity structures; the emotional batteries of EDL activism; and the persistence of organised anti-Muslim activism.

The heterogeneity of people's journeys through EDL activism

There were many commonalities across people's experiences of EDL activism: their feelings of anger and outrage, the bonds of solidarity that they forged, their shared loathing of the Left, the liberal elite and (militant) Muslims, and so forth. Yet there were also important differences. As described in Chapter 2, EDL activism meant different things to different people: some activists, particularly those who had come to the EDL from traditional far right groups, had 'wandered'[2] into the EDL in the hope that it would provide them with an avenue for the pursuit of long-held racist and xenophobic agendas, yet many others had previously had quite unremarkable political ideas, and there was little in their life histories, other than friends or relatives taking an interest in the EDL, to differentiate them from the many thousands of people in the United Kingdom with similar anxieties and apprehensions who have never become involved with organised anti-Muslim activism. This latter group of activists tended to cling fiercely to their non-racist identity. Similarly, while all the activists I knew were attracted by the 'buzz' of the EDL and its demonstrations, for some the buzz was very much about 'kicking off', while others found violent incidents and public disorder at demonstrations unnerving, stressful, and even traumatic, undermining their feeling of belonging to the group.

Recognising this variety has important implications. It should encourage us to be cautious of attempts to distil explanations of the emergence of and participation in groups like the EDL down to just one or two 'key factors'. As Flecker (2007, 6) argues in his discussion of the European far right, where there is clearly 'more than one main path of attraction' to a group or set of political groups it becomes somewhat 'futile [to] argue over *the* reason' (emphasis in the original) for their expansion.

Awareness of the variation across different activists' experiences should also inform our thinking about how to respond to groups such as the EDL. While some people involved in these groups may feel intimidated by hostile counter-protests or large-scale policing, others actively seek out such encounters, finding them exciting and emotionally rewarding on multiple levels, and while some would probably never take up an opportunity to sit down and engage in dialogue with policy makers and representatives from other parts of society, there are others who will and would even welcome the opportunity to do so. Understanding the heterogeneities in groups such as the EDL enables us to lean more strategically on the tension points within the group and to develop response strategies that are less likely to generate the kind of 'backfire effects' (Hess and Martin 2006) that I have described in the previous chapters, whereby attempts to challenge the EDL actually reinforce activists' commitment and for some act as a stimulus towards the adoption of more radical tactics. A key task for researchers and analysts working on groups such as the EDL should be to map these heterogeneities and explore how different segments of their activist communities evolve over time and relate to one another.

The ideological structures of EDL activism

In his book *Contentious Politics,* Charles Tilly (2008, 14) proposes that it is useful to imagine social movement actors as being more like a jazz ensemble than an orchestra: while participants may have a limited array of pieces that they can play, they are nonetheless able to choose which they play and in what order and are liable to improvise as they do so. While Tilly uses this metaphor primarily to describe the evolution of tactical repertoires, it is also a useful way to think about ideological structures, at least in groups such as the EDL. The core narrative about the Islamification of Britain[3] and the liberal elite's failure to respond effectively to the looming threat posed by (militant) Islam has provided a sequence of bass chords sustained not only by the group's national leaders, but also by the majority of activists at all levels of the movement. The activists that I knew were however prone to improvisation around these chords: during conversations with me and with other activists, there was a constant stretching of this narrative as they segued from commentaries about (militant) Islam to a range of other issues and anxieties about immigration, overpopulation, economic insecurity, crime and (in)justice, paedophilia and so forth. As described in Chapter 4, part of the resonance and power of the EDL protest narrative derives from the way it can intersect with discourses about other anxieties, moral panics and perceived injustices. However, they always eventually worked their way back to the underlying organising idea of the group – the bass chords that held the ensemble together – usually pointing out as they did so that 'Of course, those are just my views and not the views of the group'. As of early 2015, there has been little sign of any initiative from within the EDL to develop a more general ideological programme, and any moves to expand their focus to other issues have gained little traction.[4]

This highly circumscribed definition of their cause had a number of implications for EDL activism. As described in Chapter 4, it was central to some activists' efforts to distance themselves from the established far right and also helped them to negotiate and manage some of the obvious ideological tensions that ran through the activist community. However, their identification as a single-issue group also placed limits on the EDL, and for some activists this became a source of frustration. Activism changes people: ideas and interests are likely to evolve as a result of interactions with fellow activists, opponents, the state and an array of other actors. The EDL's identity as a single-issue group allowed little space for activists to pick up new issues without at the same time undercutting an intrinsic part of their collective identity.

In this context, it is significant that some of the groups that have emerged out of and have overlapping 'memberships' with the EDL, such as Britain First and Infidels of Britain (IOB), are articulating and mobilising around a wider protest narrative.[5] Such changes in their ideological focus are likely to have implications for who such groups mobilise against and possibly also the tactics that they adopt. As noted in Chapter 6, activists associated with 'Infidel' groups have explicitly targeted anti-fascist campaigners and Britain First took it upon themselves to intimidate anti-UKIP campaigners in the weeks prior to the 2015 general election.

Being 'proper patriots' and 'ordinary English people': the identity structures of EDL activists

As Treadwell and Garland (2011) observe, part of the allure of EDL activism is that it offers participants an opportunity to construct heroic identities. All the activists, I knew had developed self-narratives about how they were standing up for a noble cause in the face of overwhelming odds, and more generally about how their lives had been transformed by EDL activism, acquiring new interests and insights, taking on new responsibilities, finding a new purpose and becoming better and more worthy people.

Yet by and large entry into EDL activism did not entail the degree of rupture in their lives or life narratives as can sometimes be the case when joining a radical political or religious group (see Blee 2003, 35, Lofland and Skonovd 1983, Lofland and Stark 1965). Entering into EDL activism was at least as much about bringing extant identities to the fore and then gradually making them increasingly antagonistic and exclusive as it was about the construction of a new identity. While EDL activism became a focal point in their lives, there was little impulse to burning existing social bridges outside the activist community. The activists saw themselves as 'proper patriots', but they also saw themselves as 'ordinary English people', and for most, identifying as non-racist and non-far-right was an important part of this.

While it might be comforting and politically expedient to imagine activists in groups such as the EDL as 'extremists' or people somewhere way out on the margins of our society, it is also misleading. The activists I knew did develop their beliefs and emotional repertoires through interaction with one other, through engaging with the esoteric counter-jihad literature and through their hostile encounters with opposition groups and public authorities. They also developed them, however, through interactions with family, neighbours, colleagues, other parents at their son's football club and their mates in the working men's club down the road. While EDL activists found themselves criticised and shouted down with terms such as 'racist!' 'fascist!' or 'Islamophobia!', they also found what they believed to be their own ideas and arguments played back to them on a regular basis in mainstream political, media and public discourses.

While it is difficult to provide compelling evidence that generally negative representations of Muslims and immigrants in political and media discourses contribute to the emergence of groups such as the EDL, there can be little doubt that they make it much easier for the activists in such groups to explain and justify their arguments, both to themselves and to prospective new recruits.[6]

Beyond a politics of hate: the EDL's emotional batteries[7]

Our lives are characterised by a tremendous array of emotions. EDL activists are no different. Hate, anger, outrage, fear and indignation played an important role in recruitment and in sustaining participation in EDL activism. These emotions were however emergent: their focus, intensity and expression liable to change over time. The beginnings of people's journey into EDL activism were often associated with feelings of outrage, but feelings of hate usually took longer to develop, evolving out of feelings of anger, anxiety and fear as activists developed the cognitive structures and personal grievances with which to construct hate.

Participation in EDL activism also generated positive emotions. As might be expected, one of the most prominent of these was pride. As well as nationalistic flag-waving pride and pride in the EDL as an organisation, the activists also described feelings of personal pride and dignity. They experienced feelings of self-realisation and a sense of moral pride: feelings often accentuated by the sacrifices that activism entailed – the financial costs, the clashes with opponents, the time costs and in some cases the criminal records. Other emotions integral to grassroots EDL activism included feelings of solidarity and camaraderie, feelings of possibility and, as discussed in Chapter 6, their conversion into defiance and duty.

These emotions interacted with one another and myriad other emotions: gratitude towards a fellow activist who had protected them when confronted by opposition activists; amusement at a poster lampooning their left-wing critics; confusion about who to contact about the next event; relief that an adequate number of people had turned up to a demonstration; concern for an activist awaiting trial; satisfaction at hearing a statement by a politician that they believed coincided with their views; anxiety about whether their opponents would be carrying weapons; frustration about fellow activists turning up drunk to EDL events; boredom as they waited for the bus home. Expressions of anger during demonstrations helped activists to transform fear, anxiety and shame into pride and in-group solidarity. Feelings of outrage, indignation and hate were achieved, or at least intensified, through affective bonds with other activists and in reaction to their opponents' attempts to shame them with labels such as racist and fascist. Even boredom could help to consolidate solidarity if the activists went through it together.

If we want to understand how and why people become involved and stay involved in groups such as the EDL, and the decisions that activists make about what specific issues to protest about and how, it is important not to narrow our attention to focus only on their anger, hatred, resentment and indignation. We must explore more broadly how the emotional batteries of such groups work: the range of emotions, the cognitive processes and social interactions with which they are associated and how the different emotions interact with one another and enable the activists to undertake different tasks. Explaining how, why and when activists experience pride and shame in particular may take us much closer to understanding activists and how they are likely to react to different interventions.

The persistence and evolution of organised anti-Muslim activism

From the outset, the EDL faced considerable challenges: the group had scant material resources, it quickly became a pariah group, its participants had little experience of social movement activism to draw on and the activist community was clearly cross-cut with quite different and barely compatible ideas, interests and identities. While activists developed a number of strategies to manage these challenges, their capacity to do so was eventually undermined by a series of inherent tensions: activists' identification of the EDL as a single-issue group, so important for challenging accusations that they were a far right group (see Chapter 4), also limited its ability to accommodate the shifting interests of its activists; violence, or at least the threat of it, was integral to grassroots EDL activism, yet so too were attempts to disassociate with it; public recognition of the EDL brand ensured extensive media coverage and facilitated recruitment, but meant that the group tended to attract people seeking out violence and public disorder; the loose and highly devolved organisational structures facilitated the growth of the movement but also left the leaders unable to maintain group discipline and eventually lent themselves to increasingly poisonous factionalism; and the use of Facebook and other social media was both fundamental to the EDL's reach and organisational capacity but also posed challenges for group discipline and became a vector for the arguments and squabbles that did so much to corrode the social fabric of the movement. It is hard to imagine how the EDL (or any similar group) could grow and sustain itself much beyond the size that the EDL achieved during its 2010–2011 peak without becoming a fundamentally different type of organisation offering its activists a quite different project of collective world-making.[8]

Anti-Muslim protest is, however, unlikely to disappear any time soon. In spite of the decline and fragmentation of the EDL, anti-Muslim activism has persisted, albeit rarely at the scale that the EDL achieved in 2010 and early 2011. Scholars of social movements often highlight the importance of subcultures and activist scenes both in processes of mobilisation and as important outcomes of periods of intense mobilisation (Kriesi 1988, Melucci 1989, 1996, Whittier 1995, 1997). As well as appearing at times to have an almost 'autonomous capacity to motivate people' (della Porta and Diani 2006, 123) activist scenes and subcultures can help to keep ideas, beliefs, identities and styles of emoting in circulation and maintain personal and social networks even when a social movement itself enters a phase of abeyance (Billig 1978, Rupp and Taylor 1987, Taylor 1989). Whatever the group's failings,[9] the EDL has helped to generate just such an activist scene, which is likely to outlive the group: the personal and institutional Facebook networks, the blogs, the concepts now lodged in the collective consciousness articulated through the conversations that take place in these spaces, the residual affective ties, the EDL brand itself and so forth. It has also, as Lowles (2012) observes, contributed to the politicisation of a cohort of people who were not previously engaged in activism, and there is ample evidence that people who have already participated in social or political mobilisations are more likely to do so in the future than those who have not (Corrigall-Brown 2012, della Porta 2005, Gould 1995, Klandermans 1997, McAdam 1989, Whittier 1995, 1997).

A key focus for research and analysis should be how this scene evolves and how those involved in it interact with other social and political currents. It is possible that some of this cohort of activists are absorbed into more institutionalised and less hostile or aggressive forms of social or political action, although those who do pursue such a path may find that their past as EDL activists follows them into and tarnishes their future.[10] What we are also seeing is small groups or cells with their roots in this activist scene adopting more radical tactics and forging alliances with more ideologically extreme groups, such as the National Front (NF). Such moves are likely to fragment the scene even further, but may also lead to an increase in violence associated with organised anti-minority activism, at least in the short to medium term.[11]

The activities of the EDL and cognate groups since 2009 have accentuated social divisions and intensified fear and insecurity in Muslim and other minority ethnic communities (Busher et al. 2014, Harris, Busher and Macklin 2015, Rootham, Hardgrove and McDowell 2014, Thomas et al. 2014). Ironically, in doing so, they have also made it easier if anything for their Islamist opponents to recruit[12] and have left many EDL activists themselves feeling ostracised and inhabiting a lived-reality dominated by fear, insecurity, perceptions of looming disaster and the stresses of the constant sniping between their fellow activists. When looked at from outside, groups such as the EDL seem frightening, perverse and self-defeating. There is however a logic to this activism, and one that extends beyond hatred or frustration and is more intricate than a simple urge to preserve their social status by lashing out against the dangerous Other. By exploring the interactions and the patterns of beliefs and emotions that comprise activism, we can uncover this logic, enabling us to develop a richer understanding of what it is that makes these groups attractive to some people, of how activists work collectively to sustain commitment to the cause and to one another, and of how and where anti-minority activism intersects with and draws on more mainstream social and political currents.

Notes

1 See Chapter 1 for a discussion of this term.
2 To use Linden and Klandermans' (2007) terminology.
3 Or England, Europe, the West and so forth, depending on which activist was speaking and at which time.
4 As stated in a footnote in Chapter 4, on 19th July 2014, the EDL held a demonstration in Hexthorpe, South Yorkshire, about Roma immigrants, but other similar events have not followed (Harris, Busher and Macklin 2015).
5 On Britain First website, they outline policies ranging across areas such as immigration, education, constitutional reform, healthcare and the economy. Similarly, while declaring that they are not a political party, IOB, 'a consortium of Indigenous Patriots and Nationalists from all walks of life, of various age groups, and various social and economic backgrounds', still outline a 'mini manifesto' which contains items including withdrawal from the European Union, 'putting a complete halt to immigration', 'a system of assisted repatriation', the abolition of inheritance tax, and the abolition of tuition fees for 'indigenous students of this nation' (IOB Facebook page).
6 Blee (2003, 192) makes a similar point in relation to organised racism in the United States, arguing that 'The mainstay of any substantial racist movement is not the pathological individual but rather a pathological vein of racism, intolerance, and bigotry in the larger population that the movement successfully mines'.
7 See Chapter 1 and Jasper (2011, 2012).
8 As Richards (2013, 190) notes, 'In some ways, it [the EDL] is imprisoned within its own limitations as a pressure-group rather than a political party'. It may be however that its 'own limitations' were themselves necessary to sustain the group.
9 It is notoriously difficult to define success and failure for social movements because their stated aims and objectives tend to change over time, and because movement actors and their activists often pursue unstated and sometimes even subconscious aims and objectives (della Porta and Diani 2006, 223–249, Jasper 2007, 293–321)
10 This, as Bjørgo (2009) notes, is often one of the problems facing those attempting to leave 'far right' activism and engage in other forms of political action.
11 Tactical radicalisation often occurs when groups or movements experience a phase of decline. As Busher and Macklin (2014, 15) describe, a number of explanations

have been offered for this pattern: 'a sense among activists that they have failed to meet initial aims using the established tactical repertoire (Koopmans 1993); increased organizational density (Minkoff 1997); competition over diminishing resources (Tarrow 1989); a fragmentation of power that undermines movement discipline (Busher 2013); or attempts by struggling leaders to reanimate their supporters or re-establish authority'. Barker and colleagues (Barker, Johnson and Lavalette 2001, 22) have also argued that the emergence of 'relatively isolated militant groups relying on "guerrilla" actions and resources' can be understood as 'the products of a politics of angry despair, mixing radical aspirations with disappointment'. The adoption of more violent tactics often precipitates splitting within movements (della Porta 1995, Irvin 1999, Zwerman, Steinhoff and della Porta 2000).

12 Detective Superintendent John Larkin of the West Midlands Police, for example, notes that 'In some areas, we have evidence that once they [the EDL] have gone and the high-profile policing of the event has occurred, there's fertile ground for those groups who would come in to encourage people to have this [extreme Islamist] reality – this is the way white Western society sees us' ('English Defence League demos "feed Islamic extremism"', Phil Mackie, BBC, 19th November 2010, www.bbc.co.uk/news/uk-11787839

References

Barker, C., A. Johnson and M. Lavalette. 2001. "Leadership Matters: An Introduction." In *Leadership and Social Movements*, edited by C. Barker, A. Johnson and M. Lavalette, 1–23. Manchester: Manchester University Press.

Billig, M. 1978. *Fascists: A Social Psychological View of the National Front*. London: Academic Press.

Bjørgo, T. 2009. "Processes of Disengagement from Violent Groups of the Extreme Right." In *Leaving Terrorism Behind: Individual and Collective Disengagement*, edited by T. Bjørgo and J. Horgan, 30–48. London: Routledge.

Blee, K.M. 2003. *Inside Organized Racism: Women in the Hate Movement*. Paperback Edition. Berkeley: University of California Press.

Busher, J. 2013. "Anti-Muslim Populism in the UK: The Development of the English Defence League." In *The Changing Faces of Populism: Systematic Challengers in Europe and the U.S.*, edited by H. Giusto, D. Kitching and S. Rizzo, 207–226. Brussels: Foundation for European Progressive Studies.

Busher, J., K. Christmann, G. Macklin, M. Rogerson and P. Thomas. 2014. *Understanding Concerns About Community Relations in Calderdale*. Huddersfield: The University of Huddersfield.

Busher, J., and G. Macklin. 2014. "Interpreting 'Cumulative Extremism': Six Proposals for Enhancing Conceptual Clarity." *Terrorism and Political Violence*. www.tandfonline.com/eprint/XGyY3ynSqq2BXcNJnDXd/full#.VcNEZvlViko

Corrigall-Brown, C. 2012. "From the Balconies to the Barricades, and Back? Trajectories of Participation in Contentious Politics." *Journal of Civil Society* 8 (1).

della Porta, D. 1995. *Social Movements, Political Violence, and the State: A Comparative Analysis of Italy and Germany*. Cambridge: Cambridge University Press.

della Porta, D. 2005. "Multiple Belongings, Flexible Identities and the Construction of Another Politics: Between the European Social Forum and the Local Social Fora." In *Transnational Protest and Global Activism*, edited by D. della Porta and S. Tarrow, 175–202. Lanham: Rowman and Littlefield.

della Porta, D., and M. Diani. 2006. *Social Movements: An Introduction*. Oxford: Blackwell.

Flecker, J. 2007. "Changing Working Life and the Appeal of the Extreme Right: A Variety of Approaches." In *Changing Working Life and the Appeal of the Extreme Right*, edited by J. Flecker, 1–6. Aldershot: Ashgate.

Gould, R. V. 1995. *Insurgent Identities: Class, Community, and Protest in Paris from 1848 to the Commune*. Chicago: University of Chicago Press.

Harris, G., J. Busher and G. Macklin. 2015. *The Evolution of Anti-Muslim Protest in Two English Towns*. Coventry: Coventry University/The University of Huddersfield.

Hess, D., and B. Martin. 2006. "Repression, Backfire, and the Theory of Transformative Events." *Mobilization* 11 (2):249–267.

Irvin, C. 1999. *Militant Nationalism: Between Movement Party in Ireland and the Basque Country*. Minneapolis: University of Minnesota Press.

Jasper, J. M. 2007. *The Art of Moral Protest: Culture, Biography, and Creativity in Social Movements*. Paperback Edition. London: University of Chicago Press.

Jasper, J. M. 2011. "Emotions and Social Movements: Twenty Years of Theory and Research." *Annual Review of Sociology* 37:285–303.

Jasper, J. M. 2012. "Choice Points, Emotional Batteries, and Other Ways to Find Strategic Agency at the Microlevel." In *Strategies for Social Change*, edited by G. M. Maney, R. V. Kutz-Flamenbaum, D. A. Rohlinger and J. Goodwin, 23–42. Minneapolis: University of Minnesota Press.

Klandermans, B. 1997. *The Social Psychology of Protest*. Oxford: Blackwell.

Koopmans, R. 1993. "The Dynamics of Protest Waves: West Germany, 1965 to 1989." *American Sociological Review* 58 (5):637–658.

Kriesi, H. 1988. "New Social Movements and the New Class in the Netherlands." *American Journal of Sociology* 94 (5):1078–1116.

Linden, A., and B. Klandermans. 2007. "Revolutionaries, Wanderers, Converts, and Compliants: Life Histories of Extreme Right Activists." *Journal of Contemporary Ethnography* 36 (2):184–201.

Lofland, J., and N. Skonovd. 1983. "Patterns of Conversion." In *Of Gods and Men: New Religious Movements in the West*, edited by British Sociological Association, 1–24. Macon: Mercer University Press.

Lofland, J., and R. Stark. 1965. "Becoming a World-Saver: A Theory of Conversion to a Deviant Perspective." *American Sociological Review* 30 (6):862–875.

Lowles, N. 2012. "Where Now for the British Far Right?" *Extremis Blog*, 21/9/2012. http://extremisproject.org/2012/09/where-now-for-the-british-far-right/

McAdam, D. 1989. "The Biographical Consequences of Activism." *American Sociological Review* 54 (5):744–760.

Melucci, A. 1989. *Nomads of the Present: Social Movements and Individual Needs in Contemporary Society*. London: Hutchinson Radius.

Melucci, A. 1996. *Challenging Codes: Collective Action in the Information Age*. Cambridge: Cambridge University Press.

Minkoff, D. C. 1997. "The Sequencing of Social Movements." *American Sociological Review* 62 (5):779–799.

Richards, J. 2013. "Reactive Community Mobilization in Europe: The Case of the English Defence League." *Behavioral Sciences of Terrorism and Political Aggression* 5 (3):177–193.

Rootham, E., A. Hardgrove and L. McDowell. 2014. "Constructing Racialised Masculinities In/Through Affective Orientations to a Multicultural Town." *Urban Studies* Early Release, 1–17.

Rupp, L., and V. Taylor. 1987. *Survival in the Doldrums: The American Women's Rights Movement, 1945 to the 1960s*. Oxford: Oxford University Press.

Tarrow, S. 1989. *Democracy and Disorder: Social conflict, political protest and democracy in Italy, 1965–1975*. Oxford: Oxford University Press.

Taylor, V. 1989. "Social Movement Continuity: The Women's Movement in Abeyance." *American Sociological Review* 54 (5):761–775.

Thomas, P., M. Rogerson, G. Macklin, K. Christmann and J. Busher. 2014. *Understanding Concerns About Community Relations in Kirklees*. Huddersfield: University of Huddersfield.

Tilly, C. 2008. *Contentious Performances*. Cambridge: Cambridge University Press.

Treadwell, J., and J. Garland. 2011. "Masculinity, Marginalization and Violence: A Case Study of the English Defence League." *British Journal of Criminology* 51 (4):621–634.

Whittier, N. 1995. *Feminist Generations: The Persistence of the Radical Women's Movement*. Philadelphia: Temple University Press.

Whittier, N. 1997. "Political Generations, Micro-Cohorts, and the Transformation of Social Movements." *American Sociological Review* 62 (5):760–778.

Zwerman, G., P.G. Steinhoff and D. della Porta. 2000. "Disappearing social movements: Clandestinity in the cycle of New Left protest in the US, Japan, Germany, and Italy." *Mobilization* 5 (1):85–104.

Index